THROUGH A GLASS, DARKLY

ALSO BY STEFAN BECHTEL

Mr. Hornaday's War

Tornado Hunter

Dogtown: Tales of Rescue, Rehabilitation, and Redemption

Roar of the Heavens

Growing a Fortune

What Women Want (with Laurence Roy Stains)

The Good Luck Book (with Laurence Roy Stains)

Sex: A Man's Guide (with Laurence Roy Stains)

The Practical Encyclopedia of Sex and Health

Katherine, It's Time

Redemption Alley (with Bob Perry)

STEFAN BECHTEL AND
LAURENCE ROY STAINS

THROUGH A GLASS, DARKLY

SIR ARTHUR CONAN DOYLE AND THE QUEST TO SOLVE THE GREATEST MYSTERY OF ALL

ST. MARTIN'S PRESS NEW YORK

 Printed in the United States of America. For information, address St. Martin's Press, 175 Fifth Avenue, New York, N.Y. 10010.

www.stmartins.com

The Library of Congress Cataloging-in-Publication Data
is available upon request.

ISBN 978-1-250-07679-3 (hardcover)
ISBN 978-1-4668-8846-3 (e-book)

First Edition: June 2017

10 9 8 7 6 5 4 3 2 1

To my parents, Dr. Paul Moyer Bechtel (1909–1998)
and Mary Krom Bechtel (1923–2016),
whose faith never faltered

—S. B.

To my parents, Donald Eugene Stains (1917–2013)
and Shirley Greiner Stains (1922–1974)

Twilight and evening bell,
And after that the dark!

—L. R. S

CONTENTS

ACKNOWLEDGMENTS

We'd like to thank the many people who contributed to this fascinating project. Special thanks to Don Fehr, stellar agent at Trident Media Group, without whom this book would never have happened, and to Daniela Rapp, our smart editor at St. Martin's Press, for her questions and encouragement. Thanks to our readers Adam Bechtel, Lilly Bechtel, Lawrence R. Bechtel, Charles Shields, Jonathan Rintels, Matthew Carter, and Kay Ferguson. Thanks especially to Tamara Lacy, for her rivers of sweetness and her ability to read between the lines. Thanks to Ron Nagy, historian at the Lily Dale Museum, at Lily Dale (the country's oldest spiritualist community, in upstate New York), for help with archival photographs. Thanks to the many librarians who have lit our way, especially Mandi Shepp at the Marion H. Skidmore Library at Lily Dale and Kristina De Voe at Temple University. Also to Kate Mix, our tireless photo editor, for the many hours spent tracking down obscure photo permissions. (It's harder than it looks!) Thanks also to Cristina Meisner, Michael Gilmore, and the staff at the Harry Ransom Center, at the University of Texas at Austin, for help navigating through their superb archive of Conan Doyle materials, the best such collection for our purposes in the country. Many thanks to the multimedia artist Tony Oursler for the use of images from his archive. And, of course, hats off to Arthur Conan Doyle and the many other authors over the past century and a half who have contributed to world knowledge about the curiosities and conundrums of spiritualism.

AUTHORS' NOTE

"Spiritualism" has receded so far into the fogs of history that many educated people today don't even know what it means, or once meant. It meant (and still means, to its comparatively few remaining followers) that the soul is eternal and that the departed are willing and able to communicate with the living.

From the middle of the nineteenth century to the 1930s, spiritualism was a worldwide movement with millions of adherents. But if you were to consult today's online resources for some enlightenment, you'd be greeted with the foregone conclusion that it was pure bunk. And that Sir Arthur Conan Doyle, its foremost spokesperson toward the end, was a credulous old fool.

As two journalists fascinated by this extraordinary subject, we decided to approach the historical record without prejudice. We are not true believers, but it's fair to say we don't *not* believe. As we began delving into the rich archival record, we were impressed by the thoughtfulness and sincerity on the part of highly intelligent men and women—including some of the finest minds of the day. We were also impressed by their courage. Skeptics quite willfully spread lies about them and attempted to ruin their lives, but they persisted in seeking the truth. They were explorers, every bit as much as the naturalist in the jungle, the adventurer in the Arctic, the scientist in the laboratory.

We're bringing back a fair-minded report of what we found.

The record is complex, filled with blatant fraud and at the same time replete with phenomena that are eerily difficult to explain away. What the reader takes away from all this is a personal matter. Are ghosts real? You'll have to decide that for yourself.

THROUGH A GLASS, DARKLY

To Accomodate The Thousands

Who could not get Even Standing Room
in Carnegie Hall on April 21,

SIR ARTHUR **CONAN DOYLE**

HAS CONSENTED TO REPEAT HIS LECTURE,

"Recent Psychic Evidence"

At Carnegie Hall, Friday Eve., May 5
at 8:30

and Sunday Afternoon, May 7 at 3:30

When he will again show his marvellous
spirit photographs that have aroused
worldwide discussion.

To insure hearing this lecture, tickets should be purchased at once

Exclusive Management LEE KEEDICK. 437 Fifth Avenue, New York

On a triumphal lecture tour to the United States in 1922, Conan Doyle drew rapt crowds eager for news of the world beyond death. He filled Carnegie Hall six times in 1922, and three more times on a return trip in 1923.
THE HARRY RANSOM CENTER, UNIVERSITY OF TEXAS AT AUSTIN

PROLOGUE:
The Infinite Strangeness of Life

Drifts of white dogwood blossoms had just begun to show in the trees along Seventh Avenue that eerily warm evening of April 21, 1922. People waiting for tonight's performance in the main auditorium at Carnegie Hall had formed a queue that stretched all the way down Fifty-seventh to the corner of Sixth Avenue. The crowds were giddy with the balmy air, and nobody seemed to much mind the wait. After all, tonight's guest was to be none other than Sir Arthur Conan Doyle, the celebrated creator of Sherlock Holmes and one of the most famous authors in the world.

Sir Arthur and his wife, Lady Jean Doyle, three children, and two nannies had arrived in the port of New York on the ocean liner *Baltic* three days earlier, for the beginning of Doyle's triumphal speaking tour of America. The day after his arrival, Doyle had taken his family to the highest point in the city—the fifty-seventh floor of the Woolworth Building (the Empire State Building did not yet exist) to survey the busy hive of Manhattan Island. "There is a rush and roar with a brilliancy and sense of motion and power such as can nowhere else be found," he later wrote.

Many of those waiting in line tonight had come just to lay eyes on the man who brought the world the eccentric sleuth in the deerstalker hat, a surprising number of whom believed that Mr. Holmes was actually a real person. Some had written him letters at 221B Baker Street, imploring his help in some trouble or other; women offered their services as his housekeeper or even their hands in marriage. But fascination with the gaunt, haunted, cocaine-imbibing detective did not fully explain why tonight's lecture-demonstration had drawn a standing-room-only crowd of more than three thousand (and, over successive nights, would fill Carnegie Hall five more times and three times the next year, 1923). Because it was by now widely known that Sir Arthur had opened an astonishing—some said, ridiculous—new chapter in his life. The poster for tonight's event, on display across the city, summed it up:

Lee Keedick presents SIR ARTHUR CONAN DOYLE, Famous English Novelist, author of the "Sherlock Holmes" mystery series, whose investigations of Life After Death have aroused worldwide interest.

What had come to be known as "spiritualism"—the conviction that those who have passed over had the ability and the desire to make contact across the veil of death with those they'd left behind—seemed to have bewitched the Western world. Spiritualist lectures filled guild halls and auditoriums with seekers from Boston to Brittany; séances accompanied tea in upper-crust British parlors, and even in the White House; there were state and national spiritualist conventions and summer camps attended by thousands. More than two hundred spiritualist journals, some of them published weekly, had appeared on the market. Thomas Edison and Nikola Tesla were both now searching for the precise electrical frequency that would enable them to create a "ghost machine"—a device that would enable people to communicate directly with the spirit world. The movement had attracted a throng of distinguished seekers, including the Nobel laureate Pierre Curie; the evolutionary biologist and co-discoverer of evolution Alfred Russel Wallace; the Harvard lecturer and psychologist William James; Lewis Carroll; and the Irish poet William Butler Yeats.

At the same time, the movement had also attracted an opposing army of equally eminent, and equally vocal, skeptics. Ralph

Waldo Emerson branded spiritualism a "rat-revelation, the gospel that comes by taps in the wall and humps in the table-drawer." Scientists railed against this "popular madness." Preachers rained down fire and damnation on what was clearly the work of the prince of darkness. Henry David Thoreau simply dismissed all believers as "idiots." And to the naysayers' delight, it seemed that every few months another phony "medium" was unmasked.

Sir Arthur, backstage at Carnegie Hall with Lady Jean, calmly glanced over his lecture notes while a low roar arose out of the vast auditorium as the crowd settled into their seats (if they were lucky enough to get one). Now sixty-two years old, Doyle was a huge slab of a man, six feet two, fourteen stone (about two hundred pounds), with a shambling, bearlike gait and enormous hands. His intimidating physical presence was due partly to his size but also to his easy athleticism; as a young man, he had been naturally gifted at every sport he ever tried, excelling at cricket, football, boxing, golf, skiing, and even bowling. As a twenty-one-year-old third-year medical student, he'd spent six months as ship's surgeon on a whaling vessel sailing north to the Arctic, and he'd reveled in the physical exhilaration, the danger, and the manly challenge of the voyage. "I came of age at 80 degrees north latitude," he later wrote.

But now, four decades later, his drooping, walrus mustache had gone almost entirely gray, and his feet hurt. His broad shoulders were beginning to slump, and behind his steel-rimmed spectacles his blue-gray eyes were shadowed with sorrow. He was a genial man, greathearted, generous, scholarly, and kind. Some said he was a child at heart, and for that reason too credulous. He had been sweetly, devotedly in love with his second wife, Lady Jean, since the moment they met. Every spring, in celebration of their union, he would come in from the garden and hand her a single white snowdrop, the first pendulous white blossom of the receding snow. Lady Jean once told Doyle's old friend and antagonist Harry Houdini that her husband "never loses his temper and that his nature is at all times sunshiny and sweet." He hated putting on airs, despite a lifetime of astonishing accomplishment. Though he had been knighted in 1902 for a book he wrote in support of the British role in the Boer War, he refrained from signing his many books "Sir Arthur." Instead, he simply called himself "Conan Doyle."

By now, after lecture tours across the English-speaking world, Sir Arthur knew that in tonight's crowd there would likely be many who had recently been touched by the angel of death. In the decade just passed, the world had suffered not one but two tragedies of almost unimaginable proportion, and almost every family in America had an empty seat at the dinner table. In 1914, "the war to end all wars" had hurled the world into a murderous darkness. It was at that time the bloodiest conflict in human history, and also likely one of the most futile. In the first day of the Battle of the Somme, more than fifty-seven thousand British soldiers were wounded or killed on the western front. By the time the offensive was over, more than a million men lay dead in the bloody mud. Yet the offensive had succeeded in moving back the German trenches by only about six miles.

But even before the war came to a close, another grim and relentless enemy began stalking new victims. In March 1918, a soldier at Fort Riley, Kansas, reported to the infirmary complaining of a clanging headache and fever; within months, an extraordinarily virulent strain of the Spanish influenza had killed between twenty and forty million people worldwide—far more than the war. It came to be known as the Blue Death, because the sick turned blue before they died, horribly and very quickly. It seemed to strike the young and healthy first. There was no vaccine or medication to stop or even slow it. And the velocity of its spread was astonishing; it spread far more widely and with more ruthless efficiency than the Black Death of medieval Europe.

So it was perhaps not surprising that spiritualism had attracted millions of adherents by 1922. For so many, the scale of the carnage brought on by these two great calamities raised the ancient questions, and the ancient hopes. Did human personality survive death? If so, was there some way of breaching the veil that separated the living from the lost and making direct contact with loved ones? In this world of seemingly random and meaningless tragedy, was there some hope of comfort and consolation outside the confines of traditional religion?

"The subject of psychical research is one upon which I have thought more, and about which I have been slower to form an opinion, than upon any subject whatever," Doyle had written in a small book called *The New Revelation*. In fact, his interest in the subject went far back, to his days as a young doctor in his twenties, in the port city of Southsea, and now spanned forty years.

But being a reticent man, he wasn't telling the whole story. Part of his absolute conviction of the truth of human survival after death grew out of his own grief. Not long after the outbreak of the war, his beloved son Kingsley had given up his medical studies to join the Royal Army Medical Corps. Eventually, he was sent to the front, where the life span of a typical officer was a fortnight. In the Battle of the Somme, Kingsley took two bullets in the neck but narrowly survived, only to succumb later in a military hospital, a victim of the influenza pandemic. It was October 1918. He was twenty-five years old. For years afterward, Doyle could hardly speak his name without tears welling up in his eyes.

"In the presence of an agonized world," he would soon tell his audience, "hearing every day of the deaths of the flower of our race in the first promise of their unfulfilled youth, seeing around one the wives and mothers who had no clear conception whither their loved ones had gone to, I seemed suddenly to see that this subject with which I had so long dallied was not merely a study of a force outside the rules of science, but that it was really something tremendous, a breaking down of the walls between two worlds, a direct undeniable message from beyond."

This new revelation was, he said, "infinitely the most important thing in the history of the world."

Sir Arthur was well aware that his new convictions had made him the object of derision and befuddlement to throngs of people on both sides of the Atlantic. How, they wondered, had the creator of the world's most hyperrational sleuth, the master of dispassionate deductive reasoning, gone so soft in the head? How had this brilliant and accomplished man been hoodwinked by the claims of phony mediums, "spirit guides," and fairies?

Yet beneath the noisy hubbub of a mocking world, and despite all the many well-publicized fakes and frauds, Sir Arthur and his eminent colleagues had produced a long catalog of evidence that, as Sherlock Holmes once observed, "life is infinitely stranger than anything which the mind of man could invent."

But to explain how it all happened, the gaunt detective might observe, sucking pensively on his meerschaum pipe—to show what the spiritualists actually found—made for a long, long story, one that deserved to be told from the very beginning.

Conan Doyle's father, Charles, dreamy and disordered, spent his last years in a lunatic asylum, drawing pictures of fairies and elves. "His thoughts were always in the clouds," Doyle recalled.
COURTESY OF CHRIS BEETLES GALLERY, ST. JAMES'S, LONDON

CHAPTER ONE
Into the Unknown

Only a week from Shetland and here we are far into the icefields," wrote the twenty-year-old ship's surgeon in his logbook. "It has certainly been a splendid voyage. Beautiful day, wonderfully clear. Ice fields, snow white on very dark blue water as far as the eye can reach. We are ploughing through in grand style."

The date was March 20, 1880, a Saturday on the cusp of spring, and by now they were well north of the Arctic Circle. The ship, a four-hundred-ton, three-masted steam whaler, had sailed out of Peterhead, Scotland, on February 28. Just forty-five feet long, it somehow had room enough for a crew of fifty-six and a hundred tons of whale oil—that is, if all went as planned during its six months in frigid waters. But there was no guarantee of commercial success, or for that matter of survival. The voyage, involving the harpooning of fifty-ton whales in open boats, in freezing Arctic waters, was heart-stoppingly perilous. All the uncertainties of this enterprise were reflected in the ship's name: the S.S. *Hope*.

The young man looking out from the deck that day was not a seasoned seaman or even a certified doctor. He was, in fact, only a third-year medical student at Edinburgh University. Barely a week before the *Hope* was to set sail, a fellow student named Currie, who had the job, found that he could not go. So he approached the big, athletic kid in class—the Arthur with two last names: Conan (the surname of his granduncle and godfather, an editor in Paris) and Doyle. The big kid made up his mind on the spot to exchange the dismal grind of medical school for a wild adventure at sea, confessing later in his autobiography that at that age he was "wild, full-blooded, and a trifle reckless."

It turned out to be a transformative experience for him, as a writer and as a man. What possessed him to interrupt his life and take a long, uncomfortable, dangerous journey? Just this: Arthur Conan Doyle could not resist an adventure. And he never would.

IN THE coming days, Conan Doyle's Arctic adventure would get kicked up a notch. April 3 was the start of seal-hunting season, when the crews of whaling ships go scrambling out onto the ice in order to kill seals, skin them in place, and drag their hundred-pound skins back to the ship. Yes, it was "bloody work," as he confessed in the log. And perilous: Those ice fields were not the terra firma they appeared to be. "The ice is not a solid sheet, but made up of thousands of pieces of all sizes floating close to each other," he wrote. "Now in a swell those pieces alternately separate and come together with irresistible force. If a poor fellow slips in between two pieces as is easily done, he runs a good chance of being cut in two." And if he isn't cut in two, he nonetheless has about ten minutes to get out of the water before exhaustion gives way to unconsciousness and death.

For the next several weeks, they cruised roughly northward, hunting for seals and finding slim pickings as they pressed on toward the whale hunting grounds in the far north. By May 22, the *Hope* was at 80 degrees north latitude, close to the limits of Arctic exploration of the time; it was in bleak, gale-churned waters between the top of Greenland and Spitsbergen, its "great line of huge black perpendicular crags running up to several thousand feet . . . a horrible looking place," he noted in the log.

It was up there, at the top of the world, that he turned twenty-one. "I come of age today," he wrote. "Rather a funny sort of place to do it in, only 600 miles or so from the North Pole." They couldn't get much closer—the northern barrier, the edge of the polar ice cap, barred the way. In 1880, no human being had seen the North Pole. It was uncharted territory, a big blank spot on the maps. For all anyone knew, Santa Claus *did* live there.

In June, the *Hope* turned and sailed southward along the coast of Greenland's ice sheet. There Conan Doyle got his first sighting of narwhals, also known as sea unicorns for their tusks, which can grow to ten feet. One calm evening the sea was covered with them, "great brutes 15 & 16 feet long," he recorded. "You hear their peculiar 'Sumph!' in every direction. I saw one pass like a great white flickering ghost beneath the keel." But what they wanted most was the sighting of whales, and that they got on June 4.

It wasn't until June 26, however, that they caught their first whale. On July 8, they caught a second, bigger specimen, a huge "finner" whale, yielding twelve tons of oil. "It is worth quite £1,000 and has secured our voyage from being a failure," Doyle wrote.

On Monday, August 9, 1880, the *Hope* was bound for home. "A beautiful clear day with a blue sky and a bright sun," Conan Doyle noted in the ship's log. "Wind from the NE, a good strong breeze before which we are flying homeward with all sail set, and the bright green waves hissing and foaming from her bows . . . All hands on the lookout for land."

ARTHUR CONAN Doyle had grown up in a kind of genteel poverty in Edinburgh, Scotland, one of ten children, whose family and lineage were of sturdy Celtic-Catholic stock. In the cul de sac where the family lived in a modest tenement, there was a fierce feud between two groups of small neighborhood boys. Ultimately, each group put up a "champion"—the strapping Arthur being chosen as the champion of the poorer lads—and he went out to fight the champion pugilist of the other team in a bitter battle of many rounds, ending in a bloody draw.

It was prophetic, in a way. Arthur Conan Doyle would be a fighter for the rest of his life.

From a very early age, he excelled at two things. One was any sport, and the other was storytelling. It was from his mother, whom he always affectionately called "The Ma'am," that he learned his love of a good yarn. He once told Bram Stoker:

> My real love for letters, my instinct for storytelling, springs, I believe, from my mother, who is of Anglo-Celtic stock, with the glamour and romance of the Celt very strongly marked. . . . In my early childhood, as far back as I can remember anything at all, the vivid stories which she would tell me stand out so clearly that they obscure the real facts of my life. It is not only that she was—is still—a wonderful storyteller, but she had, I remember, an art of sinking her voice to a horror-stricken whisper when she came to a crisis in her narrative, which makes me gooseflesh when I think of it.

His mother's stories came down to him through the misty tangles of the Celtic past and the fog-shrouded glens of northern Scotland and Ireland, in which, in ancient times, people would gather around the fire to retell the tales that kept the people alive. These gatherings, or ceilidh, told of a tribal history of great warriors and great battles, loves won and lost, but also of a dreamlike, surrealistic world in which gnomes, elves, and fairies flitted through the glens in the half-light of dawn or twilight. Sometimes—for better or worse—they would even intersect with the affairs of men. It was an in-between world that, in the Gaelic imagination, was as real as daylight, perhaps even more vivid than "the real facts of my life." It is a world considered real in some parts of rural Scotland and Ireland to this day.

It was also a world that was to be vividly portrayed in the art of many of Conan Doyle's relatives, who shared a gift for imaginative illustration. His grandfather John Doyle developed a reputation as a sharp political satirist and caricaturist, producing the series *Political Sketches* for a London publisher. John's oldest son, James—Conan Doyle's uncle—produced an illustrated work called *A Chronicle of England*.

But it was John's second son, Richard, known as Dicky Doyle, who became the most famous artist of the clan. Dicky Doyle famously designed one of the very first covers of *Punch,* the renowned British satirical magazine. He mastered the art of elaborately decorative lettering, which seemed to hark back to the illuminated manuscripts of the early Celtic monks. But it was his fantastical illustrated books depicting the lives of elves, fairies, and woodland life-forms the Theosophists called "elementals"—illustrations for Grimm's "Fairy Ring," "The King of the Golden River," and *In Fairyland*—that seemed to create a netherworld so real it practically pranced off the page. Many years later, when Conan Doyle became embroiled in the "Cottingley Fairies" case—in which two young girls claimed to have photographed fairies beside a brook in rural England—some of Doyle's defenders remembered the vivid fairylands depicted by his uncle and the ancient Celtic storytelling traditions from which they came. In a deep Scots-Irish way, it all made sense, and Conan Doyle, despite all evidence to the contrary, was to persist in his belief in fairies until his dying day.

But it was Conan Doyle's own father, Charles, who had the most profound influence on the boy's upbringing. As a young man, Charles had been sent to Edinburgh to take a job as an assistant surveyor in the Scottish Office of Works, doing architectural drawings. Among other things, he designed a fountain at Holyrood Palace in Edinburgh and windows at Glasgow Cathedral. In truth, it was a fairly low-level civil service job that produced a pitifully small paycheck. Charles supplemented his small income by selling his eccentric drawings and watercolors, though many of them he simply gave away. In 1855, Charles married Mary Foley, his landlady's daughter, and they went on to have ten children, of whom seven survived into adulthood.

In his memoirs, Doyle remembered his childhood wistfully: "We lived in the hardy and bracing atmosphere of poverty and we each in turn did our best to help those who were younger than ourselves. My noble sister Annette, who died just as the sunshine of better days came into our lives, went out very early as a governess to Portugal and sent all her salary home. Our younger sisters, Lottie and Connie, both did the same thing; and I helped as I could. But it was still my dear mother who bore the long, sordid strain."

Though the Doyles lived in shabby circumstances, it was a family proud of its illustrious lineage; his mother was distantly related to Sir Walter Scott, and another relative, Sir Denis Pack, had commanded the Scottish forces at Waterloo. Doyle's uncle James had spent thirteen years working on a massive genealogy called *The Official Baronage of England*. His uncle Conan had traced his lineage back to the dukes of Brittany.

"From his tenderest years," Doyle's son Adrian later wrote of his father's childhood, he was surrounded by "the chivalric sciences of the fifteenth century in the bosom of a family to whom pride of lineage was of infinitely greater importance than the discomforts of comparative poverty that had come to surround them." It was one's bloodlines, one's heritage, and one's quest for chivalric greatness—in effect, one's family stories—that lifted a man's head high, even if "home" was a dreary tenement block in Edinburgh.

As the years went by, Doyle's father seemed to grow increasingly distant, adrift in his own thoughts. He was a gentle, imaginative soul who seemed completely overwhelmed by the burdens of raising a large family on next to nothing. But the world was not terribly interested in his artistic gifts or his gift for verbal whimsy. One early biographer, John Dickson Carr, wrote that "to his family he was becoming a dreamy, long-bearded stranger, with exquisite manners and an unbrushed top hat. Each day he trudged the long walk from home to his office at Holyrood Palace and back again to pat the children's heads absentmindedly, as he might have stroked his pet cats."

In his memoirs, Conan Doyle said very little about his father, though what he did say is revealing. "He had a charm of manner and courtesy of bearing which I have seldom seen equaled. His wit was quick and playful. He possessed, also, a remarkable delicacy of mind . . . [but] he was unworldly and impractical and his family suffered for it. . . . My father, I fear, was of little help to [my mother], for his thoughts were always in the clouds and he had no appreciation of the realities of life."

Eventually, Charles seemed to slip away completely, an empty top hat floating down the street. In 1885, when he was in his mid-fifties, he was admitted to a nursing home called Fordoun House, which specialized in alcoholism, then to a series of three institutions known at the time as lunatic asylums. In 1893, he died at the Crichton Royal Institution, in Dumfries, with the official cause of death listed as "epilepsy of many years' standing." But he wasn't an epileptic, nor was he insane. He was an improvident and unworldly soul who was also an alcoholic that occasionally became violent. In the Victorian era, nobody knew what to do with a person like that.

A more revealing, more sympathetic story about the fate of Charles Doyle emerged years after his death, in a sketchbook he had kept in the lunatic asylum, which had been bought at a yard sale at the country house Conan Doyle once owned.

The picture that emerges out of this little book is of a man who is charmingly odd and ineffably sad. It's a kind of carnival of whimsy, elegance, and death, filled with make-believe gnomes and fairies cavorting around real flowers, with skeletons and angels seeming to lure Charles Doyle himself—always depicted as a nattily dressed Victorian gentleman with a frock coat and a long beard—into the waiting arms of death. In one drawing, he is shown shaking hands with the grim reaper with one hand and an angel with the other. In another, picnickers in the Scottish Highlands have individual angels hovering over their heads. Charles Doyle was deathly afraid of birds, and the book is filled with them, all absolutely enormous. One early biographer, the Reverend John Lamond, observed some of Charles's pictures hanging in his son's house and noted that "they are more weird than anything Blake ever produced."

In many ways, these themes were through lines that carried on into Conan Doyle's later work, which repeatedly returned to the supernatural, the macabre, the terrifying, and the occult. And not unlike his father's sketchbook, there sometimes seemed to be nothing separating the "real" from the otherworldly.

SOMEHOW, MARY "The Ma'am" Doyle (with the help of a wealthy relative) managed to scrape together the money to send young Arthur to a Jesuit preparatory school, Hodder, when he was nine years old. He spent two mostly happy years there and then went on to Stonyhurst College, where he got a rigorous British education, complete with rapped knuckles, spartan accommodations, and a liberal helping of the classics. In school, young Arthur quickly gained a reputation for his skill at cricket and storytelling. He loved to regale his classmates with fantastical tales, borrowing his mother's gifts for the deftly drawn character and the pretzel-like plot. He later remembered how, "with an audience of little boys squatting on the floor, with their chins on their hands, I have talked myself husky over the misfortunes of my heroes. . . . I was bribed with pastry to continue these efforts, . . . which shows that I was born to be a member of the Authors' Society."

But Stonyhurst had a darker side, one that would later lead to a spiritual longing for escape from the airless Roman Catholicism into which he was born. "Nothing can exceed the uncompromising bigotry of the Jesuit theology," he later remembered in his memoirs. "I remember that when, as a grown lad, I heard Father Murphy, a great fierce Irish priest, declare that there was sure damnation for every one outside the Church, I looked upon him with horror, and to that moment I trace the first rift which has grown into such a chasm between me and those who were my guides."

In this period of spiritual disenchantment and longing, Doyle read voraciously—as he did for the rest of his life, like a man dying of thirst in the desert—John Stuart Mill, Charles Darwin, Thomas Henry Huxley, John Tyndall, Herbert Spencer, and every other major thinker of the day.

Increasingly, the solace offered by the church seemed empty. He could see the good things the church had to offer—"its unbroken and solemn ritual, the beauty and truth of many of its observances, its poetical appeal to the emotions." At the same time, there was much about it that he found "vile and detestable. If some second reformation inside the Church were to preserve the one and destroy the other, it might still make a great agent for change in the world. It is hardly likely to be so, so long as it is the unresisting servant of the little Junta of prelates in Italy."

Doyle was not alone in his growing disenchantment with the deadness, the self-aggrandizing, self-appointed hierarchy that ran the shop, and the scorn for other religions that seemed to characterize the Catholic Church. In fact, scholars have observed that one of the driving forces behind the emergence of the new "religion" called spiritualism in the Victorian and Edwardian eras was loss of faith in organized religion. As in so many other ways, Arthur Conan Doyle's life became a mirror of the grand events unfolding across the Western world during his lifetime.

At the same time, Doyle's doubts "never for an instant degenerated into atheism, for I had a very keen perception of the wonderful poise of the universe and the tremendous power of conception and sustenance which it implied." He was, more than anything else, a man devoted to seeking truth—"reverent in all my doubts"—continuously wondering about the meaning of the universe and man's place in it.

By the time he finished at Stonyhurst, and spent a year studying in Germany, Doyle had decided to become a doctor, at least partly to contribute to his family's shaky finances. He applied for and won a "bursary," or Scottish scholarship, to help pay for the four-year program, but a clerical error prevented him from getting any money at all. So he soldiered on, one more impoverished medical student in the cold, high-ceilinged lecture halls of Edinburgh University.

It was while he was still a twenty-year-old third-year medical student that Doyle published his first medical paper, a letter to the *British Medical Journal,* or *BMJ,* published on September 20, 1879. It was titled "Gelsemium as a Poison," and in retrospect it underscores Doyle's character—a budding man of science, a medical detective, and "a wild, full-blooded, and a trifle reckless" adventurer. He explained to the readers of the *BMJ* that due to neuralgia (nerve pain) he had been taking a tincture of gelseminum. (Gelseminum is made from a genus of yellow-flowering vines native to Asia and the southeastern United States, including

Carolina jasmine and so-called heartbreak grass. It contains an alkaloid poison similar to strychnine.)

Because a little bit seemed to help, Doyle "determined to ascertain how far one might go in taking the drug, and what the primary symptoms of an overdose might be." He prepared a fresh tincture and, over the next several days, dispassionately recorded what happened. At low doses, he experienced no effect, but at 90 minims (drops) he experienced extreme "giddiness," at 120 he developed vision problems, a mild paralysis, and a "great depression," which seemed to lessen at 150, though now he noted headaches and diarrhea. He pushed himself to 200, at which point the diarrhea became debilitating, his pulse weakened, and he quit. He calmly concluded, "I feel convinced that I could have taken as much as half an ounce of tincture, had it not been for the extreme diarrhea it brought on. Believe me, yours sincerely, A.C.D."

Once again, he was pushing things to the brink.

Of all Doyle's professors in medical school, there was one—a surgeon at the Royal Infirmary of Edinburgh named Dr. Joseph Bell—who was to leave a lasting impression and in fact change Doyle's life forever. Joe Bell was "thin, wiry, dark, with a high-nosed acute face, penetrating gray eyes, angular shoulders, and a jerky way of walking. His voice was high and discordant," Doyle remembered. But Bell, despite his somewhat eccentric manner, had one extraordinary ability. He could diagnose patients—and discern much else about them—simply through keen observation. Because Doyle had been chosen to be Bell's personal clerk, checking in patients as they came into the examining room to see him, he got to witness Bell's special gifts firsthand. In one typical case, recalled in Doyle's 1924 memoirs, *Memories and Adventures,* he ushered in a young man to see Bell (who had never laid eyes on the man before).

"Well, my man, you've served in the army," Bell announced without hesitation.

"Aye, sir."

"Not long discharged?"

"No, sir."

"A Highland regiment?"

"Aye, sir."

"A non-com officer."

"Aye, sir."

"Stationed at Barbados?"

"Aye, sir."

Then Bell proceeded to explain his method to the students gathered around him. The man was respectful but did not remove his hat. In the army, that's the custom, but he would have learned civilian ways, and taken off his hat, if he had been discharged for quite some time. He had an air of authority and was obviously Scottish. And as to his station in Barbados, his complaint was elephantiasis, which occurs in the West Indies, not Britain.

To Arthur Doyle, a keen student of human behavior, a born storyteller, and a young man seeking some direction in life, Dr. Joseph Bell was to become a life-changing figure indeed.

NOW, STANDING on the foredeck of the homebound steam whaler *Hope,* scanning the far horizon for land, Arthur Conan Doyle had no way of knowing what an extraordinary life lay before him. The whaling trip had been transformative for him. "I went on board the whaler a big, straggling youth," he wrote, but "I came off it a powerful, well-grown man." Now all he knew for sure was that filling his lungs with the last of that "dry, crisp, exhilarating air," he felt invigorated by it all. "I just never knew before what it was to be thoroughly healthy," he recalled later. "I just feel as if I could go anywhere [or] do anything." He would never forget "the peculiar otherworld feeling of the place. . . . You stand on the very brink of the unknown."

But what would come next?

He'd recently published his first short story, "The Mystery of Sasassa Valley," and was soon to publish another, "The Captain of the 'Pole-Star,'" using his experience on the whaling ship as grist for the mill. It was a fine short story, with a spine-tingling ending, and reminiscent of Edgar Allan Poe, the American writer he admired. In the story, a ship's captain seems to go mad and runs off across the ice fields pursuing the ghost of his true love. He's later found frozen to death. He had a smile on his face, "and his hands were still outstretched as though grasping at the strange visitor which had summoned him away into the dim world that lies beyond the grave."

"The Captain of the 'Pole-Star'" was the perfect story for a struggling young writer; it fit right in with a popular genre of his age. But as much as Victorians were interested in ghost stories, they were also fascinated by ghosts—ever since that night when two girls in America decided to start a conversation with "the dim world that lies beyond the grave."

The spiritualist movement began in upstate New York in 1848, when Kate and Maggie Fox claimed to communicate with the spirit of a murdered peddler by means of "rapping" sounds.
COURTESY OF MISSOURI HISTORY MUSEUM

CHAPTER TWO
"Mister Splitfoot, Do as I Do!"

It was just after dark on a chill, blustery, early spring day, with snow still lingering on the ground in the tiny hamlet of Hydesville in upstate New York—a Friday, March 31, 1848, to be exact. In this peaceable rural community, with its gentle rhythms of seedtime and harvest, and weekly attendance at Sunday services, this day seemed much like any other. But seventy-five years later, Arthur Conan Doyle was to describe it as "in truth the greatest date in human history since the great revelation of two thousand years ago." And that's because a twelve-year-old girl had the fearlessness to talk back to a ghost.

The setting could hardly have been more humble: a small wooden house on a dusty country crossroads in a town consisting of a schoolhouse, a Methodist church, and a blacksmith shop. Hydesville (so tiny it no longer exists) lay east of Rochester, then a bustling burg of about thirty-five thousand on the Erie Canal, and less than fifteen miles from the shore of chilly Lake Ontario to the north. In December 1847, a reformed alcoholic and staunch Methodist named John Fox had moved in, along with his wife, Margaret, and two youngest daughters, fourteen-year-old Margaretta (Maggie), and Kate, aged twelve. The little house was to serve as the family's temporary rental quarters while they built something more permanent on his son's farm nearby. Mr. Fox, who appears in an old engraving with glaring, protuberant eyes and what appears to be a permanent scowl, had moved from Rochester to take a job as the local blacksmith.

Not long after the family moved into the Hydesville house, they began to hear odd bumps and thumps and rustlings in the house, at first only at night. The prosaic Mr. Fox ascribed the sounds to rats or mice in the walls. But it was odd: The sounds were not really like that at all. Sometimes they sounded like furniture moving. Sometimes they were distinct knocks or raps. Sometimes the sounds seemed to come from the bedroom, sometimes from the cellar. At other times, Mrs. Fox later reported in a sworn statement, the sound was "not very loud, yet it produced a jar of the bedsteads and chairs that could be felt by placing our hands on the chairs, or while we were in bed."

Mr. Fox, seeking another down-to-earth explanation, next tried to persuade Mrs. Fox that the sounds might be coming from the hammering of a nearby shoemaker. One problem with that explanation was that the shoemaker said he never mended shoes at night. But the raps persisted, and one night Mr. and Mrs. Fox got up in their nightclothes to prowl around the house with a lit candle, searching every nook and cranny for their source. They couldn't find anything. Then there came a rap at the front door. Mr. Fox opened the door. There was no one there. He closed the door, waited until there was another rap, and flung open the door a second time. There was nothing there but the night air.

As February turned to March, the disturbances increased. Footsteps echoed through the house after everyone was in bed. Once something heavy came to lie on the legs of the girls in their bed. Chairs were moved. Then the dining table. Then, one night, Kate felt something cold on her face. By late March, the two girls had grown so alarmed that their beds were moved into their parents' ground-floor bedroom to sleep.

"On March 30th we were disturbed all night," Mrs. Fox later reported. "The noises were heard in all parts of the house. . . . We heard footsteps in the pantry, and walking down-stairs; we could not rest, and I then concluded that the house must be haunted by some unhappy, restless spirit."

The following day, Friday, March 31, the Foxes' eldest son, David, who had a farm about three miles away, dropped by his parents' house. When his mother told him about the mysterious goings-on, he smiled. "I advise you not to say a word to the neighbors about it," David told her. "When you find it out, it will be one of the simplest things in the world."

That night, the family decided to go to bed early, almost before dark, because they were all so exhausted from lack of sleep. "I had been so broken of my rest I was almost sick," Mrs. Fox recalled. But almost as soon as the family settled into bed, the knocking sounds commenced. The girls cried out, "Here they are again!"

It was a windy night, and Mr. Fox, climbing out of bed, went to check the window sashes to see if it was simply the wind rattling the windows. Kate noticed that each time her father shook a window sash, the sounds seemed to reply. Then she turned to where the noise was, snapped her fingers, and called out the words that would later ring down through the history of spiritualism in America: "Here, Mister Splitfoot, do as I do!" ("Splitfoot" was a common term for the devil.)

She snapped her fingers twice. And two raps immediately followed, apparently out of thin air.

Then Maggie chimed in.

"Now do this just as I do; count one, two, three, four," clapping her hands with each count. Four raps immediately followed.

Kate, still feeling playful, silently brought her thumb and forefinger together in the air. As many times as she did that, the raps responded. "Look, Mother," she said. *It can see as well as hear!*

Then Mrs. Fox, though shaken, asked "the noise" to count to ten. Ten raps followed.

"How old is my daughter Margaret?" Fourteen raps followed.

"How old is Kate?" Twelve raps.

"I then asked it if it was a human being that was making the noise? And, if it was, to manifest it by the same noise," continued Mrs. Fox's sworn statement (made on April 11, 1848, twelve days after the "rappings" became a conversation). "There was no noise. I then asked if it was a spirit? and if it was, to manifest it by two sounds. I heard two sounds as soon as the words were spoken. I then asked, if it was an injured spirit? to give me the sound, and I heard the rapping distinctly. . . . If the person was living that injured it? and got the same answer."

"Oh, Mother, I know what it is," Kate broke in. "Tomorrow is April Fool Day, and somebody is trying to fool us!"

But Mrs. Fox persisted in conducting her remarkable interrogation, apparently across the veil of death, with an intelligent spirit that went on to explain (by means of rapped answers to questions) that he had been a thirty-one-year-old peddler, with a family of five children, who had been murdered in the house and later buried in the basement. Finally, Mrs. Fox asked the purveyor of the sounds, whoever or whatever it might be, "Will the noise continue if I call in some of the neighbors, that they may hear it too?"

The raps responded in the affirmative.

At that, Mr. Fox snatched on some clothes and went to fetch the next-door neighbor, Mrs. Redfield. She was laughing when she walked into the house, thinking she'd have a good chuckle over some prank engineered by the girls. But "when she came, she saw that we were all amazed like, and that there was something in it," Mrs. Fox recalled.

"How old is Mrs. Redfield?" Mrs. Fox asked, and the correct number of raps immediately followed.

"How many children does Mrs. Redfield have?" Mrs. Fox asked.

Four raps followed.

Suddenly Mrs. Redfield burst into tears. Her neighbors knew only her three living children. But there had been a fourth child, Mary, who died as an infant—a loss that she still felt keenly. Mrs. Redfield rushed from the house, "very much agitated," as a neighbor later recalled, and went to get her husband, who came into the house and listened as, in response to Mrs. Fox's questions, it rapped out his age, as well as the answers to other queries, all of them correct.

Then Mr. Redfield went to get Mr. and Mrs. William Duesler, who had once lived in the house, as well as Mr. and Mrs. Hyde, Mr. and Mrs. Jewell, and a few other neighbors, who now crowded into the tiny, candlelit bedroom.

Seventy-eight years later, in *The History of Spiritualism,* Arthur Conan Doyle imagined this scene: "That rude room, with its earnest, expectant, half-clad occupants with eager upturned faces, its circle of candlelight, and its heavy shadows lurking in the corners, might well be made the subject of a great historical painting."

By now, the news of these remarkable events had begun to spread like a virus through the tiny town. People up late fishing in the Ganargua River came crowding into the house, and still more, until there was barely enough room to move. And still the "spirit" responded to questions by rapping out answers.

Eventually, the house became so crowded, and so filled with an atmosphere of expectant awe and excitement, that Mrs. Fox took the girls and left the premises. Mrs. Fox slept that night at Mrs. Redfield's house, and the girls spent the night with other neighbors. Only Mr. Fox spent the night in the house, but the rappings continued all night long. Years later, when skeptics began to claim that it was the girls themselves who had produced what came to be known as "the Rochester rappings," the eminent naturalist Alfred Russel Wallace observed that "on the night of March 31st, 1848, Mrs. Fox and the children *left the house,* Mr. Fox only remaining, and . . . during all night and the following night, in presence of a continual influx of neighbors *the 'raps' continued exactly the same as when the two girls were present.* This crucial fact is to be found in all the early records."

Mr. Duesler, bold and persistent, now took over the interrogation, probing for answers as the hushed crowd grew larger and more incredulous. Some were so frightened that they did not want to venture into the bedroom, but stood outside, listening, in the adjoining room. Though Mr. Duesler, like Mrs. Redfield, at first thought the whole business was "nonsense, and that it could be easily accounted for," now he began asking a series of increasingly specific questions. By means of the rapped responses, Duesler elicited the same story: that the "spirit" claimed to have been murdered in the bedroom about five years earlier, by someone who lived in the house, at around midnight on a Tuesday night; that its throat had been cut with a butcher knife; that it was later buried in the dirt-floored basement; and that the motive had been a robbery of five hundred dollars. In response to a question, it affirmed that a young woman named Lucretia Pulver (known to the community) had worked there at the time of the murder but that she was gone when the crime took place.

Then Mr. Duesler asked Charles Redfield to go down the narrow stairway into the cellar and stand in various places while Duesler asked the "spirit" if that was the correct spot where the body had been buried. In this fashion, after various questions went unanswered, the "spirit" rapped when Mr. Redfield stood in a certain spot, near the center of the basement floor.

A crowd of people stayed in the house all that night, so hopped-up they couldn't sleep. But by morning's light, the rapping sounds had ceased, and the house remained silent all day. Even so, as that Saturday passed and word spread to surrounding farms and villages, more than three hundred people massed in the house and surrounding yard. And at nightfall, like a teasingly delaying prima donna, the "rapping" commenced again. By then, the townspeople had appointed a committee to begin investigating the sounds. And that night a group of men descended into the dark basement, with candles, and began digging up the dirt floor in the spot the "spirit" had indicated. But it had been an unusually wet spring, and the river ran nearby; before they got three feet down, the hole began filling with water, so they had to give up.

"On Sunday morning, the second of April, the noise commenced again, and was heard throughout the day by all who came there," Mrs. Fox's sworn statement went on. "I am not a believer in haunted houses or supernatural experiences. I am very sorry there has been so much excitement about it. It has been a great deal of trouble to us. It was our misfortune to live here at this time; but I am willing and anxious that the truth should be known, and that a true statement should be made."

"Trouble," to say the least. Her hair had turned white within a week.

Mr. Fox, in his sworn statement, added his own bewilderment to that of his wife: "I do not know of any way to account for these noises, as being caused by natural means. We have searched in every nook and corner in and about the house, at different times, to ascertain, if possible, whether anything or anybody was secreted there, that could make the noise, and have never been able to find anything that explained the mystery. It has caused us a great deal of trouble and anxiety. Hundreds have visited the house, so it is impossible to attend to our daily occupations." He concluded that if evidence someday indicates that a body was indeed buried beneath the cellar, "I shall have no doubt but what this is a supernatural appearance."

Mr. Fox, his wife, and his daughters were dead by the time the crucial evidence came to light half a century later. In November 1904, children playing in the basement of the local "Spook House" (as it came to be known) discovered that the east wall of the cellar had caved in and it was a false wall. Behind it stood the true outer foundation wall of the house. Between the two walls lay hidden the skeleton of a man and his tin peddler's pack.

WITHIN DAYS after the rappings began in the house in Hydesville, word of these remarkable events had spread throughout the region. Among the curious was an attorney named E. E. Lewis, who lived in the nearby town of Canandaigua. By April 11, Lewis had arrived in Hydesville and began taking sworn depositions from every adult involved in the incident, including Mr. and Mrs. Fox, the Redfields, William Duesler, and other neighbors. By late April, Lewis had printed a pamphlet about his investigation, called *A Report of the Mysterious Noises Heard in the House of Mr. John D. Fox, in Hydesville, Arcadia, Wayne County*. It offered a fifty-dollar reward to anyone who could prove that the noises were "the work of any human being."

Lewis also sought out and interviewed Lucretia Pulver, the young woman who had lived in the Hydesville house while working for a previous tenant, a Mr. and Mrs. John Bell. Lucretia Pulver told this story: Five years earlier, in 1843, she had boarded for three months with the Bells, working as a household servant in exchange for room and board. One afternoon, a peddler arrived and was invited to stay overnight (a common practice at the time). He was a man in his early thirties, dressed in a black frock coat, with gray vest and trousers. When he opened up his pack on the kitchen table, Mrs. Bell and Lucretia saw his wondrous wares—fancy dress goods, laces and braids, thread, scissors and thimbles, and sparkling small trinkets.

Afterward, Mrs. Bell told Lucretia to go home to her parents' house. But Lucretia was so taken by some of the peddler's goods she made him promise to stop by her parents' house later, on his way out of town the next morning. But the peddler never appeared, and when she'd returned to the Bells' house three days later, the peddler was gone. Lucretia told Lewis that some time later, she'd gone down into the basement to fetch something and was alarmed to find herself sinking up to her knees in loose dirt. She let out a shriek of surprise. When she came back upstairs, Mrs. Bell "laughed at me for being frightened, and said it was only where the rats had been at work in the ground." Later, she testified in her statement, she had seen John Bell dragging heavy cartloads of dirt into the basement, allegedly to cover the rat holes. A couple of days later, the Bells abruptly announced that they were going away for a few days, but not before Mrs. Bell had presented Lucretia with a shiny new thimble, supposedly purchased for fifty cents from the peddler.

Then the noises began. At night, the girl began to waken to strange sounds. The Bells' dog would "sit under the bedroom window and howl all night long," she testified. "I did not know what to think of the noises I have heard."

Because Lucretia's statement appeared to point an accusatory finger at John Bell, the libel-wary attorney Lewis omitted Bell's name from his pamphlet. But eventually word got back to Bell, who had moved away to a different part of the county. John Bell produced a certificate of good character, signed by forty-four people, to the effect that they "believed him to be a man of upright and honest life" and "incapable of committing the crime of which he was suspected."

Lewis also interviewed the Weekmans, who had lived in the house prior to the Fox family. Michael Weekman reported hearing a rap at the front door one night, but when he opened the door, there was no one there. A short while later, he heard the knocking again. But when he closed the door, he held on to the latch for a minute or so; then, when the rapping started again, he could feel a faint jarring of the door. But once again, when he flung open the door, no one was there. He walked around the house in the dark but could find nothing amiss.

A nineteen-year-old housekeeper named Jane Lape, who lived with the Weekmans for a time, reported an even creepier experience. "One day about two o'clock, P.M., while I was doing my work in the kitchen, I saw a man in the bedroom adjoining the kitchen. I was much frightened. I had been in the kitchen some time, at work, and knew no one had gone into that room. . . . The man stood facing me when I saw him. He did not speak. . . . He had on gray pants, black frock-coat, and black cap. . . . I knew of no person in that vicinity who wore a similar dress. . . . I was very much frightened, and left the room, and when I returned with Mrs. Weekman there was no one there. She thought it was some one who had been trying to frighten me; but we were never able to ascertain who or what it was."

As it happened, Lewis's printer was in Rochester; he was a friend of someone who knew Maggie and Kate's much older sister, Leah. (Leah had been twice widowed already; she made a living as a piano teacher.) Leah had not heard anything about the goings-on at her parents' house until the printer showed up at her door and unveiled the proof sheets of his pamphlet *A Report of the Mysterious Noises*. Leah read them and cried. Within hours, she and her daughter Lizzie and two friends were on an Erie Canal packet boat to Hydesville.

When she arrived at her parents' forlorn little saltbox on the corner, she was alarmed to find the house empty, the front door locked, the windows shuttered. She ordered the driver to take her to her brother David's farm, where she found the frightened family. Her mother sat in one of the front rooms, grimly clutching her Bible. She seemed, Leah later wrote, "completely broken down by the recent events . . . her sighs and tears were heart-rending. . . . She wished we all could die."

After a few days at David's house, Leah and her daughter Lizzie took Kate with them to Rochester to escape the growing clamor, excitement, fear, suspicion, ridicule, and rage caused by the happenings in the Hydesville house.

But within a matter of hours, something strange happened at the house in Rochester.

The rappings began again.

LEAH, LIZZIE, and Kate arrived in Rochester about 5:00 p.m. on a warm spring afternoon. Here, at Leah's pleasant rented home on Mechanic's Square, "the sun shone brightly, and the birds sang sweetly in the trees," Leah recalled in her 1885 memoir, *The Missing Link in Modern Spiritualism.* "Roses were just out, and all nature was in her loveliest hues."

Leah sat down on a sofa to savor the serenity and stillness of home. The girls had wandered out into the sunny garden. Unpacking could wait until later. Hopefully, she could simply return to quietly giving piano lessons as she had been before all this happened. Then "all at once came a dreadful sound, as if a pail of bonnyclabber had been poured from the ceiling and fallen upon the floor." (Bonnyclabber, or spoiled, curdled milk, made a glopping sound not unlike thick, coagulating blood.) The noise was repeated three times. "Oh, that dreadful sound!" Leah cried. *"What is it? What is it?"* At the same time, there was a tremendous crash, which jarred the windows and the whole house, "as if a heavy piece of artillery had been discharged in the immediate vicinity."

The noises had followed them to Rochester!

This wasn't about one haunted farmhouse anymore—or the supposed tricks of two sisters, now miles apart. As Conan Doyle noted in his *History,* "The whole course of the movement had now widened and taken a more important turn."

That was no comfort to Leah and the girls, who spent a sleepless, terror-stricken night. No sooner had Leah blown out the candle than Lizzie screamed: A cold hand had passed over her face, and another crept down her back. A box of matches was shaken in their faces. The Bible flew out from under Leah's pillow, "where I had placed it," Leah recalled, "supposing that the sacred volume would be respected." The noises lasted most of the night, and "we gave up in despair to our fate, whatever that might be."

Their fate was more uproar, night after night.

Leah concluded that her house was now haunted, just as the house in Hydesville had been, and she decided to move out as soon as she could find another place to rent. Fortunately, she found one in a day or two—a small, brand-new house on Prospect Street. But "I was particular to tell the agent that I wanted a house in which no crime was committed. . . . The agent smiled and said he 'thought that I would have no difficulty on that account.'"

Leah, Lizzie, and Kate moved in, and for the first night all was well. Leah had by now written to her mother, who had remained with her brother, David, at his farm in Arcadia, to tell her about the eerie occurrences. The next day her worried mother, with Maggie in tow, arrived in Rochester. Leah was pleased to tell her that they'd all slept well the night before in the new house.

But that night, at around midnight, everyone woke up to heavy footsteps thumping up the stairs. Then they heard the sounds of "shuffling, giggling and whispering, as if [the spirits] were enjoying themselves at some surprise they were about to give us." Moments later, according to Leah's account, their beds were lifted up almost to the ceiling and allowed to drop with a crash. Afterward, they felt themselves being patted with little hands. Finally, things quieted down, and they eventually fell asleep and slept until late the following morning. But when they woke, with sunlight flooding in the eastern windows, Mrs. Fox was distraught.

"Can it be possible?" she exclaimed. "Is it really true? How can we live and endure it?"

On that Sunday night, just before bed, there was a "tremendous knocking on the roof." Leah begged for the "spirits" to stop, to leave them alone. Then Kate felt a slap across her face. All of them saw "what seemed to be the form of a large man, lying across the foot of our bed, breathing irregularly and apparently in great distress." Just then Kate got another sharp slap across the face and sprawled across the bed, having been knocked unconscious. A mirror held close to Kate's mouth could detect no breath at all. Eventually, Kate began to moan piteously and wakened. But by then, everyone in the room was thoroughly terrified by what was happening.

Night after night, some fresh hell awaited them. Their winter provisions—apples, potatoes, turnips—in the cellar once sailed up three flights of stairs to strike them while they slept. Balls of carpet rags came out of locked chests to pelt them. Fence pickets flew through open windows. Mrs. Fox, disconsolate, would get down on her knees and pray. "What have we done? What *have we* done, that we should be so tormented? Dear children, pray to God to have mercy upon us!"

"I can't pray," Kate said, irritably. "I feel more like swearing!"

The family decided to keep these goings-on "a profound secret," telling no one except their closest friends about what was occurring in the house. They even drew the shades during the day, to keep neighbors from peering in.

However, Leah confided in her close Quaker friends, Amy and Isaac Post, who listened closely to her story but concluded that the family was "suffering under some psychological delusion," according to Leah. Then Leah invited them to come to the house at night to see and hear for themselves. Once the Posts witnessed the manifestations, they "began to think we were not so entirely deluded as they had supposed." Then they went home . . . and were alarmed to hear the mysterious rapping there, too. The Posts brought friends to witness the phenomena, and the secret got out.

One day, the family was visited by a grim Methodist minister who proposed an exorcism. He told the family in no uncertain terms that the "ghosts" were the demonic "familiar spirits" of the Bible, which Scripture warns against trifling with. The family gladly allowed the minister to make the attempt. "He walked around the room, used certain formulae supposed to be potently orthodox for the casting out of unclean spirits; but, to his astonishment, all his mummery availed nothing, and the spirits did not obey his commands," according to an 1855 account of these events by Eliab Wilkinson Capron called *Modern Spiritualism: Its Facts and Fanaticisms, Its Consistencies and Contradictions.* "He was much disappointed at the failure of his power over unseen intelligences."

Several nights later, Leah, her mother, and the girls lingered at the table after supper. It had been a long, tiring day, but the house had been unusually quiet lately. Perhaps things were returning to normal. Perhaps peace was finally returning to their lives. Perhaps they'd all be able to sleep through the night.

Then, one by one, they began exchanging glances. No one moved. In the empty parlor next to the dining room, the piano had begun sounding a doleful bass note, over and over—a death knell. They all sat there, dumbstruck, listening, until the doorbell rang. It was Isaac and Amy Post, whom Leah invited inside. She took them into the parlor, and they all stood there listening to the impossible tolling on the piano. Then Leah walked over and closed the lid, locked it, and put the key in her pocket. But the death knell continued without interruption.

Hours passed. Sleep was out of the question. They milled about the house, dreading what this latest manifestation could possibly mean, as the death dirge rang out of the locked piano without ceasing. It was about one o'clock in the morning when they heard a wagon pulling up to the side gate.

"*Whoa!*"a familiar voice yelled to the horses.

It was Stephen, Leah's sister Maria's husband. Mrs. Fox rushed to the door.

"Oh, Stephen, who is dead?" she cried. "We have had a terrible warning of death, all night."

"I've come to take you back with me," Stephen told her. "David's little Ella is deathly sick."

Stephen fed his horses, came into the house and ate something, talked a short while, and then before first light left for Arcadia with Mrs. Fox and Maggie. When they arrived at David's farm, little Ella was still alive but failing fast.

Later that day, the small child died.

The piano finally fell silent.

IN HER memoir, Leah took pains to emphasize that despite the later accusations of skeptics—who suspected it was all a fabrication dreamed up to make money or become famous—neither she, her sisters, her mother, nor anyone else in the family welcomed what was going on.

"The general feeling of our family, of all of us . . . was strongly averse to all this strange and uncanny thing," she wrote. "We regarded it as a great misfortune, as it was an affliction, which had fallen upon us; how, whence or why, we knew not." The general opinion in the neighborhood was, *These spirits are evil.* When a new neighbor moved in next door, he became enraged by the noises and obtained a warrant to have Leah and her family removed from their house. Leah's friends, including Amy and Isaac Post, rallied to her aid, and by September 1849 the family had moved yet again, this time to a "pleasant little cottage" on Troup Street.

Meanwhile, the fair-minded Isaac Post had grown increasingly interested in simply taking a sober, scientific view of the manifestations—outside religious zealotry, fear, scorn, or ridicule—with an eye toward determining, if possible, what these apparent presences were and what they might be trying to communicate, if anything. Now he had an idea that might help. He reminded Leah that her brother, David, conversed with the Hydesville spirits by using the alphabet—a painfully slow process of reciting the alphabet aloud until the spirit rapped at the correct letter and in this way spelling out a message.

"Perhaps they will explain what is wanted, if thou will call the alphabet," Isaac suggested.

So Leah tried it.

"Do you want to say something to us?" she asked, arms outstretched in the air. Immediately, there came a furious staccato of raps. Then she began calling out the alphabet, letter by letter, waiting for a rap to indicate which letter was chosen. These raps spelled out the first message from the "spirits" in Rochester:

> Dear friends, you must proclaim these truths to the world. This is the dawning of a new era; you must try not to

> conceal it any longer. When you do your duty, God will protect you; and good Spirits will watch over you.

Now, by means of tediously spelled-out letters and words, "the spirits" began transmitting direct messages, sometimes claiming to come from deceased loved ones. One came through, allegedly from Leah, Kate, and Maggie's beloved grandfather, which greatly moved them all:

> MY DEAR CHILDREN:—The time will come when you will understand and appreciate this great dispensation. You must permit your good friends to meet with you and hold communion with their friends in heaven.
>
> I am your grandfather,
> JACOB SMITH.

News of this development—that it might now be possible to communicate directly with the guiding spirits who had appeared in the Fox household, or even communicate with deceased loved ones—swept through the town like the rising wind that presages a coming storm.

"Isaac Post's store was beset, from morning until night, with inquirers who were anxious to visit us," Leah wrote. The family had to set up a committee of five people to screen the onslaught of requests. Many of the inquiries, it turned out, were silly or scurrilous: People wanted to know how to get rich, which stocks or lottery numbers to pick, how to win a suitor, how to get revenge or get rid of a spouse. These requests were always spurned by the spirits, who "seemed delighted to lead us on, and deceive the visitors who sought them in such a spirit."

But many visitors were grieving for those they had lost and longed to make contact across the veil of death, if such a thing were now possible. Though Leah's only income came from piano lessons, she had to give up teaching to serve the crowds of supplicants who appeared at the door. But she refused to accept any money for her spiritual services, feeling that it would be degrading to do so. She continued this practice for more than two years, until her financial situation became so desperate she was forced to charge people a fee for their visits.

As 1848 turned into 1849, the "spirits" began to lay out a plan for reaching a wider audience with their message of immortality. "It was constantly repeated to us that we had 'a mission to perform,'" Leah wrote. "The Spirits said, 'You have been chosen to go before the world to convince the skeptical of the greater truth of immortality.'" The Fox ladies wanted no part of this; they told the spirits they'd already done more than enough. But the spirits were getting pushy. One morning the family awoke to find four coffins drawn on the kitchen floor. The family washed off the drawings. The next morning the coffins reappeared on the kitchen ceiling. Next they appeared in the dining room, in exquisite detail—right down to the nameplates with the names and ages of the mother and three daughters, and a note: "If you do not go forth and do your duty you will soon be laid in your coffins."

Mrs. Fox was not intimidated. She left to join her husband in their newly built house in Arcadia. Kate was in Auburn, New York, staying with the family of Eliab Capron. As for Leah, her music pupils had abandoned her, and she asked the spirits, rather pointedly, "How can we live so?" So the spirits made a formal good-bye and shut off all communication for twelve days.

On that twelfth day, Eliab Capron and George Willets came calling. They were met at the door by Leah and Maggie, who were morose at the departure of the spirits. Stepping into the hallway, the men responded, "Perhaps they will rap for us, if not for you." And so they did. "Joyous sounds, all over the hall," wrote Leah. Yes, yes, very nice, but the spirits quickly got down to business: They wanted a big demonstration, in the biggest venue in Rochester—Corinthian Hall—and the people who would officiate were none other than Eliab Capron and George Willets.

"This proposition was met with an absolute refusal," wrote Capron in his 1855 recollection. They feared the ridicule that would be heaped upon them if they did so. So the spirits relented and suggested that meetings first be held in private homes. (These meetings gradually evolved into what were essentially séances, with seekers seated in a circle awaiting rapped answers to questions.) The spirits even gave very specific directions; they told Amy Post, for example, to invite sixteen persons to a Saturday night séance to hear rappings; they provided the guest list and a template for the invitation.

As for the climax, the demonstration in Corinthian Hall: The spirits said they would produce rapping sounds, then a five-member committee of investigation was to be appointed, whose members would be selected by the audience. The committee would then spend the next day conducting a rigorous inquiry, as a "step towards laying the whole matter before the world in a way that should either settle its falsity or establish its truth." Then the committee would report its findings at the beginning of a second meeting the following night.

Notices were published in the Rochester newspapers of the first meeting, scheduled for the evening of November 14, 1849, at 7:00. Tickets were twenty-five cents. An advertisement in the *Rochester Daily Advertiser* announced that "the citizens of Rochester will have an opportunity of hearing a full explanation of the nature and history of the 'MYSTERIOUS NOISES,' supposed to be *super natural,* which have caused so much excitement in this city."

That night, a restless, excited crowd of more than four hundred showed up at the hall. One newspaper reported that the crowd was "in the best possible humor," anticipating an evening of entertainment and the exposure of an absurd fraud. Because by now the finger of suspicion had repeatedly pointed at Leah and Maggie, the girls took their seats on the stage, perched nervously in front of ornate Corinthian columns and a red damask curtain. It was the first time many in the audience had gotten a look at Margaretta Fox, who by now was sixteen. A reporter for Horace Greeley's *New-York Tribune* swooned: "She is a very interesting and lovely young lady . . . [with] large dark Madonna eyes, a sweet expressive mouth, a petite and delicately moulded form and a regal carriage of the head, with an aristocratic air quite uncommon."

Also on the platform that night were five distinguished local people chosen by the spirits, including a Methodist minister named the Reverend Asahel Jervis. Referring to the supernatural source of the rapping, he said, "I know it is true, and I'll face a frowning world." Yet so certain were the editors of the *Rochester Democrat* that the committee would reveal the whole business as a hoax they had prepared a story with the headline "Entire Exposure of the Rapping Humbug" for the next morning's front page.

At the spirits' request, Eliab Capron took the podium first, to give a short introductory lecture, summarizing the mysterious events that had occurred, beginning with the eerie rapping in the Hydesville house nearly twenty months earlier. He also told the audience that he had begun to hear the sounds in his own home, in Auburn, and that several other prominent local people had also had the same experience. Capron closed by admitting that he could not explain what the mysterious noises were, but he was convinced of what they were *not*—fakery, or demons.

To be fair, the editor of a religious newspaper called *Second Advent* was also allowed to speak briefly. He earnestly announced that he had no doubt the sounds were spiritual but that they were the spirit of the devil, who was up to his old tricks "in these latter days."

Then Capron, with a dramatic flourish, announced that the spirits would demonstrate the famous "rapping" that had excited the attention of all upstate New York. First faintly, then more loudly, a ghostly rapping resounded through the hall—apparently from the floor, then the walls, then the ceiling.

At the close of the meeting, a committee of five distinguished local men was appointed. The next evening, in the second meeting at Corinthian Hall, the committee reported its findings to a restive crowd. At a secret location, without any of Leah's or Maggie's friends present, and in proximity to them, the committee members had distinctly heard the rapping sounds themselves. And though the answers to their questions "were not altogether right nor altogether wrong," the committee admitted it had "entirely failed to discover any means by which [the presumed fraud] could be done."

Murmurs of discontent rippled through the audience at the reading of this report. "Many persons," wrote Leah, "were disappointed and indignant at the discovery that it was *not a cheat*."

Leah sensed such hostility from the crowd that there was an "unmistakable willingness to proceed to violence."

The disgruntled crowd, still unsatisfied, appointed another five-person committee of discontents, including a Dr. Langworthy, as chairman. Held in a lawyer's office, this second examination involved (among other things) listening to the women's hearts with a stethoscope, but though the committee had "conclusively shown [the sounds] to be produced neither by machinery or ventriloquism," no clue was discovered that would fully explain them. All the committee members reported hearing the raps on the floor, on the wall, and on the door. Yet a third committee was appointed, this one so openly hostile it came to be known as the Infidel Committee. One man, W. L. Burtis, volunteered that he was an expert at exposing fraud and said that if he failed to figure out the trick, he would forfeit a new beaver hat. He was immediately voted onto the committee. Another man, named Kenyon, said, "If I cannot fathom the fraud, I will throw myself over Genesee Falls!" And *he* was promptly voted aboard the new committee. A committee of three ladies was also appointed, to examine the girls after they had disrobed.

The next morning, in a hotel room, Maggie and Leah were subjected to the indignity of a strip search. In that prudish age, both of them shed a few tears of humiliation. The female investigators examined their gowns, petticoats, and underwear after they'd removed them, but no "trick" could be found. Then they gave Maggie and Leah dresses of their own choosing to wear.

Next, the rest of the committee began rudely grilling the two women, "taunting us in every way," and attempting to induce the famous rapping sounds in response to questions. But to the chagrin of Maggie and Leah, and the merriment of the committee, the "spirits" remained completely silent all morning. Irreverent jokes began bouncing around the room. Maggie started to cry. They could hear the footsteps of their friends in the hall outside the locked hotel room, but their supporters were not permitted to come in, and "we felt ourselves forsaken, and disposed to give up in despair," Leah recalled. Finally, after several hours, someone suggested that they all adjourn this nonsense for lunch.

"No," Leah insisted, "we shall not stir from this room until the time for this investigation shall expire; which will be at six o'clock P.M."

So lunch was brought in; it was laid on a big table in the middle of the room. While they ate, "the party were joking and funning at our expense, when, suddenly the great table began to tremble, and raised first one end and then the other, with loud creaking sounds, like a ship struggling in a heavy gale," according to Leah's account. For a moment, everyone was silent. The table returned to the floor. Several waiters fled from the room. And then members of the women's committee threw their arms around Leah and Maggie, apparently remorseful for their doubts.

The committee chairman adjourned the meeting, but before everyone left the room, a sympathetic friend came to the door to whisper a message of warning to Leah and Maggie: If the Infidel Committee made a favorable report at Corinthian Hall that night, the girls would be attacked. Maggie had been so relentlessly harassed during the committee's investigations that day, and was so frightened by this warning, that at first she refused to go to the hall that night. But their loyal friend Amy Post told them, "Go, and I will go with you." Leah told her friend, "Amy, if you will go, I will go with you, if I go to my death." And when they questioned the "spirits," the reply came back: "Go, and God will protect you. You will not be harmed."

At the last minute, Maggie relented. "I cannot have you go without me," she said. "I must go, although I expect we will all be killed."

Several hours later, Maggie, Leah, the Posts, and a small group of their loyal supporters trooped into Corinthian Hall, now overflowing with people, to face the music. The crowd was much larger than any of the previous nights, and much louder, rowdier, and more openly belligerent. People yelled off-color jokes at the comely, uncomfortable Maggie and referred to both sisters as "witches." One friend of the Fox family's had already discovered a bucket of hot tar hidden in a stairwell.

This time, the committee's chairman gave a much more thorough report than the previous two but in the end had to admit that the committee members had failed to discern how the trick was accomplished. Neither Mr. Burtis nor Mr. Kenyon could explain it, even though they'd clearly heard the sounds, like everyone else. Alas, neither one of them offered to forfeit a beaver hat or take a plunge over Genesee Falls.

Summing up these four meetings at Corinthian Hall in Rochester, Conan Doyle later observed, "So long as the public looked upon the movement as a sort of a joke, it was prepared to be tolerantly amused. But when successive reports put the matter in a more serious light, a wave of blackguardism swept over the town."

Now, in response to the unsatisfying report from the last committee, the mood of the crowd shifted from angry discontent to naked rage. In fact, according to Leah's memoir, the crowd quickly began turning into a "howling mob, who were predetermined to assault us." A lawyer named Josiah Bissel, apparently the ringleader of the riot, had passed out firecrackers to men and boys in the crowd beforehand. At an agreed-upon moment, before the committee had even finished its report, Bissel leaped onto the stage and raised his cane as a signal to set off the free-for-all. The hall exploded with the sound of firecrackers, howls, and yelling. People jumped into the aisles, brandishing clubs. The hall was engulfed in "stamping, shrieking and all kinds of hideous noises," according to Isaac Post.

But no sooner was the signal given than "a fine, large, respectable-looking gentleman sprang onto the platform and took a seat between myself and my sister," Leah wrote. Thinking he was one of the ruffians, Leah demanded that he not lay a finger on Maggie.

"I am your friend," the man said calmly. "I'm the Chief of Police. Look, these men in front are all my men. They have come to protect you."

He quietly told Josiah Bissel that if anyone were taken into custody, it would be him. Leah and Maggie were hustled out a back door of the hall, leaving the pandemonium behind.

THEN, AS now, people seemed to take away from these improbable events what they brought to them. The mysterious manifestations were like Rorschach tests of preexisting beliefs. Whether you mocked them, feared them, belittled them, or believed, your reaction often said more about you than the phenomena themselves.

There were plenty of people—men, mostly, for reasons we'll get into later—who were determined to dismiss it as *a humbug.* Among the fanciful explanations was a declaration by three doctors at the University of Buffalo (in 1850, it wasn't exactly a scientific powerhouse) that the girls produced the knocking by cracking their knee joints. This theory was scorned by medical men of far greater fame, including Conan Doyle, but the great French physiologist Charles Richet put it best. "This infantile explanation," he wrote in 1920, "that we smile at today was well received by scientists who probably had never heard the raps which cause wood to vibrate sometimes loudly, sometimes with musical rhythm, and have nothing in common with the snappings of a tendon."

Nonetheless, that's one of the explanations you'll read today on Wikipedia. If *something out there* caused all the racket, what was it? Most clergymen of the day hastened to say the following: They were evil spirits! The devil himself! Mister Splitfoot! Other deep thinkers said there must be something in nature, "an imponderable agent," that connects all matter in the universe. Or it was a manifestation of what the twentieth century would call the subconscious mind. A few decades later, late-Victorian occultists claimed the phenomena were caused by living persons, acting at a distance. Possibly they were "great souls from Atlantis, incarnated into the bodies of North American Indians," or members of the Hermetic Brotherhood of Luxor!

But a whole lot of Americans were ready to agree with Leah Fox. These were truly the spirits of the departed, and what had just happened was nothing less than "the birth-throes of a new truth."

By the end of the 1800s, the spiritualist community of Lily Dale was part summer camp, part church, part Oracle at Delphi. Spiritualism had become a major movement and shared many ties with the woman's suffrage movement.
COURTESY OF LILY DALE MUSEUM

CHAPTER THREE
The Spiritual Wildfire

In the spring of 1850, Eliab Capron somehow persuaded Mrs. Fox to take her three daughters to New York City in order to "proclaim these truths to the world." Ever since hosting Kate Fox at his house the year before, Capron had been conducting his own séances in his hometown of Auburn, New York, in the Finger Lakes region. He summarized his experiences in the pamphlet *Explanation and History of the Mysterious Communion with Spirits: Comprehending the Rise and Progress of the Mysterious Noises in Western New-York, Generally Received as Spiritual Communications,* which was given a long front-page treatment in the *New-York Tribune* that January 18. The *Tribune* was published by the abolitionist and future presidential candidate Horace Greeley. Alone among the newspaper editors of New York, he was open-minded about spiritualism. When Mrs. Fox and her daughters arrived at Barnum's Hotel on Broadway on June 4, 1850, their first visitor was Horace Greeley.

Two nights later, they conducted one of the most famous séances in American history. They were invited to the home of a New York clergyman, the Reverend Dr. Griswold, "who has been incredulous from the first," said a June 8, 1850, *Tribune* article, which ran under the headline "An Evening with the 'Spirits.'" Among the guests waiting for them were James Fenimore Cooper (author of *The Last of the Mohicans*), the poet William Cullen Bryant, the editor Nathaniel Parker Willis, and the historian George Bancroft, as well as other clergymen and doctors—all in all, a roomful of the leading lights of New York in those days. And they were as shrewdly skeptical as any New York dinner party of today.

The Foxes arrived at a little past 8:00 p.m.—Mrs. Fox, Leah, Maggie, and Kate—and the two younger sisters sat at a table, inviting others to join them in a tight circle. Then, for at least half an hour, nothing happened; that's perfectly normal in séances, but this was New York, and "the company gave obvious symptoms of impatience." Finally, faint sounds began to be heard under the floor, around the table, and in various parts of the room. They increased in loudness and frequency until the sisters asked, "Will the spirits converse with anyone present?" At first the spirits seemed pointedly unenthusiastic. At long last the gentlemen in the room took turns playing a sort of mental charades with the spirits, who would correctly guess a person they would silently fix in their mind.

Fifth in line was James Fenimore Cooper. His questioning, as recorded by the *Tribune*'s George Ripley, went like this:

> "Is the person I inquire about a relative?"
> Yes, was immediately indicated by three distinct knocks.
> "A near relative?"
> Yes.
> "A man?"
> No answer.
> "A woman?"
> Yes.
> "A daughter? A mother? A wife?"
> No answers.
> "A sister?"
> Yes.
> "How many years since her death?"
> At this the spirit slowly knocked fifty times.
> "Did she die of consumption?"
> No answer to this and many other diseases named.
> "Did she die by accident?"
> Yes.

"Was she killed by lightning? Was she shot? Was she lost at sea? Did she fall from a carriage?"

No answers.

"Was she thrown from a horse?"

Knock knock knock.

Cooper then stopped the questioning and told the room that he indeed had a sister who "just fifty years this present month was killed by being thrown from a horse." Evidently, the evening left a deep impression: On his deathbed a year later, Cooper left instructions to tell the Fox family, "They have prepared me for this hour."

The circle broke up, for the hour was late, but several gentlemen asked the Fox sisters to stand in another part of the room. "The knockings were now heard on the doors, at both ends of the room, producing a vibration on the panels which was felt by everyone who touched them," noted the article. "The ladies were at such a distance from the door in both cases, as to lend no countenance to the idea that the sounds were produced by any direct communication with them." The party then went downstairs into a parlor, where the sounds caused "sensible vibrations in the sofa."

The *Tribune* offered no explanation for the mysterious noises. It staunchly defended the Fox sisters, who clearly wowed the crowd: "The manners and bearing of the ladies are such as to create a prepossession in their favor." But if the knockings are made by spirits of the departed, "why do they come [on] such an unusual journey, on an unprofitable errand? At the utmost they only exhibit their credentials, but bring no messages." Having been left with more questions than answers, the *Tribune*'s Ripley concluded with a nonconclusion: "We wait for further disclosures."

Many Americans were not waiting around. Seemingly overnight, spiritualism in America was a vastly popular grassroots movement, and the Fox sisters, although the most visible emblem of the movement, were by no means its leaders. During that summer of 1850, as they toiled away on Broadway, the weekly *Spirit Messenger* was being started in Springfield, Massachusetts;

Eliab Capron said his town of Auburn, New York, housed a hundred mediums; and Cincinnati was about to hear its first raps, courtesy of a Mrs. G. B. Bushnell. Soon thereafter, "detailed instructions for the formation of circles appeared in print," notes the Harvard Divinity School professor Ann Braude in her landmark study, *Radical Spirits*. "Most advised a maximum of twelve investigators, equally divided between men and women, seated close together around a table, hands either joined or laid on the table. They stressed the necessity of harmony among the circle's participants." Many circles opened with the singing of familiar hymns. In many ways, spiritualism was ideally suited to a young democracy. You didn't need money or class distinction or special permission. All you needed were friends, family, and a parlor table. Séances were social. And, in a time before electricity, they offered something to do when the sun went down.

And so, away it went: By 1853, dozens of spiritualist titles had appeared in print, from *The Celestial Telegraph* to *The Science of the Soul*. By 1854, thirteen thousand people signed a petition asking the U.S. Senate to appoint a scientific committee to investigate spirit communication. And by 1855, Henry J. Raymond, a founder of *The New York Times,* said of spiritualism's influence, "In five years it has spread like wild-fire over this Continent, so that there is scarcely a village without its mediums and its miracles."

Meanwhile, the Foxes went back to Barnum's Hotel, where they spent the summer conducting séances three times daily, from 10:00 to 12:00 each morning, then from 3:00 to 5:00 in the afternoon and from 8:00 to 10:00 each night. "The dear spirits are doing wonderful things," Kate wrote in an early letter to Amy Post back in Rochester. "The piano was sweetly played upon by spirit fingers, the guitar was played then taken up and carried above our heads. . . . We have convinced many skeptical people." But the pace was grueling; soon enough it got old—and the sisters were so young. Conan Doyle quoted Emma Hardinge, the great American historian of spiritualism, recalling in her autobiography that she paused "on the first floor to hear poor, patient Kate Fox, in the midst of a captious, grumbling crowd of investigators, repeating hour after hour the letters of the alphabet, while the no less poor, patient spirits rapped out names, ages and dates to suit all comers." He then shook his head, in effect, saying that they lacked a "wise mentor at the elbow of these poor pioneers. . . . Worst of all, their jaded energies were renewed by the offer of wine at a time when at least one of them was hardly more than a child." Writing this in the 1920s, he knew how badly the Fox sisters' story would end.

JUST AS a wildfire needs dry conditions, spiritualism needed a receptive audience. What prepared the way? This passage from Eliab Capron's *Explanation and History of the Mysterious Communion with Spirits* explains how insubstantial spirits can make very substantial rapping sounds:

> Again we are asked how a *spirit* can rap so as to make an audible sound. The spirits say they do not rap, but produce the sounds by will. We have examined a number of clairvoyants on this subject and all agree in this. We put a boy, who had no knowledge of the matter at all, neither was he noted for a remarkable degree of intelligence, into a magnetic sleep, and turned his attention to the subject. He was clairvoyant and said he could see *who* made the sounds. We asked him how the persons looked. His answer was, "they look light—just like gauze; I can see right through them." Well, how do they make the sounds; do they rap? "No! they don't rap or strike at all." When after looking earnestly for a time he said: "they want it made, and it is made wherever they want it." This was his simple way of telling what other clairvoyants have told in language somewhat different, but amounting to the same thing. This is the best explanation we have ever been able to obtain.

The reader of today has no idea what Capron is talking about . . . put into a magnetic sleep? But Capron's readers of 1850 did understand; they knew all about mesmerism.

Mesmerism is named after Franz Anton Mesmer, the son of a

German forester who married a wealthy widow, patronized Mozart, studied medicine in Vienna, then fled to Paris, where, in 1779, he published a pamphlet unveiling his pet theory of "animal magnetism." He believed that a mysterious magnetic fluid connects our bodies with the earth and the planets and that if the free flow of this fluid gets obstructed, illness is the result. One of his followers in Paris, the Marquis de Puységur, developed the mesmeric trance (or magnetic "sleep") in order to alleviate pain and cure disease.

The trance was induced by making "passes." Typically the patient would be in a sitting position, and during this sitting (in French *séance*) the mesmerizer would stare into the patient's eyes while running his hands from the crown of the head downward across the face and down the front of the body. The hands came as close to the body as possible without actually touching the patient. In a few minutes—or more, depending on the patient's suggestibility—the patient would lapse into a somnambulistic state.

During this trance, the patient felt no pain and could undergo an operation without the crude anesthesias of the day (alcohol and opium). But much more intriguing was the fact that some people, when mesmerized, could see hidden objects or distant lands. They were suddenly *clairvoyant*—French for "clear-sighted." While in trance, common laborers spoke languages they had never learned and recited snatches of poetry; young ladies witnessed shipwrecks occurring hundreds of miles away.

By the 1830s, French mesmerists were exporting their wonders to Britain and America, and they brought their most suggestible patients with them. The most famous mesmeric patient of the era was Alexis Didier. He could identify the contents of sealed documents and describe faraway landscapes. One notable scene, recounted in Alison Winter's book *Mesmerized,* describes a private party in London at which one Colonel Llewellyn gave Didier a small box resembling a surgical instrument case and asked him to identify its contents. In a scene later recounted by the London surgeon John Elliotson, Didier held it in his hands and slowly gave the following:

"The object within the case is a hard substance."

"It is folded in an envelope."

"The envelope is whiter than the thing itself." (The envelope was a piece of silver paper, Elliotson later noted.)

"It is a kind of ivory."

"It has a point at one end."

"It is a bone."

"Taken from a body—from a human body—from your body."

"The bone has been separated and cut, so as to leave a flat side." (The bone, which was a piece of the colonel's leg, and sawed off after the wound, was flat toward the part that enclosed the marrow, Elliotson later wrote.)

Here Didier removed the piece of bone from the case, and placed his finger on a part, and said that the ball struck *here,* pointing to a spot. "It was an extraordinary ball, as to its effect," Didier told the colonel. "You received three separate injuries at the same moment." (That was the case, Elliotson confirmed, for the ball broke or burst into three pieces and injured the colonel in three places in the same leg.)

"You were wounded in the early part of the day, whilst charging the enemy," Didier went on.

In 1838, Elliotson gave demonstrations of mesmerism at the hospital of University College London, where he was senior physician and professor. In the audience was his friend Charles Dickens. They were to become lifelong friends (Elliotson was godfather to Dickens's second son). And Dickens developed a lifelong interest, becoming a mesmeric "operator" in the process. While on a visit to Pittsburgh in 1842, he first tried his powers on his wife. Within six minutes of passes about her head, she became hysterical. Two minutes later, she fell asleep. Dickens was quite pleased with his newfound power, and he magnetized whoever would consent to it. In 1845, he wrote, only half jokingly, "I have the perfect conviction that I could magnetize a Frying-Pan."

But displays of mesmerism weren't confined to private parlors or the amphitheaters of medical schools. Everywhere in Britain and America, traveling mesmerists of the 1840s put on road shows. Patients were placed into a magnetic sleep, and in that insensate state they endured electric shocks, pistols fired next to their ears, and fingers held directly above the flame of a candle. While this amazed most members of the audience, a few were angered; they claimed fraud. They thought they were being hoaxed. At a lecture in Norwich, England, one furious doctor suddenly took out a lancet and ran it deeply into the patient's finger *under the nail into the quick*. While the boy gave no expression of pain at the time, he "suffered a good deal after he was awakened." That reaction was another prelude to spiritualism: Some observers took offense and became irrational, insisting that if fraud were possible, then ipso facto fraud occurred.

When spiritualism came along, proponents of mesmerism weren't exactly pleased. Take the case of John Bovee Dods, a former Universalist minister who'd been lecturing on mesmerism for fifteen years. In April 1851, he traveled to Auburn, New York, to deliver a series of ten lectures in which he desperately tried to roll back the tide. *It's all mesmerism, folks!* "The spirits of our departed friends in a future world have nothing to do with this matter," he told his audience in Auburn's city hall. When a medium writes or speaks while in trance, "he obtains all his knowledge from the same source that all mesmeric and psychological subjects do, and this is, *not from spirits,* but from the instincts of the involuntary powers of the mind in the back brain." Yes, he said, we've all heard about the medium who merely *thinks it* and a table tips thirteen times. "But do you not understand, that mesmeric clairvoyants have done this in thousands and thousands of instances, and so often repeated, that the experiment has become stale? For who does not know, that a person who involuntarily falls into the mesmeric state, is in communication with surrounding nature, and with all persons of a certain nervous temperament in sympathy with his own, even though thousands of miles distant, and, for aught we know, throughout the globe—and receives impressions from their brains."

But try as he might, mesmerism was shattering into pieces—like the musket ball that hit Colonel Llewellyn in his leg. The ability to put someone in a trance became hypnotism, after the Scottish surgeon James Braid produced similar results by dangling a shiny object. Surgeons were only too happy not to share their operating rooms with mesmerists once a Boston dentist in late 1846 discovered ether vapor to be an effective anesthetic. As for the idea that the magnetic operator could dominate the patient's will—a notion that always gave mesmerism the strong whiff of sexual scandal—it lived on at least as a plot device in novels like George du Maurier's *Trilby* and Conan Doyle's short story "The Parasite." (And it lives today in the expression "he made a pass at her.") Finally, the uncanny psychic effects, together with the fancy French lingo, became part of spiritualism. Most people accepted the idea that young girls who saw through walls, or who could see into other people's bodies as if their skin were a sheet of glass, were aided by discarnate spirits rather than their own "back brains." In the end, even John Bovee Dods had to agree and changed his tune after his daughter Jennie became a medium.

TRAVELING MESMERISTS weren't the only group who were threatened by the spiritual wildfire. Most clergymen—not all, but most—thundered about the "moral abominations" that came from contacting demonic spirits. And the more they thundered, the more they motivated their rebellious parishioners to investigate a neighbor's "spirit room." Emma Hardinge, in her 1870 history, *Modern American Spiritualism,* wrote, "It would be difficult to determine which was the most effective form of propaganda for the spread of the belief, namely, the zealous enthusiasm of its admirers or the bitter persecution of its antagonists."

In part, their rancor betrayed their defensiveness. The various denominations and sects of Protestantism competed against one another for faithful congregants to fill their pews. And they all faced the headwind of a radically independent populace. Despite the mythmaking of today's politicians, America never had a glorious past as a nation of brave, strong, pious, churchgoing Christians. When George Washington was president, no more than 15 percent of Americans were active church members.

But another chunk of their animosity was due to this: Spiritualism was a movement of, by, and for women. Yes, there were a few "addle-headed feminine men," as a detractor put it, but most of the movement's leaders—including its mediums—were women. And to their detractors' horror, they actually let women *speak in public.*

It's difficult to imagine today, but a woman in the mid-nineteenth century simply could not get up and speak in front of a "promiscuous assembly," which was the current phrase for a group of both men and women. The few bold women who did so were criticized for promoting "degeneracy and ruin." If they got that far: When the suffragist Lucy Stone graduated from Oberlin College in 1847, her classmates unanimously elected her to deliver the commencement address, but the school forbade it, insisting that a male professor read it for her instead.

Even the most reluctant young student of American history knows that the women's rights movement started in 1848 in the little town of Seneca Falls in upstate New York. But those early feminists were wary of crossing this taboo. When the historic Seneca Falls Convention of 1848 adjourned, the participants agreed to reconvene in Rochester two weeks later. The arrangements committee proposed that a woman preside over that Rochester convention, but Lucretia Mott and Elizabeth Cady Stanton—two household names in the history of women's rights in America—firmly opposed it as "a most hazardous experiment." They wanted Lucretia's husband to do the honors. Finally, they relented, allowing Abigail Bush to take the chair. Bush later described herself as "born and baptized in the old Scotch Presbyterian church . . . [whose] sacred teachings were 'if a woman would know anything let her ask her husband at home.'"

The spiritualists helped to change all that. At their large public gatherings in the 1850s, a man might well act as a master of ceremonies, as Eliab Capron did at Corinthian Hall. But the main attraction was a trance speaker, a woman like Cora Hatch or Achsa Sprague, who delivered an inspirational address while in a mediumistic trance. And although it was shocking to see a woman speaking on a public platform, it was somehow less of a shock if she was young and pretty and, unconscious of her own eloquence, could spend an hour speaking in verse about the next world. *She* wasn't giving the lecture—because, after all, what woman could possibly do that? No, the spirits were talking *through* her. So it was more acceptable, but it broke the ice and helped pave the way for women to assume public roles in America after the Civil War.

It's a curious fact that both the spiritualist movement and the women's rights movement began in the same year, 1848, less than four months and twenty-five miles apart. Pure coincidence? Not at all. Dissident Quakers supplied the critical mass for both groups. Besides Amy Post, who was the Fox sisters' protector and mentor, there was the Quaker preacher Lucretia Mott, and Mary Ann McClintock provided the parlor table on which the 1848 Declaration of Sentiments was written in preparation for Seneca Falls. Susan B. Anthony was born into a Quaker family. Abigail Bush, who presided over the Rochester convention, was not a Quaker, but she was a close friend of Amy Post's and one of the earliest witnesses of the new spiritual manifestations. A few days after the Fox sisters arrived in Rochester in 1848, Abigail Bush visited Amy Post and the Foxes, and they retreated to a bedroom where Abigail heard the raps for the first time. She became a lifelong spiritualist.

The household names among suffrage leaders—Lucy Stone, Susan B. Anthony, Elizabeth Cady Stanton, Lucretia Mott—were not committed spiritualists, but all had close friends and relatives who were. Later in her life, Susan B. Anthony would travel every summer from her home in Rochester to Lily Dale, the spiritualist camp in western New York that still functions as a summer retreat, to mount the rostrum for its annual Woman's Day. She would talk strictly of worldly matters, notably her ongoing campaign to get the right to vote, but she was among friends, usually a couple thousand of them, who came out to cheer her on. Lily Dale records show that she was still mounting the rostrum in late August 1905, when she was eighty-five years old. That was her last visit; she died the following spring, more than a decade before the passage of the Nineteenth Amendment.

The official history of the early women's movement, the *History of Woman Suffrage,* edited by Elizabeth Cady Stanton and Susan B. Anthony, acknowledged the ties that later historians chose to ignore. "The only religious sect in the world . . . that has recognized the equality of woman is the Spiritualists," it noted. "They have always assumed that a woman may be a medium of communication from heaven to earth, that the spirits of the universe may breathe through her lips."

Not all suffragists were spiritualists, but all spiritualists were early feminists, and they all also agitated for the abolition of slavery. The three movements were intertwined. The Posts' home in Rochester was one of the main depots of the Underground Railroad; one of their beneficiaries and close friends was Frederick Douglass, who stayed in Rochester and published the antislavery newspaper *The North Star* from 1847 to 1851. He never warmed to spiritualism, but he did speak at the convention in Seneca Falls. Most other prominent abolitionists embraced (or at least respected) spiritualism, including William Lloyd Garrison. Garrison attended a séance with Leah Fox in 1854 at which a bell rang by itself and a walking stick slithered, snakelike, around his feet. One of the visiting spirits identified itself as Jesse Hutchinson, a member of an abolitionist singing group, and as the group sang his song "The Old Granite State," he kept time with his raps. Garrison and the entire group came away believing in the reality of spirit agency.

ON THE *early morning of April 9, 1855, the steam packet* Africa, *from Boston, was drawing into Liverpool docks. Most of the passengers showed natural exultation, but among them was one who seemed to have no pleasant prospects in view. This was a youth some two and twenty years of age, tall, slim, with a marked elegance of bearing and a fastidious neatness of dress, but with a worn, hectic look upon his very expressive face, which told of the ravages of some wasting disease. Blue-eyed, and with hair of a light auburn tint, he was of the type which is peculiarly open to the attack of the tubercle. An acute physician would probably have given him six months of life in our humid island. He had hardly a relation in the world. His left lung was partly gone.*

The youth depicted in this scene loosely quoted from Conan Doyle's *Edge of the Unknown* is Daniel Dunglas Home. Born in Scotland, D. D. Home was adopted by an aunt in America when he was nine. Raised in Connecticut, he was a gentle, soft-spoken child. When he was seventeen, his aunt threw him out of the house anyway; tables and chairs went airborne as he entered a room. Left to fend for himself, he conducted séances around New England in the early 1850s, and according to the letters of first-hand witnesses his séances were marked by luminous spirit hands and tables that rocked and tilted. A small group of supporters in America raised the money to send him to Britain as a spiritualist missionary. Yes, D. D. Home was a medium—"the greatest on the physical side that the modern world has ever seen," said Arthur Conan Doyle decades later in his last book, a 1930 collection of essays, *The Edge of the Unknown*.

The scene at Liverpool docks is a condensed version of Conan Doyle's own words; it's a re-creation of the fateful moment that D. D. Home arrived in Britain, and spiritualism came to Britain with him. Yes, he had been preceded by another American medium, Mrs. Hayden, in 1852, but he had much more impact. The reason is the unusual versatility of his psychic power, said Doyle. "We speak usually of a direct voice medium, of a trance speaker, of a clairvoyant, or of a physical medium, but Home was all four." He truly was "stranger than fiction," which was the title of an 1860 article about him in William Makepeace Thackeray's *Cornhill Magazine*. (Thackeray himself attended Home séances in both England and America.)

Arriving in England, Home was to earn his reputation as the consummate houseguest, staying several months with the family of Thomas Rymer, a rich solicitor in the London suburb of Ealing. There he would give séances to friends of his host, and all distinguished callers for that matter, offering his abilities for free—he never charged money—to hundreds of the curious and the skeptical and the famous: On July 25, 1855, the poet Robert Browning and his wife, Elizabeth Barrett Browning, visited Ealing for a séance with D. D. Home. She had been deeply interested in mesmerism and spiritualism for more than a decade. Robert? Not so much. Two days earlier, their friends Sir Edward Bulwer-Lytton and his son, Robert, had attended a séance at Ealing; Robert Bulwer-Lytton wrote to her afterward of his experience.

So they went into the séance with potentially different attitudes and emerged with a very sore subject in their marriage.

Everyone there had a different take on the evening, but all agreed that a wreath had been placed on Mrs. Browning's head. The wreath of clematis had been woven by D. D. Home and the Rymers' daughter earlier that day. So what's controversial about that?

We know that Robert Browning came away from the evening in a peevish mood. In a letter written shortly thereafter, he mocked the voice of the Rymers' dead child, disparaged the banalities of the spirit voices, and didn't trust any of the physical manifestations—the spirit hand, the tipping table, the self-playing accordion. "On reviewal the exhibition seems the sorriest in my recollection," he wrote to a friend.

We also know that Elizabeth Barrett Browning came away thinking she'd just met "the most interesting person in England." On August 17, she wrote to her sister Henrietta with a fairly gushing description and a warning: "When you write to me don't say a word on the subject—because it's a *tabooed* subject in this house—Robert and I taking completely different views, and he being a good deal irritated by any discussion of it." She proceeds to tell her sister,

> We were touched by the invisible, heard the music and raps, saw the table moved, and had sight of the hands. Also, at the request of the medium, the spiritual hands took from the table a garland which lay there, and placed it upon my head. The particular hand which did this was of the largest human size, as white as snow, and very beautiful. It was as near to me as this hand I write with, and I saw it as distinctly. I was perfectly calm! . . .
>
> I think that what chiefly went against the exhibition, in Robert's mind, was the trance at the conclusion during which the medium talked a great deal of much such twaddle as may be heard in any fifth rate conventicle. But according to my theory (well thought-out and digested)

> this does not militate at all against the general facts. It's undeniable, and has been from first to last, that if these are spirits, many among them talk prodigious nonsense, or rather most ordinary commonplace.
>
> For my own part I am confirmed in all my opinions. To me it was wonderful and conclusive; and I believe that the medium present was no more *responsible* for the things said and done, than I myself was.

Clearly she's trying to let Home off the hook for something there at the end. What had Home done that was so terrible? As it turns out, the wreath was a *poet's crown,* and Robert Browning was jealous that the spirits were crowning Elizabeth, not him!

Here's Home's version of the incident, told years later in his memoir *Incidents in My Life*:

> During the séance this wreath was raised from the table by supernatural power in the presence of us all, and whilst we were watching it, Mr. Browning, who was seated at the opposite side of the table, left his place and came and stood behind his wife, towards whom the wreath was being slowly carried, and upon whose head it was placed, in full sight of us all, and whilst he was standing close behind her. . . .
>
> It was the remark of all the Rymer family, that Mr. Browning seemed much disappointed that the wreath was not put upon his own head instead of his wife's, and that his placing himself in the way of where it was being carried, was for the purpose of giving it an opportunity of being placed upon his own brow.

Making matters worse, the spirits then asked everyone to leave the room, including the Brownings, while a private message was given to Mr. Rymer. Mr. Browning seemed quite hurt by this, and he supposedly said he "was not aware that spirits could have secrets."

Two days later, Robert Browning wrote to Mrs. Rymer requesting a second séance, but it didn't fit into the family's schedule. When they visited the Brownings a few days later, hoping to make amends, it went very, very badly, according to Home.

> We were shown into the drawing-room, and he, advancing to meet us, shook hands with Mrs. Rymer; then, passing by me shook hands with her son. As he was repassing me I held out my hand, when, with a tragic air, he threw his hand on his left shoulder, and stalked away. My attention was now drawn to Mrs. Browning, who was standing nearly in the centre of the room, and looked very pale and agitated. I approached and she placed both her hands in mine, and said, in a voice of emotion, "Oh, dear Mr. Home, do not, do not blame me. I am so sorry, but I am not to blame."

What sort of domestic hell had they wandered into? Robert Browning had a brief argument with Mrs. Rymer, during which he rocked back and forth in his chair "like a maniac." They got up to leave, and Home again shook hands with Mrs. Browning, "who was nearly ready to faint."

Robert Browning carried on a vendetta against D. D. Home for the rest of his life. Shortly after Mrs. Browning died, in 1861, he published the poem *Mr. Sludge, "the Medium,"* a thinly veiled attack on Home; it's about a medium who's been caught producing fraudulent manifestations. Conan Doyle called it "a long poem to describe an exposure which had never taken place." As for the incident in the drawing room, Browning's own version of it years later portrayed himself as the dashing hero, telling Home, "If you are not out of that door in half a minute I'll fling you down the stairs."

D. D. Home left England later that year, traveling to Florence, where he exorcised a ghost in a haunted house and was attacked by an assassin with a knife that struck his door key rather than his heart. He was warned by the spirits that he would lose his powers for a year, and he did. In Paris, the gifts came back redoubled; the emperor Napoleon III was convinced of Home's powers. Home then returned to England in 1859, the same year in which a Mary Doyle of Edinburgh gave birth to a rather large infant whom she named Arthur.

The fantastic success of Sherlock Holmes as a literary creation was something Conan Doyle came to hate. He thought Sherlock would be forgotten, but spiritualism would live forever.
PICTORIAL PRESS LTD / ALAMY STOCK PHOTO

CHAPTER FOUR
The Invention of Sherlock Holmes

In the late summer of 1881, at the age of twenty-two, Arthur Doyle graduated from Edinburgh Medical School. His diploma somewhat pompously conferred the title "Master of Surgery," although, being a temperamentally modest man, he was quick to admit that his surgical skills were far from masterful. As if to acknowledge his lack of proficiency, he sent his mother a sketch of himself holding up his newly minted diploma with the sinister caption "License to kill!"

In the rush to finish up his medical studies, he almost forgot that he'd applied for a berth as ship's surgeon on another voyage, this one a trip to West Africa on a dirty old tub called the *Mayumba.* At the last minute, he got a telegram accepting his application, hastily packed, and once again found himself at sea, ministering to the medical needs of thirty passengers. The voyage lasted three months, during which time he learned enough details about the sailor's life to fill a few more salty short stories, such as "J. Habakuk Jephson's Statement" and *The Firm of Girdlestone.* He also penned a pithy little ditty called "Advice to a Young Author":

> *First begin*
> *Taking in.*
> *Cargo stored,*
> *All aboard.*
> *Think about*

Giving out.
Empty ship
Useless trip!

It was in the spring of 1882, when he was back in England, that he received an intriguing telegram from a remarkable man he'd met in medical school. George Turnavine Budd was half genius, half scoundrel, a formidable rugby forward who came from a famous medical family. He was a man, Doyle later wrote, "born for trouble and adventure" whose life was filled with alarming explosions and wild escapades that often landed him in a fight or in jail. For some reason, the two men had always hit it off, and now Budd wanted to know if Doyle would care to join him in his new medical practice in the seaside town of Plymouth, on the south coast of Devon. Budd said he had a fabulously successful practice going, promising Doyle a guaranteed salary of three hundred pounds (about fifty thousand dollars in today's money) a year. Though it all sounded too good to be true, it was the best offer Doyle had on the table, so he moved to a small rented flat in Plymouth to become a real, practicing doctor.

But he soon discovered that Budd's "practice" revolved around a simple, misleading idea: The consultations were completely free; patients just paid for their medicines. So crowds of patients were flocking to his door for "free" medical care, then being sold overpriced drugs in what Doyle described in his memoirs as "a heroic and indiscriminate manner." In effect, Budd was running what would now be called a pill mill. His medical practice was just another wild escapade, though this one was highly lucrative. Doyle lasted a couple of months as Budd's medical partner (much to his mother's relief; she had always been suspicious of the man). Mulling over this bizarre, two-month-long joyride, Doyle mentally began turning the whole thing into a novel, and in 1895 *The Stark Munro Letters* told the whole crazy story in thinly fictionalized form, as a series of letters.

Now, casting about, Doyle decided to move to another coastal town, Southsea, a charming little Victorian seaside resort on the southern coast of Portsea Island. He knew absolutely no one there, but he decided to establish a practice of his own—this time, an honest one. He rented another tiny flat with one spare room for examinations, furnished it with battered yard sale furniture, and hung out a shingle. Then he waited for the occasional patient to show up at his door. Most of the time, though, he simply waited—his "waiting room" became the place where he waited—so in the meantime, as was to become his lifelong habit, he began filling up the hours by writing stories and selling them to London magazines such as *The Cornhill* and *The Strand*.

He later admitted that most of these stories were "feeble echoes of Bret Harte," an American writer he admired, but he was able to sell them without much trouble, and his output was prodigious. Over the next several years, his published stories began bringing in a modest supplemental income, though he never dreamed they would ever produce an actual living wage. Eventually, though, it dawned on him that because he sometimes sat in his office for the entire day with "never a ring to disturb my serenity," he was in an ideal situation. "As long as I was thoroughly unsuccessful in my professional venture there was every chance of improvement in my literary prospects."

Shortly after his arrival, he invited his nine-year-old brother, Innes, to come live with him, and the two bachelors, almost like father and son, shared Doyle's cozy flat at Bush Villas until Innes went on to boarding school.

In March 1885, Conan Doyle was asked by a medical colleague to examine a twenty-five-year-old man named Jack Hawkins, who was having convulsions due to cerebral meningitis, at the time an incurable disease. Young Hawkins had been living in uncomfortable circumstances with his twenty-seven-year-old sister, Louise, and another younger sister, after the death of their father. Because of the seriousness of the young man's case, because Conan Doyle was a sort of gentleman's gentleman who could not bear to see someone suffer, and because he had a spare upstairs bedroom, he offered to let Jack Hawkins stay in his house while he attempted to alleviate his suffering. The young man moved in, but in spite of all Doyle's efforts within a few weeks he died. The funeral was held out of Doyle's house. As it happened, in the course of this grievous loss, for which Doyle took personal responsibility, he began to develop a tender relationship with the boy's sister Louise, known as Touie. She was a soft-spoken woman with wispy brown hair and green eyes who was two years older than Conan Doyle.

They began taking long walks together, discovering each other and the many things they had in common. One was that she had an older brother, named Jeremiah, who had been in a mental institution for seventeen years and was also a gifted artist. Just about this same time, Arthur got the news that his own father had been transferred to another asylum, euphemistically called Sunnyside, that he had smashed a window and tried to escape, and that he claimed "he was getting messages from the unseen world."

These tortured relationships helped to knit Arthur and Touie together, and on August 6, 1885, she and Doyle were married. "No man could have a more gentle and amiable life's companion," he later wrote.

Meanwhile, though he now found himself comfortably nested in a sweet, supportive marriage, and increasingly secure financially, he also felt spiritually lost.

"I cannot look back on those years with any spiritual satisfaction, for I was still in the valley of darkness," he wrote in his memoirs, published in 1924. "I had ceased to butt my head against what seemed to be an impenetrable wall, and I had resigned myself to ignorance upon that which is the most momentous question in life—for a voyage is bleak indeed if one has no conception to what port one is bound." Overall, he described his inner spiritual life at that time as being "conscious of a vague unrest, of a constant want of repose, of an emptiness and hardness which I had not noticed in life before."

He had rejected the comforts and rituals of the Catholic Church. The worldly philosophers like Thomas Huxley and Herbert Spencer did not seem to offer any real hope of meaning in human life, just "survival of the fittest" and agnosticism. He had been trained in the methods of science but found no lasting comfort there either. Even so, he hadn't abandoned all hope—he did not believe in an anthropomorphic God, a jolly Santa Claus in the sky—but like Thomas Carlyle, Johann Wolfgang von Goethe, and the American transcendentalists, Doyle turned to Nature as the supreme manifestation of the divine. He believed "in an intelligent Force behind all the operations of Nature—a force so infinitely complex and great that my finite brain could get no further than its existence." It all seemed rather distant and impersonal, a spirituality of stars and galaxies rather than love and comfort. Wasn't there something more out there?

At the time, of course, spiritualism—a religion, a new branch of science, or a woolly-headed mania, depending on one's point of view—was in the very air. It was discussed and debated in public forums, and everybody knew somebody who was a spiritualist or something close to it. But Doyle wasn't buying it. He'd read in the papers about the exposure of phony mediums and deplored the simplemindedness of people who got suckered in as much as the venal manipulations of those who exploited them. "I had at that time the usual contempt which the young educated man feels towards the whole subject which has been covered by the clumsy name of Spiritualism," he wrote. "I found myself, like many young medical men, a convinced materialist as regards our personal destiny."

As to whether the human personality might survive bodily death, that he considered "the greatest nonsense upon earth." "When the candle burns out the light disappears. When the electric cell is shattered the current stops. When the body dissolves there is an end of the matter." Besides, he added, "each man in his egotism may feel that he ought to survive, but let him look, we will say, at the average loafer—of high or low degree—would anyone contend that there was any obvious reason why *that* personality should carry on?"

Even so, Arthur Conan Doyle had a lively, restless intellect, he was deeply alive, and he continued to puzzle over the knottiest of the existential questions: What is this all about? What is the nature and purpose of existence? Can the divine intercede in human life? Are there "principalities and powers," as the Bible says, at work in our lives of which we have little or no understanding?

When the young Dr. Doyle met a local Southsea architect named Joseph Henry Ball, who seemed to share his interest in exploring the inexplicable, the two of them set up a small experiment of what would now be called remote viewing. With Ball sitting in front of him and with his back turned, Doyle would draw figures on a piece of paper while attempting to communicate the images mentally through "thought-transference." The result was that "again and again, sitting behind him, I have drawn diagrams, and he in turn made approximately the same figure." Here was a curious anomaly that seemed to be outside the known laws of science—action at a distance, without any measurable sensory contact between the two people at all.

"And if mind could act upon mind at a distance, then there were human powers which were quite different to matter as we had always understood it," he wrote years later in a book called *The New Revelation,* thinking back over his early days as a still-skeptical student of spiritualism. "I had said that the flame could not exist when the candle was gone. But here was a flame a long way off the candle, acting upon its own. The analogy was clearly a false analogy. If the mind, the spirit, the intelligence of man could operate at a distance from the body, then it was a thing to that extent separate from the body. Why then should it not exist on its own when the body was destroyed?"

He decided to keep exploring, because after all "I had always sworn by science and the need of fearless following wherever the truth might lie." And so, for many years to come, "in the leisure hours of a very busy life," he continued to devote attention to what he was coming to believe was the most important subject in human history.

In 1886, Doyle went to the home of Major General Alfred Drayson, one of his patients, a brilliant amateur astronomer who was a fellow member of the Portsmouth Literary and Scientific Society. General Drayson had been participating in a series of "table tipping" sessions. A small group of people would sit around a dining-room table with their hands lightly on the tabletop. After a time, the table seemed to vibrate or sway, then tap with one leg. Answers to questions were spelled out through the tedious process of reciting the alphabet and then writing down the letter indicated by a table tap. Doyle was sport enough to sit through at least twenty of these sessions, but in the end he was unimpressed, concluding, "I am afraid the only result that they had on my mind was that I regarded these friends with suspicion." It seemed to him that the sitters were moving the table, whether consciously or not; that the "messages" were mostly empty platitudes; and that he never heard anything that could be considered actual, verifiable evidence of some discarnate intelligence.

Nevertheless, he kept up his acquaintance with General Drayson and kept on reading, widely and hungrily, as he would for the rest of his life. He read the early and influential two-volume *Spiritualism* by John Worth Edmonds, who had been a judge of the Supreme Court of New York, and George T. Dexter. Edmonds claimed to have been able to keep in contact with his wife for many years after her death. "I read the book with interest, and absolute skepticism," Doyle wrote. He read Robert Dale Owen's *Footfalls on the Boundary of Another World* and Daniel Dunglas Home's *Incidents in My Life.* He read another book by Monsieur Jacolliot, chief judge of the French colony of Chandernagore, in India. Though Jacolliot was a skeptic of spiritualism, he conducted a series of experiments, carefully controlled against fraud, with native fakirs, or Hindu religious ascetics. He found that the fakirs seemed to have paranormal powers similar to those of European mediums, causing tables to tip, plants to grow rapidly, and articles to move at a distance. They claimed these powers had been handed down to them from time immemorial, from the ancient Chaldeans. This impressed Doyle, because these were the same phenomena being reported from spiritualists in the Western world, but from an entirely different culture and geographic location. The Europeans could not claim, as they often did, that it was all just American fraud and vulgarity.

Doyle, perhaps too readily impressed by pedigree, also took note of the caliber of some of the people who had become spiritualists—Alfred Russel Wallace, the great biologist and co-discoverer of evolution; Camille Flammarion, the famous French astronomer; Sir William Crookes, the British chemist and physicist, among many other distinguished people. The opinions of these men were not as easily dismissed as those of the credulous masses.

BUT THE credulous masses were soon to receive a stunning blow to their convictions. On the morning of Sunday, October 21, 1888, stagehands at the three-thousand-seat Academy of Music auditorium, in New York City, trundled a few select pieces of heavy Victorian furniture onto the stage to create "a bare and somber drawing room scene," in keeping with the tone of that night's much-anticipated presentation. And it promised to be a barn burner, because Maggie and Kate Fox, whose mysterious "rappings" had touched off the whole spiritualist mania almost exactly forty years earlier, were now said to be taking the stage to renounce spiritualism entirely. The whole thing, they now claimed in a series of inflammatory letters to the New York papers, had been a fraud.

As soon as the doors were opened at the Academy of Music that evening, throngs of people crowded into the hall—spiritualists and anti-spiritualists, the press, the idly curious, and those simply itching to see a fight. "The great building was crowded and the wildest excitement prevailed at times," *The New York Herald* reported. When Maggie walked onstage, pale, somber, and dressed in black, she was greeted with cheers and hisses, the *Herald* reported. The intervening years had not been terribly kind to the once-comely girl. She appeared to have aged far beyond her fifty-five years; personal setbacks, poverty, ill health, and years of alcohol and drug abuse had taken their toll.

Standing in front of the expectant crowd, Maggie "put on her glasses, curtsied to the audience, and read slowly and in a voice trembling with emotion her confession," the paper said.

"That I have been chiefly instrumental in perpetrating the fraud of Spiritualism upon a too confiding public, most of you doubtless know," she began. "The greatest sorrow of my life has been that this is true, and though it has come late to my day, I am now prepared to tell the truth, the whole truth and nothing but the truth, so help me God!"

The audience responded with more cheers and more hisses.

Maggie maintained that the fraud had begun in all innocence, as a child, when she was unable to distinguish between right and wrong. But now that she was an adult and bathed in the light of God, "I am at last able to reveal the fatal truth, the exact truth of this hideous fraud which has withered so many hearts and blighted so many hopeful lives."

The next morning, the *New York World* ran a front-page illustrated story, covering four columns, about what happened next. A plain wooden table, on four short legs, like a sounding board, was brought out onto the stage. Maggie removed her right shoe and put her foot on the table. Then "the entire house became breathlessly still, and was rewarded by a number of little short, sharp raps—those mysterious sounds which have for more than forty years frightened and bewildered hundreds of thousands of people in this country and Europe."

A worldwide movement, with millions of adherents, appeared to have been triggered by a child cracking her toe.

Spiritualists were aghast at Maggie's recantation, of course. In a hastily arranged private meeting to assess the damage and discuss strategy, an old spiritualist who had known Maggie since 1850 tried to make it all go away by saying that she was "an ill, mentally unstable woman, whose use of stimulants and drugs makes her word undependable and of no account." But the damage had already been done. News of her "confession" swept across the country.

Still, the consternation and excitement did not last too terribly long. By now the Fox sisters had become old news. Spiritualism had long ago moved on from its origin story and also from its vaguely unstable founders. So when, a year later, Maggie Fox went public with yet *another* shocking announcement—this time recanting her recantation—it was too much for many but the most devoted spiritualists to follow.

"Would to God that I could undo the injustice I did the cause of Spiritualism when, under the strong psychological influences of persons inimical to it, I gave expression to utterances that had no foundation in fact!" she moaned, in a story that appeared in the *New York Press* in November 1889.

This time, she explained, she was *really* telling the truth. The year before, she had falsely claimed that the rappings were a fraud because the materialist enemies of spiritualism had offered her money to say that, and she was so desperate for cash that she had accepted their bribe. Also, she added, having converted to Catholicism, she had begun to worry that the various manifestations might be the work of the devil.

"When I made those dreadful statements I was not responsible for my words," Maggie said this time. "My belief in the philosophy and phenomena of Spiritualism is unshaken. Its genuineness is an incontrovertible fact."

But by now almost no one was listening. The publisher Isaac Funk, who had conducted psychic sessions with Maggie, later wrote, "So low had this unfortunate woman sunk that for five dollars she would have denied her mother."

Both Maggie and Kate, ridiculed and discredited, now seemed to sink into the oblivion born of a kind of shunning. Kate eventually died of a stroke and end-stage alcoholism, in a shabby apartment in New York City, on July 2, 1892. Maggie, in similarly desperate straits, put an ad in *Banner of Light* asking spiritualists to help contribute to her care. All of $86.80 came in.

Eventually, Maggie wound up bedridden in a tenement house on Ninth Street, in lower Manhattan. A physician from the Medico-Legal Society of New York, a woman named Dr. Mellen (who was not a spiritualist), attended to her for several hours a day. And she made a curious observation.

"Mrs. Fox Kane [her married name] was unable to move hand or foot," Dr. Mellen was quoted as saying in a published account called *Rappings That Startled the World*. "There was not a closet in the place nor any other hiding place of any kind. And yet the knockings were heard now through the wall, now through the ceiling, and again through the floor. They were heard in response to questions [a] woman put to her guide, as she expressed it. And she was as incapable of cracking her toe-joints at this time as I was."

Maggie slipped away on March 8, 1893. She was given a respectful burial by the few spiritualists who remembered her.

DOYLE BEGAN visiting mediums and participating in séances, and some of the messages that came through, he noted archly in his memoirs, "were not always absolutely stupid." Others appeared to be completely bogus. One long, detailed message came through from a spirit who said he had died in a fire in a theater at Exeter and asked that Doyle write his family, in a place called Slattenmere, in Cumberland. Doyle dutifully did so, and the letter came back, "appropriately enough, through the dead letter office."

Was it all nonsense and clumsy fraud?

Doyle took up the matter with General Drayson, whom he greatly respected. Drayson explained that "the truth is, every spirit in the flesh passes over to the next world exactly as it is, with no change whatsoever. This world is full of weak or foolish people. So is the next." In Drayson's view, Doyle had stuck his head into the next world, in amateurish séances with no particular aim, and had drawn the attention of a few "naughty boys" on the other side, who fed him blather and nonsense. "Go forward and try to reach something better," the general advised. So Doyle kept trying. By now, he wrote, "I was still a skeptic, but at least I was an inquirer."

He found his way into more sober séances, with more reputable mediums, and was sometimes astonished by long, anguished, remarkably detailed stories from "spirits" who claimed to have crossed over. Even so, despite the detail, Doyle wondered, "what proof was there that these statements were true? I could see no such proof, and they simply left me bewildered."

Though he was usually too poor to hire his own medium, one

day he hired an old man who had a reputation for psychic power. The old man came to Doyle's flat and, surrounded by a small group of people, went into a heavy-breathing trance. Then he gave each person a message. When he turned to Doyle, he said abruptly, "Do not read Leigh Hunt's book." Doyle was startled: Earlier that same day, he'd been wondering whether or not he should read a book by the English essayist Leigh Hunt. Once again, there it was—some seemingly inexplicable bit of evidence, a glimmer of starlight from afar, that suggested a world outside the known world of rationality and science. Doyle took this as proof of telepathy (though nothing more) and in 1887 went to the trouble of writing a short piece about the incident for the spiritualist newspaper *Light*. It was the first time he would go public as a student—though still an agnostic one—of the new "science" of spiritualism.

In 1893, Doyle's father, Charles, passed away in the Crichton Royal Institution, a sad, gentle ghost in a lunatic asylum. Three weeks later, Doyle joined the British Society for Psychical Research (SPR). By now, he had become preoccupied with studying the claims of spiritualism and began to associate with eminent men who were also deeply involved in spiritualist studies. In the SPR, he was to meet such celebrated men as Sir Oliver Lodge, a physicist who held key patents in the development of radio; Arthur Balfour, who later became prime minister of the U.K.; and F. W. H. Myers, a classics scholar turned scientist who wrote a number of important books about psychic research, including *Phantasms of the Living* and the massive two-volume *Human Personality and Its Survival of Bodily Death,* in which Myers argues that any model of the human mind must encompass not just normal psychological processes but also the shadow realm of the paranormal—telepathy, mediumship, even psychokinesis (the movement of objects at a distance). Doyle called the book "a great root book from which a whole tree of knowledge will grow."

Unlike the all-too-credulous "New Age" devotees of the 1960s, who seemed willing to hitch their star to any passing fancy, Arthur Conan Doyle and his colleagues of the late nineteenth century were serious and sober-minded men.

(Which is not to say that they were not sometimes fooled by phony mediums and quacks of one sort or another.) They were asking the most profound questions that humans had ever asked and attempting to subject ephemeral phenomena to the sort of scientific proofs that were rarely if ever applied to religious beliefs. It was "*proof* of immortality" that they were searching for, and it would distinguish spiritualism from the old religions, Doyle came to believe. In that sense, spiritualism would come to represent not a frightened, Luddite retreat from the era of enormous, sometimes bewildering technological and scientific progress—radio, the telephone, the telegraph, electric lights—but an answer to it.

If communication with the dead could be proven, spiritualists believed, theirs would become the world's first scientific religion.

AT THE same time as Doyle was delving deeper and deeper into the mysteries of spiritualism—and, it's fair to say, encountering the frauds and flimflams that often surrounded it—he was also pursuing a literary career.

And now, quite to his own surprise, it was beginning to look as though the literary life might supplant the life of a doctor. It might even pay better.

In a grainy black-and-white Movietone film, recorded not long before his death in 1930, Doyle responded to the two questions that people had asked him over the course of his long, highly public life. One had to do with how he had gotten interested in so-called psychic phenomena and spiritualism in the first place—a subject that was to consume most of his time and energy during the latter days of his life. The other thing, of course, had to do with the creation of Sherlock Holmes, the eccentric sleuth of 221B Baker Street.

Seated in a garden with his little dog, nattily attired in suit, tie, vest, and boater—a Scottish gentleman down to his watch fob—Doyle chuckled a bit when he explained that, curiously enough, both things had developed at about the same time in his life, when he was a young, not-very-successful doctor in

Southsea. It was *not* true, as many people later said of him, that his interest in spiritualism began after the death of his son Kingsley, in 1918. It had in fact begun decades earlier, as a young man in his twenties, with General Drayson's table-tipping experiments, his own vast reading, and his own direct experience with mediums and séances.

It was during those same early days in Southsea that he had also developed an appetite for reading detective stories, he told viewers of the Movietone film. He was especially fond of the three Edgar Allan Poe stories, including "The Murders in the Rue Morgue," that featured the crafty sleuth C. Auguste Dupin. Poe was, in fact, the undisputed father of the modern detective story—a "model for all time," as Doyle put it. But Doyle had a problem with most detective stories that appeared in pulp magazines. "I was a young doctor at the time, and of course I had scientific training," he said. "It always annoyed me that the detective always seemed to get at his results by some sort of lucky chance or else it was not quite explained how he got there. . . . That didn't seem to me quite playing the game, and I thought he was bound to give his reasons, why he came to his conclusions. So I began to think of turning scientific methods as it were onto methods of detection."

It was then that he remembered old Joe Bell, his surgery professor in medical school, with his extraordinary ability to diagnose a patient with little more than eerily astute observation—a fleck of mud on the shoe, a telltale bruise on the knuckle, a revealing mannerism.

"Naturally I thought if a scientific man like Bell were to get into the detection business, he wouldn't do these things by chance, he would build the thing up scientifically. So having once conceived that line of thought, you can well imagine that I had, as it were, a new idea for a detective, and one which interested me to work out."

Thinking of a fictional disguise to wrap around Joe Bell, he began to imagine a gaunt detective named "Sherrinford Hope," a collector of rare violins, a worldly philosopher, and a man with his own chemical laboratory. Eventually, he changed the name of his hero to Sherlock Holmes, at least partly due to his admiration for the doctor-philosopher Oliver Wendell Holmes, whom he had long admired. Mr. Holmes strutted onto the world's stage for the first time in 1887, in a short novel called *A Study in Scarlet.* The illustrations, oddly enough, were by none other than Charles Doyle, still confined to the lunatic asylum. (Though they weren't very good, they depicted Sherlock Holmes as having a beard like himself, almost as if he *wished* he were Holmes.) Doyle, who was twenty-seven years old when he wrote it, had dashed off the novel in less than three weeks. The title came from Holmes's description of the story's murder investigation as his "study in scarlet"—"There's the scarlet thread of murder running through the colourless skein of life, and our duty is to unravel it, and isolate it, and expose every inch of it." (The story, originally called "A Tangled Skein," had been repeatedly rejected until being accepted by *Beeton's Christmas Annual,* where it appears to have been barely noticed at all. In fact, had Doyle not kept writing about Sherlock Holmes, the man in the deerstalker hat would probably have vanished without a trace.)

But Doyle had another clever idea, this one about marketing: the idea of serializing the stories, each one complete in itself, but with the central character of Holmes carrying through them all. He sold the idea to *The Strand Magazine,* and in 1891 Sherlock Holmes began making monthly appearances in the magazine, in "A Scandal in Bohemia," "The Red-Headed League," "A Case of Identity," and many others. (In all, there are fifty-six stories and four short novels in the Sherlock Holmes "canon.")

"I thought of a hundred little dodges as you may say," Doyle recalled in the Movietone film, "little touches by which [Holmes] could build up his conclusions, and then I began to write stories on those lines. At first they attracted very little attention, but after a time . . . they began coming out month after month . . . people began to recognize that it was different than the old detective, that there was something there that was new. And they began to buy the magazine and it prospered and so I may say did I, and we both came along together and from that time Sherlock Holmes took root."

It was a typical Arthur Conan Doyle comment—a modest, understated aside. He hated pretensions. He did not mention that Sherlock Holmes would eventually become one of the most famous fictional creations in all of modern popular literature.

"I've written a good deal more about him than I ever intended to do," Doyle went on, "but my hand has been rather forced by kind friends who continually wanted to know more and so it is that this monstrous growth has come out of what was really a comparatively small seed. The curious thing is how many people around the world are perfectly convinced that [Holmes] is really a living human being. I get letters addressed to him; I get letters asking for his autograph. Letters addressed to his rather stupid friend Watson, and I even had ladies saying that they'd be very glad to act as his housekeeper. One of them when she heard that he had turned to the occupation of keeping bees wrote to say she was an expert in segregating the queen, whatever that may mean, and that she was evidently predestined to be the housekeeper of Sherlock Holmes."

It was the summer of 1891, the same year Sherlock began his long run in the pages of *The Strand,* that Doyle was walking to work one day when he felt himself gripped by an icy nausea. He staggered back home to bed, where he suffered an incapacitating attack of influenza. Only three years earlier, his sister Annette had died of the flu, shortly before Doyle's growing literary success might have lifted her out of her life as a governess in Lisbon. Now, "weak as a child and as emotional, but with a mind clear as crystal[,] . . . I surveyed my own life, I saw how foolish it was to waste my literary earnings in keeping up an oculist's room in Wimpole Street, and I determined with a wild rush of joy to cut the painter [rope] and to trust for ever to my power of writing. I remember in my delight taking the handkerchief which lay on the coverlet in my enfeebled hand, and tossing it up to the ceiling in my exultation.

"I should at last be my own master. No longer would I have to conform to professional dress or try to please anyone else. I would be free to live how I liked and where I liked. It was one of the great moments of exultation of my life."

By the end of the nineteenth century, some of the most eminent scientists in America, Britain, and Europe took part in séances in order to explore psychic phenomena. This is a retouched photo of an 1898 Paris séance in which the famous medium Eusapia Palladino levitated a table. Noted at the top: "without threads."

THE ARCHIVES OF TONY OURSLER

CHAPTER FIVE
The Science of the Unseen

"No self-respecting scientist believes in the paranormal," says Kristen Wiig's character, Erin Gilbert, in the 2016 remake of *Ghostbusters*. She's taking the conventional line because she's up for tenure at Columbia University, where she's a physics professor. But she loses her job after her villainous dean sees her on social media screaming "Ghosts are real!" after she's been slimed by the ghost of Gertrude at the Aldridge mansion.

As a depiction of the problems faced by psychical research, that scene is actually right on the mark. No, not the part where the ghost vomits ectoplasm: Some mediums exude it, but not ghosts, and it's grayish white, not lime Jell-O green. More to the point: There were scientists a century ago, some of them very eminent, who hoped that science could explain the mysteries produced in the séance room. Unfortunately, they had to endure more than a gentle demurrer from their colleagues; they had to endure outright lies and slander, and one, James Hervey Hyslop, was hounded out of his faculty position at . . . Columbia University. Really. Were their hopes misplaced? Probably. Science depends on being able to repeat a finding, again and again, before it's declared true. It's about controlling the variables. And that is simply impossible in the séance room. Results are never replicable, strictly. The experimenter isn't in charge. Even the medium isn't in charge. The spirits decide if and when they'll come through, and what they'll do when they get here. Lord Rayleigh, who won the Nobel Prize for his discovery of the gas argon and became chancellor of Cambridge University, also spent nearly half a century sitting with the most powerful mediums of his era; he died in 1919 still unsure of what he'd seen. In the end, he lamented, "We are ill equipped for the investigation of phenomena which cannot be reproduced at pleasure under good conditions."

But their hope was understandable, especially given the scientific advances of their day. Science was already exploring the unseen; the dazzling inventions of the late nineteenth and early twentieth centuries were based on research into the submicroscopic world of electricity, radio waves, X-rays, and atoms. Surely some of their newfound theories could explain how a wreath of clematis floated through the air and came to rest on the head of Elizabeth Barrett Browning.

Maybe the scientific method couldn't be applied to séances, but Arthur Conan Doyle and his generation could apply a scientific *attitude.* That attitude called for an open-mindedness about what we don't know and keen observation to arrive at something we *do* know. That was the real strength of spiritualism, said Doyle; the movement was "the most serious attempt ever made to place religion upon a basis of definite proof. . . . It was founded upon the rock of actual personal observation."

Seen in that light, Doyle's interest in spiritualism was not some baffling quirk of the man who invented Sherlock Holmes. There was no inherent contradiction. It was simply Doyle being Doyle: ever the detective in everything he came across. As his first biographer, the Reverend John Lamond, wrote, "Above all, *he could discern the value of evidence.*"

That's why he welcomed science into the séance room: "Each honest inquiry can only strengthen the cause of truth. The more light, the more understanding," he wrote in 1920. "But let it be real Science which comes to us, not prejudice and ill will, which judge a case first and examine it afterwards. That is not Science, but the very antithesis of Science."

THE FIRST scientist to systematically investigate spiritualism was Robert Hare, a chemist and professor emeritus at the University of Pennsylvania. He was famous both in Europe and in America for inventing the oxyhydrogen blowpipe, an early version of today's welding torch. He was already seventy when spiritualism was sweeping America, and he was comfortably retired after writing more than 150 academic papers. In the summer of 1853, he wrote a letter to his local paper, the *Philadelphia Inquirer,* criticizing the "popular madness" of the day. As he explained later in his book *Experimental Investigation of the Spirit Manifestations,* "I had been brought up deaf to any testimony which claimed assistance from supernatural causes."

When challenged by an earnest believer, he visited a few spirit circles, was impressed by the integrity of one medium in particular, and so set out to determine whether the rapped messages "could be made without mortal aid." He came up with a kind of Rube Goldberg contraption of wheels, weights, and pulleys he named the spiritoscope. He thought it would prove that the tables at séances were tipped by the humans around them. "The result was not as he expected," said the naturalist Alfred Russel Wallace in his first writing on spiritualism, *The Scientific Aspect of the Supernatural,* "for however he varied his experiments he was in every case only able to obtain results which proved that there *was* a power at work not that of any human being present. But in addition to the *power* there was an *intelligence,* and he was thus compelled to believe that existences not human did communicate with him."

Hare's first visit from a spirit was that of his father, Robert senior. When the spirit of his deceased sister came through, he asked for the name of their English grandfather's business partner, who'd died seventy years before. She nailed it. And so, having received these and other "evidential" messages, he became a convert and wrote his 460-page book, *Experimental Investigation,* which was published in 1855—and promptly scorned by his fellow scientists. "The brave report . . . led to a disgraceful persecution," Doyle wrote in his *History of Spiritualism.* The American Scientific Association "howled down Professor Hare when he attempted to address them, and put it on record that the subject was unworthy of their attention." The association then turned its attention to a far worthier topic: why cocks crow between midnight and 1:00 a.m.

Hare's research should have been lauded, not scorned, said Doyle. He flatly stated, in a 1920 essay, "From the hour of the Hare report there has been no excuse for the human race."

Nonetheless, the human race kept coming up with more excuses and turned a deaf ear to the research of Wallace, the chemist Sir William Crookes, and others. In a more organized effort to stop the madness, several British scientists and academics formed the Society for Psychical Research in 1882. They put up their own money to investigate psychic phenomena, they announced, "in the same spirit of exact and unimpassioned inquiry which has enabled science to solve so many problems." The founders included the physicist Sir William Barrett and the Cambridge philosophy professor Henry Sidgwick; one of the initial members was the mathematician Charles Lutwidge Dodgson, better known as Lewis Carroll. Doyle finally joined the organization in 1893.

We'll let William James take it from here. James, the older brother of the novelist Henry James, played a principal role in establishing psychology as a field of study; he's widely acknowledged as the father of American psychology. In an essay, "What Psychical Research Has Accomplished," he opened on this engaging note:

> According to the newspaper and drawing-room myth, soft-headedness and idiotic credulity are the bond of sympathy in the Society, and general wonder-sickness is its dynamic principle. A glance at the membership fails, however, to corroborate this view. The president is Prof. Henry Sidgwick, known by his other deeds as the most incorrigibly and exasperatingly critical and sceptical mind in England. The hard-headed Arthur Balfour is one vice-president, and the hard-headed Prof. J. P. Langley, secretary of the Smithsonian Institution, is another. Such men as Professor Lodge, the eminent English physicist, and

> Professor Richet, the eminent French physiologist, are amongst the most active contributors to the Society's "Proceedings"; and through the catalogue of membership are sprinkled names honored throughout the world for their scientific capacity. In fact, were I asked to point to a scientific journal where hard-headedness and never-sleeping suspicion of sources of error might be seen in their full bloom, I think I should have to fall back on the "Proceedings" of the Society for Psychical Research.

James wrote that in 1892, ten years after the Society for Psychical Research was founded. In another ten years, Balfour would be Britain's prime minister, and Lodge would be knighted for his scientific achievements. In a little more than two decades, Charles Richet would win the Nobel Prize.

William James didn't include himself in the pantheon, but he did play a key role in psychical research. He contributed to the society's *Proceedings,* and he was president of the SPR in 1894 and 1895. He was a founding member of the American branch in 1885. But most of all he introduced to the world one of the most remarkable (and most documented) mediums of all time, Leonora Piper. Her mediumship transformed arch-skeptics into true believers. Arthur Conan Doyle devoted ten pages of his *History of Spiritualism* to her. "Mrs. Piper," as she was commonly known, was a major milestone in Doyle's own thirty-year spiritual journey "from the left of negation to the right of acceptance," to use one of his favorite phrases.

SHE WAS born Leonora Evelina Simonds in Nashua, New Hampshire, in late June 1859—one month later than Conan Doyle. Great mediums are born, not made, and one of her first psychic experiences occurred when she was eight. She was playing outside when she felt something smack her right ear; it was followed by a hiss that turned into the name Sara. Leonora ran into the house, hysterical. She told her mother, "Aunt Sara said she wasn't dead but with you still." She was so upset that her mother, whose sister was indeed named Sara, noted the day and time in her diary. Several days later, they heard from Sara's husband: Sara had died, unexpectedly, right about the time Leonora ran into the house.

Leonora grew into a tall, fair-haired, dignified young woman and married William Piper, a Boston shopkeeper, when she was twenty-two. Two years later, in 1884, she gave birth to her first child, a daughter named Alta. She suffered from abdominal pain afterward, and William Piper's parents persuaded her to visit a blind healing medium. On her second visit, the medium placed his hands on her head, and she lost consciousness. In a trance, she got up from her chair, went to a table in the center of the room, scribbled a note, and handed it to Judge Frost, an elderly jurist who was waiting his turn for a sitting. When she came out of her trance, Judge Frost told her it was a message from his son who'd died in an accident thirty years earlier. The private message was, he told her, "the most remarkable I ever received."

Shortly afterward, the young Mrs. Piper began granting sittings to friends and family in her suburban Boston home (at that point she and William still lived with his parents in Arlington Heights). The modus operandi was always the same. Shortly after she sat in her armchair, her eyeballs rolled upward and her face became contorted; occasionally, she tore at her hair. Then she began talking in voices quite unlike her own. Usually there was one primary voice—that of the "control," a spirit who takes over the medium's body and acts as a gatekeeper in the other world, maintaining order among the other spirits who want to communicate and fending off random low-level spirits who simply want to make mischief. (As Doyle had been warned by General Drayson back in Southsea, there are plenty of "naughty boys" on the other side.) When Mrs. Piper emerged from her trance, the convulsions resumed, much to the alarm of many sitters. Notably, all this took place in broad daylight. Mrs. Piper was strictly a "mental" medium, not a "physical" medium. There was no need for darkness, no need for the medium to sit in a cabinet or behind drawn curtains in a corner of the room. There were no ringing bells or flying trumpets or levitating tables. But sometimes there were messages from dead relatives.

All the while, Mrs. Piper was clueless as to their contents. As she later described her trances to her daughter Alta,

> I feel as if something were passing over my brain, making it numb. . . . I feel a little cold, too, not very, just a little, as if a cold breeze passed over me, and people and objects become smaller until they finally disappear; then, I know nothing more until I wake up, when the first thing I am conscious of is a bright, very very bright light, and then darkness, such darkness. . . . I see, as if from a great distance, objects and people in the room; but they are very small and very black.

As her reputation grew during the year 1885, and friends of friends came to visit, she granted a sitting to a widow named Eliza Gibbens, who happened to be the mother-in-law of William James.

Eliza was amazed by the medium's knowledge of her family members, their names and their lives. So she sent her daughter Margaret to Mrs. Piper with a sealed letter from a friend in Italy. Mrs. Piper, holding the sealed envelope in front of her, described the writer, where she was, and why she'd moved across the Atlantic. That was impressive: Even if she could have seen the letter, it was written in Italian. With Margaret on board, they told her sister Alice, James's wife. Alice was disconsolate over the recent death of their young son, Herman. Maybe some comfort could be found.

And so, on a soft autumn late afternoon in 1885, William James and his wife first entered the front parlor of Mrs. Piper's in-laws. He'd warned Alice beforehand, *Don't tell her our names. Don't tell her anything,* just as Eliza and Margaret had not revealed their identities. As Mrs. Piper sat in her armchair with her head turned sideways, she drifted into a trance and began murmuring names. Niblin became Giblin became Gibbens. Names, more names. Then she asked about a dead child. A boy. A small one. Herrin? No, Herman.

William James was so intrigued that he came back for eleven more sittings and sent twenty-five other people to see her, all under pseudonyms. Fifteen of them heard, at their first sitting, names of deceased relatives and facts about them that the most brilliant detective couldn't have uncovered. The following spring, James submitted a brief account to the SPR's *Proceedings*. Although he initially assumed that her "hits" were the result of lucky guesses or knowledge of the sitters' identities, he wrote, "I now believe her to be in possession of a power as yet unexplained."

James had to move on with his other work; he was, after all, teaching the nascent subject of psychology at his alma mater, Harvard, and he was trying to wrap up his magnum opus, the two-volume *Principles of Psychology*. So he handed over the primary investigation of Mrs. Piper to the world's sharpest hotshot in the business of exposing fraudulent mediums: Richard Hodgson.

Hodgson was the son of an Australian wool importer who'd gotten his law degree in Melbourne but decided not to practice law and instead showed up at Cambridge to study poetry and philosophy. He impressed his philosophy professor, Henry Sidgwick, who decided to send Hodgson on a little mission. In late 1884, Hodgson went to Madras, India, on behalf of the SPR (and on Sidgwick's own dime) to unmask Madame Blavatsky, the leader of the Theosophical Society. She claimed that spirits wrote messages to her on letters that mysteriously appeared in the tiny drawers of her Indian shrine. Hodgson found out how that worked: The drawers also opened onto Madame Blavatsky's bedroom on the other side of the wall. As he slipped away from Madras with this and other insights, the shrine mysteriously burned to the ground. The subsequent SPR report called her "one of the most accomplished and interesting imposters in history."

Hodgson returned to England and soon tackled yet another spiritualistic practice that was ripe for fraud: slate writing. He angered many prominent spiritualists when he concluded that it was all a con and that "nearly all professional mediums are a gang of vulgar tricksters." Alfred Russel Wallace was especially peeved and openly wondered when the SPR would get down to actual psychical research instead of scouting for frauds or coming up with an endless array of suspicions when no fraud was found.

Yes, Hodgson had made a name for himself. So it might have been an ominous moment for spiritualism when he landed in Boston in 1887, having been sent by Sidgwick to be chief investigator for the American branch of the SPR; he assumed from the start that Mrs. Piper was a fraud. He went to his first sitting with her on May 4, 1887, revealing neither his name nor his reason for being in America. It was curious, very curious, that this simple Boston lady knew so much about his life back in Australia. Actually, *she* didn't; as noted above, she would awake from her trances recalling nothing. It was her control, "Phinuit," who did the talking. Phinuit claimed to be a French doctor who died about 1860; he spoke in a gruff voice, freely mixing English with French, Negro patois, and Yankee slang. (He delighted in slang, once cheerfully repeating a sitter's expression, "Put that in your pipe and smoke it.") He would diagnose diseases and prescribe herbal remedies. But mostly he would relay messages from the other side.

Hodgson's notes from his first sitting with Mrs. Piper read, in part,

> Phinuit began, after the usual introduction, by describing members of my family.
>
> "Mother living, father dead, little brother dead." [True] Father and mother described correctly, though not with much detail. In connection with the enumeration of the members of our family, Phinuit tried to get a name beginning with R, but failed. [A little sister of mine, named Rebecca, died when I was very young, I think less than eighteen months old.]
>
> "Four of you living besides mother." [True]
>
> Phinuit mentioned the name "Fred." I said it might be my cousin. "He says you went to school together. He

> goes on jumping-frogs, and laughs. He says he used to get the better of you. He had convulsive movements before his death, struggles. He went off in a sort of spasm. You were not there." [My cousin Fred far excelled any other person that I have seen in the games of leap-frog, fly the garter, &c. He took very long flying jumps, and whenever he played, the game was lined by crowds of schoolmates to watch him. He injured his spine in a gymnasium in Melbourne, Australia, in 1871, and was carried to the hospital, where he lingered for a fortnight, with occasional spasmodic convulsions, in one of which he died.]
>
> Phinuit described a lady, in general terms, dark hair, dark eyes, slim figure, &c, and said that she was much closer to me than any other person: that she "died slowly. Too bad you weren't with her. You were at a distance. It was a great pain to both of you that you weren't there. She would have sent you a message, if she had known she was going. She had two rings; one was buried with her body; the other ought to have gone to you. The second part of her name is–sie." [True, with the exception of the statement about the rings, which may or may not be true.]

The lady's name was Jessie, a fact later revealed by Hodgson's biographer, Alex Baird. She was the one true love of his youth, but their relationship had to end in 1875 because her parents objected to his reluctance to embrace their Methodist faith. (No wonder he ran off to Cambridge.) In his second sitting, Phinuit said Jessie was good friends with his sister, and his sister told him about her death. In his sixth sitting, Phinuit said Jessie's left eye is brown, but her right eye has a spot of light color in the iris. Hodgson asked Phinuit how he knew about the eye. Phinuit said she was standing right there, showing him.

Oh, and Phinuit said Jessie wanted to be sure he kept that book of poetry he'd given her and that her family returned to him after her death. Hodgson said nothing. But the book, Tennyson's *Princess,* was on his shelf in his Boston apartment.

Who *was* Phinuit, and how did he know these things? William James suspected that Phinuit was a secondary personality buried in Mrs. Piper's subconscious and this secondary personality had telepathic ability—the ability to read the minds of sitters in front of her. But if that were so, how did it know things the sitter *didn't* know? In one sitting, Phinuit told Hodgson that his sister back in Australia would soon be giving birth to a fourth child, a boy. That came true. But Hodgson didn't even know his sister was expecting.

The only other explanation, of course, was outright fraud. Mrs. Piper didn't seem as if she had the means to hire spies to find out all this stuff. But just to be sure, Hodgson hired detectives to trail her and her husband and make inquiries. They found nothing, but when she found out about it, she upbraided Hodgson, and then James, telling them respectable people didn't have detectives following them around town. It was humiliating. She threatened to quit the research program. James tried to make light of it; he implored her to see its "comic side."

Fortunately, James won her over. Luckily, he didn't have to tell her that Hodgson had been putting ammonia under her nose and pinching her until she bruised to check the genuineness of her trances. Once she passed all these tests, Hodgson arranged to put Mrs. Piper under contract to the SPR in the beginning of 1888. She would give roughly three sittings a week for his research; he would bring in visitors. They would come in anonymously and yield no personal information; he would sit in a corner and glare at them if they did. Once he yelled at a visitor for leaving her wet umbrella in the umbrella stand—because it *could* be used to carry in a note, you know! Hodgson, already a pretty intense guy, was becoming obsessed. That probably had a lot to do with the nature and quality of the sittings: Some of them were remarkable, and he wanted nothing to mar the results.

In 1889, Hodgson and James devised another test of Mrs. Piper's powers. They would remove her to a totally new environment to preclude any possibility of secret spies or talkative servants. Accordingly, she was invited to visit England for three months, beginning in November 1889. She stayed twice in Liverpool with Oliver Lodge and his wife, twice in Cambridge with the Sidgwicks, and twice in London. She allowed Lodge to examine her mail and search her baggage (she was getting used to this). It mattered not: The twenty-one sittings she gave under Lodge's roof were the most successful of the entire trip.

On December 24, 1889, only Lodge, his wife, Mary, and a shorthand reporter were present at a remarkable sitting involving a gold watch. Here are Lodge's notes, later published in the *Proceedings*:

> It happens that an uncle of mine in London, now quite an old man, and one of surviving three out of a very large family, had a twin brother who died some twenty years ago. I wrote to ask if he would lend me some relic of his brother. By morning post I received a curious old gold watch, which this brother had worn and been fond of; and that same morning, no one in the house having seen it or knowing anything about it, I handed it to Mrs. Piper when in a state of trance.
>
> I was told almost immediately that it had belonged to one of my uncles—one that had been very fond of Uncle Robert, the name of the survivor—that the watch was now in possession of this same Uncle Robert, with whom he was anxious to communicate. After some difficulty and many wrong attempts Dr. Phinuit caught the name, Jerry, short for Jeremiah, and said emphatically, as if a third person was speaking, "This is my watch, and Robert is my brother, and I am here, Uncle Jerry, my watch."
>
> Having thus ostensibly got into communication through some means or other with what purported to be a deceased relative, whom I indeed had known slightly in his later years of blindness, but of whose early life I knew nothing, I pointed out to him that to make Uncle

> Robert aware of his presence it would be well to recall trivial details of their boyhood, all of which I would faithfully report.
>
> He quite caught the idea, and proceeded during several successive sittings ostensibly to instruct Dr. Phinuit to mention a number of little things such as would enable his brother to recognize him. . . . "Uncle Jerry" recalled episodes such as swimming the creek when they were boys together, and running some risk of getting drowned; killing a cat in Smith's field; the possession of a small rifle, and of a long peculiar skin, like a snake-skin, which he thought was not in the possession of Uncle Robert.

Lodge checked with Uncle Robert, who confirmed all but the killing of the cat. But another brother, Frank, clearly recalled the cat-killing incident in Smith's field. These details were nowhere to be found among Oliver Lodge's memories, making telepathy inadequate as an explanation.

The following day was Christmas, and, yes, they did make Mrs. Piper work on Christmas, those scrooges. Twice. When Lodge sat with his brother Alfred, Phinuit announced that their dead relatives were worried about the health of Oliver and Alfred's sister. Phinuit struggled to get her name; finally, he asked for a pencil, and Mrs. Piper wrote "Nellie." Phinuit said Aunt Anne wrote it. It was indeed their sister's nickname.

She earned her thirty shillings that day.

"I took every precaution that I could think of," Lodge wrote many years later in his memoir. All in all, Mrs. Piper's Christmas visit left him "thoroughly convinced, not only of human survival, but of the power to communicate under certain conditions, with those left behind on the earth."

When Mrs. Piper returned to Boston with her two daughters in February 1890, she was exhausted from the sittings, the constant scrutiny, and the enforced isolation. She wanted no part of any experiments for the rest of the year. But Hodgson had more than enough material for his next big report to the SPR. Those who were looking for another exposure along the lines of Madame Blavatsky were disappointed: Mrs. Piper's trances were genuine. As for Phinuit, well, that was fishy; no such doctor's death could be tracked down in France. So Hodgson, along with James and Richet, attributed his character to a secondary personality. But as-yet-unexplained supernormal forces were the causeways of information. And in his *Proceedings* report, finally published in 1892, he left the door open with a brief mention of recent research, where nothing other than a hypothesis of "embodied human intelligence" (that is, the survival of human personality) could explain things.

That's because of a dramatic change during the sitting of March 22, 1892. A new "control" appeared, a young man named George Pellew, who had been killed a few weeks earlier while riding his horse on the ice in Central Park. He had been a Harvard grad with a law degree who wrote editorials for the New York *Sun*. He had once met Hodgson and told him that if he died first and was "still existing," he'd get in touch. At that March 22 sitting, Hodgson brought Pellew's friend John Hart. Phinuit announced, early on, that "George" was present. Phinuit gave George's full name, as well as the names of several close friends—including Hart, who was supposedly sitting anonymously. Phinuit then told Hart that the studs he was wearing used to be Pellew's and that Pellew's parents gave them to Hart after the funeral. George, through Phinuit, asked Hart to bring some mutual friends, Jim and Mary Howard, to a future sitting, and he described conversations with their fifteen-year-old daughter, Katharine. All this was true, and it was way past telepathy.

When Jim and Mary Howard came three weeks later, Pellew took over Mrs. Piper's body and spoke directly.

> **George**: Jim is that you? Speak to me quick. I am not dead. Don't think me dead. Give my love to my father and tell him I want to see him. I am happy here, and more so since I can communicate with you.
> **Jim**: What do you do, George, where are you?

> **George**: I am scarcely able to do anything yet. I am just awakened to the reality of life after death. I could not distinguish anything at first. I was puzzled, confused. . . . Your voice, Jim, I can distinguish with your accent and articulation, but it sounds like a big bass drum. Mine would sound to you like the faintest whisper.
> **Jim**: Our conversation, then, is something like telephoning?
> **George**: Yes.
> **Jim**: By long distance telephone?
> **George**: (Laughs)
> **Jim**: Were you not surprised to find yourself living?
> **George**: Greatly surprised. I did not believe in a future life. It was beyond my reasoning powers. Now it is as clear to me as daylight.

In this and in many sittings over the next few years, George Pellew came across as his full-blown former self. When Katharine attended a sitting, he teased her about her "horrible" violin playing, as he always did. He discussed secrets with Jim. He identified pictures of the Howards' summer home. He was so domineering as a control that Phinuit complained about him. Out of the 150 sitters who were introduced to him, he recognized the 30—and only the 30—with whom he'd been acquainted in the flesh. This was no secondary personality, and he flatly said so.

As George Pellew asserted more control, Mrs. Piper's trances changed. She became more of a trance-writing medium. Several pillows were placed on a table in front of her, and she turned her head to the left so she could breathe. About thirty seconds after she slipped into a trance, her right hand would rise up. Blank sheets were placed to her right, along with four or five soft-lead pencils. Hodgson would place a pencil in her hand and tear off the sheets as she filled them with writing. At times, Phinuit would be communicating via voice while George Pellew sent messages through the hand. In fact, at a sitting in early 1895 Hodgson reported that Phinuit was speaking and George was writing with one hand while yet a third spirit, a deceased sister of a sitter, wrote with the other hand—all simultaneously, on different subjects.

Phinuit made his last appearance as a "control" in early 1896, and George Pellew gradually relinquished his role the following year. But Hodgson had enough to write "A Further Record of Observations of Certain Phenomena of Trance," three hundred pages of evidence, for the June 1898 issue of the *Proceedings*. In it, he clearly put himself among the spiritualists: The communicators through Mrs. Piper were indeed the surviving spirits of the deceased. This was an extraordinary moment, especially for the spiritualists like Dawson Rogers of the London Spiritualist Alliance, who remembered him somewhat differently, long ago: "He was a very Saul persecuting the Christians." As for Doyle, it was the single biggest piece of evidence until the messages delivered through Lily Loder-Symonds in late 1915 cemented his conviction of spirit survival.

In 1898, James Hervey Hyslop took the place of Richard Hodgson as Mrs. Piper's chief investigator. The son of a stern fundamentalist Presbyterian farm family in Xenia, Ohio, Hyslop was a professor of logic and ethics at Columbia, having previously taught at Lake Forest, Smith, and Bucknell. And he had been estranged from his late father, Robert, because of his doubts. In his first sitting with Mrs. Piper, Hodgson introduced him as his "four times friend" who'd requested four sittings. Even though he'd waited outside until Mrs. Piper was in a trance, he came in wearing a black mask over his face. In the second sitting, Mrs. Piper announced that a new spirit was in the room: Robert Hyslop. Over four sittings, Hyslop said the ghost of his father described 205 incidents, of which 152 were verified. But never mind the numbers: "I talked with my discarnate father with as much ease as if I were talking with him, living, through the telephone."

Hyslop and Hodgson worked amiably together for the next several years, right until the day Hodgson dropped dead on the handball court of the Union Boat Club. It was December 20, 1905, and he was only fifty. Mrs. Piper had a dream that night; she was entering a tunnel and a figure raised his hand to block her way. The hand looked like Hodgson's. The morning paper brought the news of his death.

A month later, a message came through during a sitting with Alice James and her son Billy. It was Hodgson. "Is that Mrs. James and Billy? God bless you! I have found my way, I am here, have patience with me. All is well with me. Don't miss me. Where's William?"

By February, Hodgson was communicating with Hyslop through Mrs. Piper; they were "keeping up a conversation at their accustomed level through the mouth and hand of this entranced woman," Doyle wrote. "It is a wonderful, almost an inconceivable situation, that he who had so long been examining the spirit who used the woman, should now actually *be* the spirit who used the woman, and be examined in turn by his old colleague."

Mrs. Piper returned to England in late 1906 for more séances with Oliver Lodge. At the eighth sitting, Hodgson announced himself, and Lodge said, "Very glad to see you." Hodgson gave a characteristic reply: "Here's ditto." And then he asked, "Do I understand that Mrs. Piper is in England?"

In 1909, G. Stanley Hall, the president of Clark University, asked William James for permission to have six sittings with Mrs. Piper. Granted permission, he and his assistant Amy Tanner promptly got to work. When Mrs. Piper was in trance, they dripped camphor into her mouth to see if she was faking the trance. No, she didn't wake up, but the next morning blisters covered her mouth and tongue. Next, he placed an instrument on her arm that slowly screwed a weight against her skin. Again, the trance was not disturbed, but her daughter Alta was, when her mother lost the use of her arm for several days. All this so that Hall could triumphantly announce that Mrs. Piper's spirits were a joke and that spiritualism was "the ruck and muck of modern culture." In pursuit of his ideology, Hall had physically abused Mrs. Piper.

After the Hall episode, Leonora Piper had seen enough science.

She continued with private sittings but kept a low profile. When Arthur Conan Doyle came to America in 1922, she traveled to

New York to hear him speak at Carnegie Hall and went backstage afterward, along with a hundred other well-wishers. She was among "the few whom I really welcomed . . . a gentle, elderly woman."

Elderly as she was, she was active psychically into the 1920s and beyond. In 1925, Sir William Barrett, a physicist and founder of the SPR, was about to have tea with a family friend, a Mrs. Jervis, who had recently visited America and sat with Mrs. Piper. He wrote to Mrs. Jervis telling her to come to tea on May 28, but he died on May 26.

In mid-June, Mrs. Jervis got a letter from Mrs. Piper. She wanted to pass along a message from Sir William: "Tell Mrs. Jervis I am sorry I could not keep the appointment."

The public had begun to wonder: How could Conan Doyle, creator of the world's most rational sleuth, have been suckered into the silliness of spiritualism?

PICTORIAL PRESS LTD. / ALAMY STOCK PHOTO

CHAPTER SIX
"Some Splendid Starry Night"

Arthur Conan Doyle seemed to write about everything that ever happened to him, and everything he ever thought about or imagined, so it's a bit of a mystery why he left no written record of precisely what occurred on the evening of March 15, 1897. But he would remember that day for the rest of his life. Because that was when he first met Miss Jean Leckie, the love of his life, his second wife, his lifelong companion, and his spiritual soul mate.

He was just shy of thirty-eight; she was twenty-three and lovely, with great bolts of auburn hair, green eyes, alabaster skin, and a look of vaguely bored late-Victorian refinement. She came from a distinguished Scottish family that traced its lineage back to the thirteenth century and included the Scottish folk hero Rob Roy Macgregor. She had a fine mezzo-soprano voice and was an expert horsewoman.

Apparently, she and the urbane Dr. Doyle, the well-known author, hit it off immediately.

There was just one problem, of course.

He was still married.

Touie was the most devoted and affectionate woman a man could ask for, but Doyle's letters and papers suggest that he did not love her in the way he quickly came to love Jean Leckie.

By comparison, Touie's family, her interests, even her physical appearance, now seemed homely and commonplace. By now, Touie was also a semi-invalid, having been diagnosed with tuberculosis several years earlier. Doyle took her on several health trips to the Alps, in the hope of clearing her weakened lungs, but she seemed to grow ever more delicate, and dependent, as the disease progressed.

Given these circumstances, a less principled man might have lunged into a sexual affair with the comely Miss Leckie (if she were willing) or arranged some excuse to abandon poor Touie. But Conan Doyle did neither. Available written records, both public and private, are in agreement that over the next ten years, until Touie's death in 1906, there is no evidence that he and Jean had a secret amorous affair or that he turned away from his wife. (Doyle and Jean *did* develop an ever-deepening platonic relationship, however, making contact by letter, telephone, and in person.) When Touie's lungs finally succumbed to the tuberculosis infection, Doyle wrote to his mother, "I tried never to give Touie a moment's unhappiness; to give her every attention, every comfort she could want. Did I succeed? I think so. God knows I hope so."

A year after Touie's death, Doyle and Jean were married, in St. Margaret's Church, Westminster. It was September 18, 1907, and though the wedding was a private family affair, it was reported around the world. The Buenos Aires *Standard* ran the headline "Sherlock Holmes Quietly Married." Having been knighted five years earlier (for a book he wrote in support of the British role in the Boer War), Doyle was now "Sir" Arthur Conan Doyle, and his new wife became "Lady Jean." Together they stepped into one of the happiest periods of Sir Arthur's life.

By now, Doyle's literary fame had spread across the English-speaking world, courtesy of Sherlock, but also because of his historical nonfiction and medieval tales such as *The White Company* and *Sir Nigel*. The incoming fan mail turned into a deluge. Though he generally wrote forty or more letters a day, according to John Dickson Carr, an early biographer who had access to his private papers, he hired a full-time secretary to help manage his personal affairs.

Meanwhile, he now set about renovating and greatly expanding his country house, called Windlesham, in Crowborough, East Sussex. It became a stately manor house, with five gables, towering chimneys, a red tile roof, and sumptuous English gardens. Eventually, he and Jean came to employ eight servants to tend the house and grounds. The billiard room, which ran the entire length of the house, was so vast that more than a hundred couples could dance in it, once the furniture was moved back. In 1912, the British Medical Association actually held its annual meeting at Windlesham. No longer a penniless, obscure, small-town doctor who scribbled stories in his empty waiting room, now Sir Arthur was a titled, wealthy, literary aristocrat. He and Lady Jean began entertaining lavishly at Windlesham. And now the children began to arrive, first Denis, then Adrian, then Jean, a tomboy nicknamed Billy. (Including Mary and Kingsley, from his first marriage to Touie, Doyle had five children.)

Yet in his daybooks and personal papers, and sometimes in his literary work, Doyle kept obsessively returning to the fundamental questions about the nature of human life and the possibility of the personality's survival after death. He also kept experimenting for himself, sitting with mediums, holding table séances, and continuing to read from the voluminous outpouring of books and periodicals concerned with spiritualism. At the same time, he'd become deeply engrossed in British politics, and even ran for Parliament, twice, but was defeated. (His friend William Gillette, reading about Doyle's increasingly public presence in British political life, wrote to him, "My dear fellow, what singular tastes you have! Why all this energy? Is it not much better—like me—to care for nothing?")

One night his brother Innes remarked offhandedly, while visiting him at Windlesham, "You know, Arthur, it would be strange if your real career should prove to be political and not literary."

Arthur, busy writing a letter, immediately shot back without looking up, "It will be religious."

The comment was so sudden, and so unexpected, they both burst out laughing.

ON JUNE 28, 1914, a disordered young Serbian nationalist named Gavrilo Princip pulled out a pocket-sized pistol and shot Archduke Franz Ferdinand, heir to the throne of the

Austro-Hungarian Empire, and his wife, Sophie, as they passed by in a motorcade in Sarajevo, Bosnia. With astonishing speed, the assassination set in motion a chain of events that was to lead to what came to be called the Great War, and later, more sadly, "the war to end all wars." By the time it ended, in 1918, more than seventeen million people lay dead, twenty million had been wounded, and much of Europe lay in smoking ruins.

There was hardly a family on the Continent that had not lost someone, and Sir Arthur's family was no exception. Lady Jean's brother Malcolm, who was serving as a military doctor, was killed in the retreat from Mons in August 1914, barely three weeks after the war began. In the coming days, Sir Arthur's nephew Oscar Hornung would be killed in the trenches. So would his sister's husband Leslie Oldham.

It was at Mons, in those first days of the war, that the British public began to realize that defeating the German army would be far more difficult than anyone had hoped—that this confused conflict might turn into a long, bloody slog rather than a quick, glorious, decisive victory. The Battle of Mons was the first major action of the British Expeditionary Force, in which the British fought to hold the line against the advancing German First Army. Though the British fought valiantly, inflicting far more casualties than they suffered, they were ultimately forced into a hasty, humiliating retreat, which turned into a rout when the French army also retreated, exposing the British flanks to attack.

A few weeks later, in September 1914, a short story called "The Bowmen," by the Welsh author Arthur Machen, appeared in a British newspaper. Machen imagined a soldier at the Battle of Mons calling on Saint George to dispatch bowmen from the Battle of Agincourt (a decisive British victory in the Hundred Years' War, in 1415) to overwhelm the German army. The story was written in the first person, as if it were true, and not clearly marked as fiction. It became instantly popular and was widely reprinted. From there the tale quickly took on a life of its own. People became convinced the story was true. Reports began to circulate that German soldiers had been found at Mons with arrow wounds. That shining multitudes had been seen intervening between the two armies at the decisive moment of battle. A priest reprinted the story as a pamphlet, with supporting evidence to show that there had actually been what came to be known as the "Angels of Mons." The angel story made its way into Sunday sermons, as proof of divine favoritism toward the British. In some versions, Joan of Arc even appeared on the battlefield.

Arthur Machen finally published a book-length version of the story, with a long preface explaining that it was all mere fiction. But to no avail. It was emblematic of those times, when the world seemed to have descended into bloody darkness, that this story (and others, about ghosts and apparitions seen at Flanders field and elsewhere) spread like a contagion and could not be stopped.

People were simply desperate to believe.

Eventually, the Society for Psychical Research conducted a thorough study of these "angel" rumors. Regarding firsthand accounts, it reported, "we have received none at all, and of testimony at second-hand we have none that would justify us in assuming the occurrence of any supernormal phenomenon." All of it, the SPR concluded, was little more than hopeful fantasies which "prove on investigation to be founded on mere rumour, and cannot be traced to any authoritative source."

MEANWHILE, BY November 1916, while the war raged on and the death toll seemed to climb beyond counting, Sir Oliver Lodge published a book called *Raymond; or, Life and Death*.

The distinguished Sir Oliver was one of Conan Doyle's most respected friends and colleagues. In fact, they had been knighted together in 1902 and spent much of the ceremony discussing spiritualism. Lodge's book made an enormous impression on Doyle.

The book concerned a series of eerie events that surrounded the death of Lodge's twenty-six-year-old son Raymond, who was killed in action in the trenches of Flanders, near Ypres, on September 14, 1915. Lodge had been knighted for his contributions to science and held several key early patents in the development of radio. He was also deeply interested in the question of life after death and was a founding member of the Society for Psychical Research. Lodge had also been a colleague of

F. W. H. Myers, another founder of the SPR and the author of several important books about spiritualism, including *Phantasms of the Living* and *Human Personality and Its Survival of Bodily Death.*

Before he died in 1901, Myers had promised to attempt to communicate across the dark chasm of death once he reached "the other side." But for fourteen years, none of the mediums in England or America had received any messages from him (or any purporting to be from him). Then, on August 8, 1915—a month before Raymond's death—Oliver Lodge received a curious message from Alta Piper, the daughter of the American medium Leonora Piper, who had been giving a sitting in New Hampshire. Not knowing quite what it all meant, but believing it had been directed at Oliver Lodge, Alta Piper sent him the text of her mother's séance, which had been conducted at the request of a Miss Robbins. In it, Mrs. Piper channeled a personality calling itself "Richard Hodgson," her old investigator from the 1890s.

In the text of this sitting, Hodgson is dealing with some minor matters of personal significance to Miss Robbins, when suddenly he seems to shift gears.

"Now Lodge, while we are not here as of old, *i.e.* not quite, we are enough to take and give messages. Myers says you take the part of the poet, and he will act as Faunus."

Miss Robbins: "Faunus?"

Hodgson: "Yes. Myers. Protect. He will understand. What have you to say, Lodge? Good work. Ask Verrall, she will also understand. Arthur says so."

Miss Robbins (confused): "Do you mean Arthur Tennyson?"

Hodgson: "*No. Myers* knows. . . . Myers is straight about Poet and Faunus."

To the ordinary person, including those present at the séance, all this meant next to nothing. But Lodge, when he received the text from Alta Piper, sensed that the allusion was probably to some scene or quotation from classical literature. (Myers had been a classical scholar, as well as an accomplished poet.) Lodge also knew that "Verrall" referred to the classical scholar and spiritualist Margaret Verrall, of Newnham College, part of the Cambridge nucleus of the SPR. (Her deceased husband, Arthur, was also a renowned classicist.) Lodge contacted her to ask, "Does *The Poet and Faunus* mean anything to you? Did one 'protect' the other?"

Mrs. Verrall replied promptly, saying that "the reference is to Horace's account of his narrow escape from death, from a falling tree, which he ascribes to the intervention of Faunus, the guardian of poets." She added that "the passage is a very well-known one to all readers of Horace" and that a falling tree was a common symbol of death. In other words, Myers seemed to be telling Lodge to prepare himself for a great blow but that he, Myers, would do everything he could to ease the pain.

Five weeks later, on September 17, Lodge and his wife received the telegram from the War Office that every English family dreaded, informing them that Second Lieutenant Raymond Lodge, their youngest son, had been struck and killed by shell fragments while leading his company back from an expedition to one of the communication trenches at the front.

Lodge came to believe that his old friend Myers had been trying to warn him of Raymond's impending death and to shield him from the blow by demonstrating that both he (Myers) and Raymond still lived.

On September 25, Lady Lodge arranged a séance with a different medium, in England (Mrs. Leonard), for a distraught friend who had just lost two sons in the war, within a week of each other. Mrs. Lodge was a complete stranger to the medium. But during this sitting, in which words were spelled out by means of tilts of a table, the message came through: "TELL FATHER I HAVE MET SOME FRIENDS OF HIS."

Mrs. Lodge asked, "Can you give any name?"

The answer came back: "YES. MYERS."

Two days later, on September 27, Lady Lodge had a sitting with a Dutch medium, Mr. A. Vout Peters (also as a complete stranger). Peters's "control," named Moonstone, quickly came through, giving an accurate description of Raymond. Then he described "a man, a writer of poetry, on our side, closely connected with spiritualism. He was very clever . . . he has communicated several times. This gentleman who wrote poetry—I see the letter M—he is helping your son to communicate. . . . This is so important that . . . I want to go slowly, for you to write clearly every word: NOT ONLY IS THE PARTITION SO THIN THAT YOU CAN HEAR THE OPERATORS ON THE OTHER SIDE, BUT A BIG HOLE HAS BEEN MADE."

That same day, Oliver Lodge had his first séance with Mrs. Leonard (who did not know or recognize him), and when a voice came through, apparently that of Raymond, he said, "I have met hundreds of friends. I don't know them all. I have met many who tell me that, a little later, they will explain why they are helping me. I feel I have got two fathers now. I don't feel I have lost one and got another; I have got both. I have got my old one, and another too—a *pro tem* father."

Later sittings indicated that the father figure was F. W. H. Myers and, Lodge came to believe, that Myers was honoring his promise to protect Raymond on the other side.

The Dutch medium Vout Peters also told Lady Lodge that a group photograph had been taken of Raymond and several other officers, at the front, shortly before Raymond's death. "Moonstone" said that Raymond "is particular that I should tell you this. In one you see his walking-stick" (here the medium tucked an imaginary walking stick under his arm).

At the time of this séance, Sir Oliver and Lady Lodge did not know of the existence of such a photograph. Lodge made inquiries to see if he could locate such a picture, or even confirm that one had been taken, but came up with nothing. Then, two months later, on November 29, 1915, the mother of one of Raymond's fellow officers (whom the Lodges did not know) sent Mrs. Lodge a short note:

> DEAR LADY LODGE—My son, who is an M.O. to the 2nd South Lancs [Raymond's unit] has sent us a group of officers taken in August, and I wondered whether you knew of this photo and had had a copy. If not may we

> send you one, as we have half a dozen? I hope you will forgive my writing to ask this, but I have often thought of you and felt so much for you in yr. great sorrow.
>
> B. P. CHEVES

Oliver Lodge eagerly replied that he would love to have a copy and then attended a series of séances, asking detailed questions about the photograph *before* it arrived in the mail.

In séance, "Raymond" said that in the photograph he was sitting down, that somebody was leaning on him and he was rather annoyed by this, and that there were a dozen or more men in the picture. He added that in the background there were "lines" pointing down.

The photograph arrived in Oliver Lodge's mailbox on December 7. It showed twenty-one officers arranged in three rows. Behind the group was a low building, with conspicuous vertical, downward-pointing lines, from external trusses on the roof. Raymond was seated in the front row, with a walking stick laid across his lap. Another officer, seated behind him, had his hand on Raymond's left shoulder and appeared to be leaning against him. He was the only officer in the photograph who was in this position, and Raymond appeared to be slightly annoyed, with his face a little screwed up, his body leaning away.

OLIVER LODGE's book about Raymond was only one of many experiences and influences that seemed to push Sir Arthur closer to committing to the claims of spiritualism. But when, precisely, did Sir Arthur "convert" to this new revelation, stepping over the line that separated his previous life as an interested but guarded dilettante into a new, much more precarious public life as a zealous, fully committed missionary for the cause?

It appears to have been sometime between the fall of 1915 and the following January. At the time, one of Lady Jean's dear friends, Lily Loder-Symonds, who had been a bridesmaid at the Doyles' wedding, had been quite ill and came to live in the Doyle household at Windlesham. Loder-Symonds had become a devoted spiritualist after three of her brothers were killed at the

Battle of Ypres. She appeared to have the gift of automatic writing, in which (either in trance or in a fully conscious state) she appeared to "channel" the spirits of the dead, scribbling down messages from them in longhand on paper. When she began receiving messages from her deceased brothers, describing the circumstances of their deaths in detail, Conan Doyle was initially skeptical. He pointed out that all or most of the particulars of the battle at Ypres could have been culled from newspaper reports.

But his attitude changed one day when, apparently as a test, he asked Loder-Symonds to give him details about an extremely personal conversation he had had with Lady Jean's brother Malcolm (now deceased) many years earlier. To his astonishment, she was able to replay this private, long-ago conversation with remarkable accuracy. There was no possible way she could have known about this conversation, Doyle believed; any rational explanation seemed more far-fetched than one presuming psychic abilities unknown or unacknowledged by science. Even if the details had been conveyed by means of telepathy, that, too, was a form of mysterious psychic ability. According to at least one Doyle biographer, Charles Higham, "at that instant, he decided that Spiritualism was genuine." According to another biographer, Martin Booth, this most likely occurred after September 1915, when Doyle wrote to *The International Psychic Gazette,* in response to someone seeking solace from grief, "I fear I can say nothing worth saying. Time is the only healer." But it had to have occurred before January 1916, when Loder-Symonds died.

On November 4, 1916, the spiritualist journal *Light* published a short but earnest essay by one A. Conan Doyle—his official "coming out" party as a spiritualist. He summed up his new convictions in a single sentence: "In spite of occasional fraud and wild imaginings, there remains a solid core in this whole spiritual movement which is infinitely nearer to positive proof than any other religious development with which I am acquainted." For Doyle, the accumulation of evidence from multiple sources was so strong that it could now be considered proven. The phenomena had passed from the stage of being "a parlor game," was just now emerging from being "a debatable scientific novelty," and was beginning to take shape as the foundation of "a definite system of religious thought."

From both sides of the "partition" that separates this world from the next one, he wrote, people of integrity and high intellect were trying to break through to the other side, while spirits on the other side were doing the same. Both were "beating down the partition, and [we can] hear the sound of each other's picks." Someday soon, spirit communication would be acknowledged as a breakthrough comparable to the birth of Christ but not in conflict with Christianity, a revelation that would provide believers with "an utter fearlessness of death, and an immense consolation when those who are dear to us pass behind the veil."

The following year, in October 1917, Conan Doyle gave his first public lecture on spiritualism, to the London Spiritualist Alliance, sharing the podium with Sir Oliver Lodge. And by now, Conan Doyle was not alone: Though at first Lady Jean had been alarmed by her husband's explorations into the shadowy world of the occult, considering it to be "uncanny and dangerous," she had by now seen enough firsthand evidence that she, too, became convinced of the reality of spiritualism.

Now no longer would either one of them be a dabbler or a stander in the doorway of the great questions concerning human survival after bodily death.

They had become true believers.

FOR CONAN Doyle, the severest test of his newfound convictions would come only a few weeks before the end of the war. But it also led to the most exalted moment of his life.

In 1916, during the Battle of the Somme, Doyle's beloved son Arthur Alleyne Kingsley (known as Kingsley), who was serving in the Army Medical Corps, took two bullets in the neck. In some ways, this serious but nonfatal wound was a lucky chance: In a single day during the bloodbath of the Somme, in an assault on the German trenches, 19,240 British soldiers were mowed down by machine-gun fire. (The worst day, by far, in British military history.) To Doyle's great relief, Kingsley managed to recover in a military hospital. Later he returned to active service, but because doctors were in such short supply, he was recalled to the medical school at St. Mary's Hospital. It was there that he became one of the millions of victims of the Spanish flu that swept across the world. He died on October 28, 1918, less than a month before the war ended. (Doyle's brother Innes was also to die in the flu epidemic four months later.)

When Doyle got the news about Kingsley's death, in a telegram from his older daughter, Mary, he was preparing to give a lecture on spiritualism. He decided not to cancel the talk but carried on as planned, later saying that he could never have done that without the inner serenity provided by his spiritualist convictions.

Still, Kingsley's death was a staggering blow. He was such a gallant young man, so gentle, so principled, so reserved, a brave soldier, and a fine officer who would have made a splendid doctor. "He was a very perfect man—I have never met a more perfect one," Doyle wrote to Lady Jean, after viewing his son's gray body in the morgue.

It was almost a year later, on the evening of September 7, 1919, that Sir Arthur gave a spiritualist lecture in a guildhall in the town of Portsmouth, on the British seacoast about sixty miles south of London. Also on the platform that night was the somewhat improbable figure of a Welsh coal merchant from Merthyr Tydfil named Evan Powell. But Powell, with his unkempt hair and his ill-buttoned waistcoat stained with coal dust, was also, according to Doyle, an extraordinarily gifted medium, shuttling messages between the "land of mist" and the earthly world. Doyle was impressed with Powell because he did not accept any money for his mediumship, and because he only lent his psychic services to occasional clients, Doyle believed his powers were "free from that deterioration which comes from over-strain." In *The History of Spiritualism,* Doyle opined that "on the whole, Evan Powell may be said to have the widest endowment of spiritual gifts of any medium at present in England." He was also "a kindly, good person worthy of the wonderful gifts entrusted to him."

Those gifts included moving objects at a distance (psychokinesis), "psychic lights," and direct voice phenomena, sometimes including the eerie ability to "channel" more than one voice at a time. He had given many sittings at the British College of Psychic Science.

After Doyle's lecture that night, Powell offered to give a private sitting for Sir Arthur, Lady Doyle, three spiritualists, and a well-known film producer named Harry Engholm, who was "intellectually convinced" of the reality of spiritualism but had never seen it in person.

Before the sitting began, "Mr. Powell insisted upon being searched, and was then bound by me to a wooden armchair," Doyle wrote later in an article called "A Wonderful Séance," which appeared in the spiritualist journal *Light* at Christmas 1919. Then Doyle "cut six lengths of stout twine, and tied the medium in six places to the arms and legs of the chair. So thoroughly was this done, that at the end of the sitting it was quite impossible to loosen him, and we were compelled to cut him free." Powell was bound hand and foot to prevent fraud, of course, but also "for his own protection," Doyle explained, "since he cannot be responsible for his own movements when he is in a trance."

Next a small megaphone, circled with luminous paint to make it visible in the dark, was placed on the floor beside the medium. The attendees arranged themselves in a semicircle, holding hands, surrounding Powell but not touching him. And then the lights were turned out and the room was in total darkness (a customary practice that always drew the scorn of skeptics). The séance sitters could hear Powell's breathing grow loud and labored as he sank into a trance. Then a voice, quite unlike Powell's normal voice, spoke up. (Powell, being Welsh, had a distinct accent, and his voice was "gentle and musical," but the new voice—that of Powell's "control," named Black Hawk, was "deep, strong and virile," Doyle reported.) Black Hawk greeted the company with good-natured kidding, calling Doyle "Great Chief" but also addressing each person by name. Then the medium slipped into silence and there was the sound of snoring.

A short while later, Doyle reported seeing the luminous band of the megaphone lift into the air and circle around the sitters' heads, sometimes slowly, sometimes swiftly, but always as smoothly as if it were attached to the end of a string. Then it vanished. Shortly afterward, it returned, this time with a handful of flowers taken from the mantel and shoved into the narrow end of the megaphone. This was passed around the room so that everyone could smell the flowers, "with an accuracy which showed that whoever held them could see very plainly where we were." Then, most surprising of all, a heavy wooden pedestal that Doyle estimated to weigh forty or fifty pounds was moved from the corner of the room to the center of the circle, lifted off the ground, and balanced gently on top of Doyle's head, then rubbed lightly down the edge of his cheek. "An examination had shown us that the heavy crown of this pedestal was balanced upon a single loose screw in a wide socket, so that any careless handling would have sent it down with a terrific effect upon our skulls. . . .

"Then came what to me was the supreme moment of my spiritual experience. It is almost too sacred for full description, and yet I feel that God sends us such gifts that we may share them with others," he wrote.

Suddenly there was a whispered voice in the darkness.

"Jean, it is I!"

Lady Doyle felt a hand on her head and cried, "It's Kingsley!"

"*Father!*" the voice whispered earnestly.

"Dear boy, is that you?" Conan Doyle asked, scarcely able to believe it was true. He had the sense that there was a face very close to his own. He could hear someone breathing.

In a voice that sounded very much like Kingsley's voice, the entity replied in a very intense whisper, *"Forgive me!"*

"There was never anything to forgive," Conan Doyle replied. "You were the best son a man ever had."

Then a large, strong hand rested on Sir Arthur's head and gently bent it forward. Then he felt a soft kiss just above the brow.

"Tell me, dear, are you happy?" Sir Arthur asked.

There was a silence, and Doyle feared his son was gone. Then, softly, in a sort of sighing voice, came the words "Yes, I am *so* happy!"

While this remarkable conversation was in progress, Doyle was dimly conscious that the medium, across the room, seemed to be simultaneously channeling a second voice. Harry Engholm, the film producer, later wrote of this: "Whilst Sir Arthur and his boy were carrying on a conversation of a very private and sacred nature, I was suddenly addressed by a very dear old friend, a well-known newspaper correspondent, in terms and on a subject that left no doubt in my mind as to who the unseen personality was."

Several times later in his life, Conan Doyle would have what he believed to be direct communications with Kingsley. But none of them compared with the unearthly thrill of this moment.

LATER IT was alleged that when Conan Doyle emerged from this séance, he declared, "Sherlock Holmes has died!"

Whether or not this actually happened, it was clear that from now on he was no longer an author of detective stories but a missionary for the cause of spiritualism. In those years of "universal sorrow and loss," he wrote at the end of his autobiography, "it was borne in upon me that the knowledge which had come to me . . . was not for my own consolation alone, but that God had placed me in a very special position for conveying it to that world which needed it so badly."

From now on, he pledged, he would share the good news of the soul's eternal survival, no matter its personal cost to him and his family, no matter its financial cost, and no matter how much ridicule would be heaped upon him.

And in the years to come, there would be plenty.

Essentially, he would be seated in the public square wearing a dunce cap, pelted with rotten tomatoes, and scorned by many of the same people who once bought his books and considered him one of Britain's leading literary lights.

But who could argue with the evidence he had seen with his

own eyes? He summed it up, as a kind of personal confession and recitation of faith, in *Memories and Adventures*:

> I have clasped materialized hands.
>
> I have held long conversations with the direct voice.
>
> I have smelt the peculiar ozone-like smell of ectoplasm.
>
> I have listened to prophecies which were quickly fulfilled.
>
> I have seen the "dead" glimmer up upon a photographic plate which no hand but mine had touched.
>
> I have received through the hand of my own wife, notebooks full of information which was utterly beyond her ken.
>
> I have seen heavy articles swimming in the air, untouched by human hand, and obeying directions given to unseen operators.
>
> I have seen spirits walk round the room in fair light and join in the talk of the company.
>
> I have known an untrained woman, possessed by an artist spirit, to produce rapidly a picture, now hanging in my drawing-room, which few living painters could have bettered.
>
> If a man could see, feel and hear all this, and yet remain unconvinced of unseen intelligent forces around him, he would have a good cause to doubt his own sanity. Why should he heed the chatter of irresponsible journalists, or the head-shaking of inexperienced men of science, when he has himself had so many proofs?

For Doyle, the matter had been proven beyond the shadow of a doubt. Now he wished only to discern the majestic mystery that lay around him and share its eternal reassurance with the world. Striking an achingly high note—and one that laid himself open to even more attack and ridicule—he concluded his little book *The New Revelation* with a beatific vision written by an English poet and spiritualist named Gerald Massey:

Spiritualism has been for me, in common with many others, such a lifting of the mental horizon and letting-in of the heavens—such a formation of faith into facts, that I can only compare life without it to sailing on board ship with hatches battened down and being kept a prisoner, living by the light of a candle, and then suddenly, on some splendid starry night, allowed to go on deck for the first time to see the stupendous mechanism of the heavens all aglow with the glory of God.

By the time he was sixty, Conan Doyle wrote almost exclusively about spiritualism, having spent a lifetime moving, as he said, "from the right of negation to the left of acceptance." He wrote Sherlock Holmes stories and other fiction just to keep some money coming in.
SUEDDEUTSCHE ZEITUNG PHOTO / ALAMY STOCK PHOTO

CHAPTER SEVEN
The Saint Paul of Spiritualism

The event would be nothing more than two men arguing for a couple of hours, but all twenty-four hundred tickets were sold out a month in advance. Surely there were better things to do on a Thursday night in London. Regardless, a crowd filed into Queen's Hall on March 11, 1920, to attend a clash of opinions billed as "The Truth of Spiritualism."

Arguing in its defense was, of course, Sir Arthur Conan Doyle. He had been spiritualism's defender in chief for three years now, bringing to it "a combative and aggressive spirit which it lacked before," if he did say so himself. He'd written *The New Revelation* and *The Vital Message* and several dozen articles and letters. He and Lady Jean had been crisscrossing Britain, giving lectures to packed halls, often five nights a week, and addressing a total of 150,000 people, he estimated. And he was relishing the role: In January 1919, he had written to his mother, "Someone has called me 'The Saint Paul of the New Dispensation.' Where are we getting to!!"

Nonetheless, he was particularly anxious about this debate. He knew it wouldn't be just another hall full of admiring souls in Hastings. It would be a confrontation. And he hated confrontation. "I go into battle in good heart," was his rather melodramatic choice of words to his mother a few days beforehand. "This will in a way be the most important night of my life so I pray you to think of me."

His adversary was Joseph McCabe, a Franciscan priest who'd

left the Church Militant to become a militant atheist. Consider the irony: A former friar argues for a godless universe, while the creator of the supremely rational detective Sherlock Holmes claims that we can talk to the dead. It was a surreal scene befitting the new century. But more than that, McCabe's appearance that night signaled a new opposition to spiritualism. This rising opponent wasn't the stuffy Church of England or irate Nonconformists. It was loss of faith itself. World War I had brought on so much death and misery that millions of people now had no patience for blather about the hereafter and a loving God.

As Queen's Hall filled that night, each man was backed up by his chosen supporters onstage with him: fifty spiritualists to Conan Doyle's right, fifty atheists to McCabe's left. They sat glaring at each other as the evening's moderator, Sir Edward Marshall Hall, a famous defense attorney and former MP, quickly got down to business. "This is a serious debate," he warned the audience in his brief opening remarks. "Both these gentlemen are in earnest."

McCabe was up first, and he began his forty-minute segment with a theme sure to please his supporters: Religion was all well and good when humans believed the world was flat and the sun revolved around the earth, but with the advent of modern astronomy "man found himself living on one tiny speck in an illimitable material universe." The result: "The old creeds began to grow dim." We've grown up, he said. "Millions are fast falling from this dream of an eternal home." But wouldn't you know it: "Just when men are beginning to wonder if at last religion is doomed, there comes this portentous phenomenon we are discussing in the shape of spiritualism. I do not wonder that my opponent takes it to be a new religion, a new revelation."

But there's one big problem with this new religion, said McCabe: "It was born of a fraud. It was cradled in fraud. It was nurtured in fraud. It is based to-day to an alarming extent all over the world on fraudulent performances." And with that line, he got his first sympathetic laughter from the crowd. He spent the next half hour poking fun at D. D. Home, at Sir Oliver Lodge, and at Sir Arthur Conan Doyle, and he got lots more laughs.

After saying Doyle "has lived in clouds, in a mist," McCabe ended his opening speech on a somewhat different note. To great cheers from the audience (or half of it, anyway) he said,

> I submit to you in conclusion: let us be satisfied with this great broad earth which we do know and can control. Here is a world with mighty problems—a world with mighty resources. Here is a world which in its great tasks is fit to absorb the energy and devotion of every living man and woman on its surface. Let us leave that cloudy, misty, disputable, misleading world, and let us concentrate upon this earth upon which we live.

This argument—*let's take each world in its turn*—had been a rejoinder since the dawn of spiritualism. As a practical matter, spiritualism involved so much time and effort—for what reward? Horace Greeley was at the end of his life agnostic on the whole matter but wrote in his autobiography, "Those who discharge promptly and faithfully all their duties to those who 'still live' in the flesh can have little time for poking and peering into the life beyond the grave. Better attend to each world in its proper order." He wrote this in 1868, a few years after Henry David Thoreau's famous reply on his deathbed when asked if he was ready to meet his Maker in the next world: "One world at a time." In the twentieth century, this attitude gained in popularity as a more secular world offered more distractions (from motorcars to Mae West) and then more pressing perils. Later, Conan Doyle would say it himself, although ruefully: "When the whole world is living vividly here and now there is no room for the hereafter."

How did Conan Doyle reply to forty minutes of McCabe? By brandishing a notebook. "I have in this little book . . . the names of 160 people of high distinction . . . people who, to their own great loss, have announced themselves as Spiritualists. . . . These are folk who have taken real pains and care to get to the bottom of the subject. They have not been to one séance . . . or two or three, like Mr. McCabe. Many have studied for twenty or thirty years, and been to hundreds of séances." Yes, Doyle admitted, there are fraudulent mediums; he called them "hyenas" and said, "I think that to deceive the living by imitating the dead is the most horrible crime a man could commit." But many, many other mediums are honest people who suffer for their gifts. You don't hear about them, said Doyle: "The trouble is that you never hear of mediums unless they get into trouble." To which the audience shouted, "Hear, hear!"

He then launched into a defense of the mediums McCabe had mocked, and told stories of respected people he knew and their visits with mediums who established contact with dead relatives. Doyle claimed he knew "more than a hundred" such cases personally. "If I have had more than a hundred," he continued, "how many thousands and tens of thousands there must be in the country," a flourish that drew cheers from the crowd. "That is what our opponents will never admit—the enormous cumulative evidence of all these cases."

Then he got personal. He told of a séance in Wales in which he was visited by the spirit of his younger brother, who had died in the great flu epidemic of 1918.

> Four spirits came to me in succession, each of them making their identity perfectly clear. The fourth was my brother. When I asked for a name he gave "Innes." The name published in his obituaries was John Francis, and Innes was his third name, used only by intimates. Besides my wife and myself, I do not think there was a person in Wales who could have known this. I at once began talking family matters with him, exactly as if he were alive. His widow is in ill health in Copenhagen, and we discussed her condition. I asked him if he thought psychic or magnetic treatment could avail. He answered by the two words, "Sigurd Frier," or "Trier." I could not catch it, and he repeated it twice. Mr. Southey, an ex-J.P. of Merthyr, with his daughter, was on my left, and my wife was on my right. They all made note of the words. Next day I wrote to a young Danish friend in London, and asked him if they had any meaning. He re-

> plied that it was the name of a well-known psychic in Copenhagen. Now I will swear to you that I did not know that there was a Spiritualistic Society in the whole of Denmark. As to the Welsh people who formed the circle, they could not have known that the conversation was going to Copenhagen. Now, if that entity, who stood in front of me in the dark, who talked in my brother's manner, who discussed family matters intimately, and who knew more about the surroundings of his widow than I did, was not my brother, I ask you, who was it?

Half the audience knew the answer. The other half didn't care.

The two men spent the next hour bickering over the details of their early remarks. McCabe got in one last plea for his one-world-at-a-time argument: "This movement is one vast, mischievous distraction of human energies from the human task that lies before us today." (Prolonged cheers.) And Doyle, as ever, was the earnest defender of those who must suffer in silence: "I am sure [McCabe] would not have talked so lightly of this matter if he had known, as I know, the consolation it has brought to thousands and thousands of people." (Prolonged cheers.)

The debate was a draw, but McCabe had gotten under his skin. Three months later, in June 1920, Doyle sat down and wrote "A Drastic Examination of Mr. Joseph McCabe," in which he meticulously answered all the objections that McCabe tossed about. But Doyle went beyond proofs: McCabe was an arrogant killjoy who told outright lies and who did so "in short snip-snap sentences," as if that were the final word on the matter. "Everyone who differs from him is a fraud, a fool or a drunkard," Doyle noted of the man's debating style. As for the one-world-at-a-time argument, that's fine for a healthy man on a fine summer day, "but how about the poor wretch who lives in a garret in a London winter with cancer of the bowels!"

Strangely, that's just how Joseph McCabe died thirty-five years later: broke and alone in London. The cause of death was pneumonia following prostate cancer. It was winter.

SHORTLY AFTER the McCabe debate, Sir Arthur and Jean decided to say yes to the requests of spiritualist groups in Australia to bring their missionary work to the island continent. They both felt obliged to go. "God had given us wonderful signs," he wrote, "and they were surely not for ourselves alone." In his leadership role, he had access to the best mediums in the world, and by that point he and Jean had been in séances where they spoke face-to-face with a total of eleven friends and relatives "who had passed over, their direct voices being in each case audible, and their conversation characteristic and evidential—in some cases marvellously so." He would spread the word. So on August 13, 1920, the seven of them—he, Jean, the three kids, a nanny, and a secretary—got on the *Naldera,* a slow boat to Australia. They wouldn't see the Australian coastline until the morning of September 17, more than a month later. On the return voyage in February, he would put the month of travel time to good use: He sat on deck with a writing pad on his knee composing his memoir of the trip, *The Wanderings of a Spiritualist.*

Years of practice had turned Conan Doyle into a masterful public speaker, so the large audiences turning out for him were not disappointed. A newspaper in Adelaide, the *Register,* described him as having a "big arresting presence" at the podium, with a clear delivery that was plain, humble, and sincere, rather than theatrical. At times, he would jab a finger in the air for emphasis or twirl his glasses "during moments of descriptive ease." It added, "He did not dictate, but reasoned and pleaded, taking the people into his confidence with strong conviction and a consoling faith." He could improvise when heckled. At the start of his first speech in Sydney, one protester near the door shouted "Anti-Christ" several times before being put out. Doyle went on to describe how his son Kingsley had come back to him during a séance, and challenged anyone to say that it was a devil who visited him. Someone in the audience yelled, "It was!" Conan Doyle only laughed and replied that if the devil went around imploring people to practice unselfishness as the true way to make spiritual progress, then the devil didn't know his job.

In between lectures, the Doyles attended séances with local

spiritualists. One of these, in Melbourne, was a "rescue circle." These séances attempt to help dead people's souls who are still earthbound and who don't know where they are or how to make progress in the next life. Here is Doyle's description of a typical rescue séance:

> A wise spirit control dominates the proceedings. The medium goes into trance. The spirit control then explains what it is about to do, and who the spirit is who is about to be reformed. The next scene is often very violent, the medium having to be held down and using rough language. This comes from some low spirit who has suddenly found this means of expressing himself. At other times the language is not violent but only melancholy, the spirit declaring that he is abandoned and has not a friend in the universe. Some do not realize that they are dead, but only that they wander all alone, under conditions they could not understand, in a cloud of darkness.
>
> Then comes the work of regeneration. They are reasoned with and consoled. Gradually they become more gentle. Finally they accept the fact that they are spirits, that their condition is their own making, and that by aspiration and repentance they can win their way to the light.

At the rescue circle attended by the Doyles, there appeared a dead cleric who didn't understand why he wasn't in the sort of heaven he'd preached about, a sailor who'd gone down on the *Monmouth* ("We never had a chance. It was just hell"), and a Gurkha who thought he was still in the war and charged about the circle, upsetting the medium's chair. Then came the apostolic gift of tongues as two of the ladies broke out into a conversation in the Maori language.

Also while in Melbourne, he had two séances with the medium Charles Bailey, who had the rare gift of producing *apports* at his sittings. (The word is French, "something brought.") Such phenomena were uncommon, which may be just as well, because it's so hard to believe that spirits can take physical objects from thousands of miles away, pass them through walls, and produce them in the middle of the séance table. Conan Doyle had himself witnessed *apports* at séances with General Drayson back in Southsea in the 1880s, but it put him off. "So amazing a phenomenon, and one so easily simulated, was too much for a beginner," he wrote of his early reaction in *The History of Spiritualism*. "Even the Spiritualist can hardly credit it until examples actually come his way." Often the séance goer is silently presented with a strange object not of his choosing, but the London medium Mrs. Guppy actually took requests. At one of her séances, the great naturalist Alfred Russel Wallace requested a sunflower, and a six-foot specimen—roots, dirt, and all—fell at his feet.

Charles Bailey had a reputation for producing an amazing array of objects under amazingly rigid conditions. At one particular series of six sittings, the doors and windows were secured and the fireplace blocked; Bailey was stripped naked and placed inside a bag and then inside a cage of mosquito curtain. While in trance he produced a total of 138 articles, including 87 ancient coins, 8 live birds, 18 precious stones, 2 live turtles, a leopard skin, an Arabic newspaper, and 4 nests. On a different occasion, he produced a young live shark, tangled in wet seaweed, which flopped around on the séance table. This was a guy Doyle had to see.

The first séance was so-so; the second proved better. Doyle and the others searched Mr. Bailey to be sure he carried nothing into the room with him. Then they placed him in a corner of the room, drew the curtain, lowered the lights, and waited.

> Almost at once he breathed very heavily, as one in trance, and soon said something in a foreign tongue which was unintelligible to me. . . . In English the voice then said that he was a Hindoo control who was used to bring apports for the medium, and that he would, he hoped, be able to bring one for us. "Here it is," he said a moment later, and the medium's hand was extended with some-

> thing in it. The light was turned full on and we found it was a very perfect bird's nest, beautifully constructed of some very fine fibre mixed with moss. It stood about two inches high and had no sign of any flattening which would have come with concealment. In it lay a small egg, white, with tiny brown speckles. The medium, or rather the Hindoo control acting through the medium, placed the egg on his palm and broke it, some fine albumen squirting out. There was no trace of yolk. "We are not allowed to interfere with life," he said. "If it had been fertilized we could not have taken it." These words were said before he broke it, so that he was aware of the condition of the egg, which certainly seems remarkable.
>
> "Where did it come from?" I asked.
>
> "From India."
>
> "What bird is it?"
>
> "They call it the jungle sparrow."

Later in that same séance, Doyle asked another spirit control to explain *apports* and just how an object can be transported from thousands of miles away. The spirit gave a rough analogy of water turned into steam, and the invisible steam can be conducted elsewhere and condensed into water again. That's the best explanation Doyle got; he took the nest and eggshell to a local museum and was told they weren't native to Australia. If a supernatural explanation seemed far-fetched, so did the explanation of fraud. "I had an Indian nest. Does anyone import Indian nests?" Much less Indian nests with fresh eggs? "The matter is ventilated in papers, and no one comes forward to damn Bailey forever by proving that he supplied them." So, as skeptical as Doyle still was about the subject, he couldn't join the long line of Bailey's doubters.

If you don't believe any of this, take a trip to Stanford University. There, in the archives, are twenty-six gray boxes filled with miscellaneous *apports* (papyrus, seeds, rocks, a Roman lamp, arrowheads, sharks' teeth, a tortoise shell, a Chinese ink block, a human shoulder blade) and slates with spirit messages scrawled on them. One slate has a message from the spirit of the university's namesake, Leland Stanford Jr., to his uncle Thomas Welton Stanford: "My dear uncle I am pleased to meet you here this morning." Welton Stanford was the youngest brother of the founder, Leland Stanford; he immigrated to Melbourne in 1859 and got rich by selling real estate and importing Singer sewing machines. He married, was widowed, and became an active spiritualist, hosting countless séances with Charles Bailey. Welton Stanford left his collection of Bailey *apports* to the university upon his death in 1918, two years too soon to meet Sir Arthur Conan Doyle. They would have enjoyed each other's company.

BARELY A year after their return to England, the Doyles were off again: this time to America. It would prove to be another record-breaking tour; he would lecture at Carnegie Hall for six nights. He would go up to Boston, down to Philadelphia and Washington, then take the train out to Buffalo, passing by Hydesville and musing about the Fox sisters as they chugged past. He would lecture in Detroit and Toledo and Chicago and attend séances with America's best mediums along the way before returning to New York, meeting up with Houdini, playing a joke on the magicians' club, and finally having a séance with Houdini in Atlantic City that began to convince Doyle that Houdini harbored a deep secret: He was, in actuality, one of the most powerful mediums of his day.

"Who was the greatest medium-baiter of modern times?" Doyle would later write. "Undoubtedly Houdini. Who was the greatest physical medium of modern times? There are some who would be inclined to give the same answer."

On April 9, 1922, they reached New York harbor. Doyle was met by a dozen members of the press, who came on board the *Baltic* even before it docked. "They pinned me in a corner and were showering questions upon me," he wrote. "They got to the heart of things at once." He told them that the psychic movement, which he had come to America to champion, was "the most serious attempt ever made to place religion upon a basis of definite proof." Okay, said the reporters, but what does all this séance stuff have to do with religion? As Doyle himself echoed their question in the early pages of his memoir *Our American Adventure*: "What religion could there be in a jumping table or a flying tambourine?"

He'd been answering that question for a few years now, and his answer was always the same: All the physical phenomena of spiritualism—the flying tambourines, tilting tables, raps, bells, and *apports*—were nothing in themselves. They were simply calling attention to the existence of the afterlife. They were like "telephone bells," he liked to say. It's the message that matters. Don't stand there wondering what makes the phone ring; *answer the phone!*

It's difficult for us to imagine the harrowing effect of World War I, but it was, to quote the opening line of Doyle's 1919 tract *The Vital Message,* "the most frightful calamity that has ever befallen the world." Many shrugged it off as being the latest chapter in the long, sad saga of man's inhumanity to man. Not Sir Arthur. To him, there was a lesson to be learned. "If our souls, wearied and tortured during these dreadful five years of self-sacrifice and suspense, can show no radical changes, then what souls will ever respond to a fresh influx of heavenly inspiration?"

That fresh influx, he believed, came in the form of all the psychic phenomena of the last seventy years. God was giving us fresh proof that, yes, we *will* live forever. And the voices reaching us from the other side of the veil were telling us that life over there was infinitely happier for most souls; furthermore, all souls were involved together in an eternal spiritual refinement—it was truly a communion of the saints. "Unselfishness, that is the keynote to progress," he wrote in *The New Revelation*. "Realize not as a belief or a faith, but as a fact which is as tangible as the streets of London, that we are moving on soon to another life, that all will be very happy there, and that the only possible way in which that happiness can be marred or deferred is by folly and selfishness in these few fleeting years."

The Doyles settled in at the Ambassador Hotel on Park Avenue, and the next morning more members of the press came to visit. Promptly at 11:00 a.m., eighteen reporters marched into his sitting room, "about a third of them ladies," he noted with surprise. As they fired questions at him, soon enough the topic got around to the afterlife. Would there be whiskey and cigars? Would there be marriage? Would there be golf? They were fishing for a funny angle, and he could just imagine their editors' plans for a brassy headline the next day.

In his memoir, Doyle repeated one exchange in particular that made the papers. "All ordinary decent people will find themselves in Paradise after death," Sir Arthur insisted optimistically.

"I believe everyone in this room will go there," he added, indicating the eighteen reporters present.

The reporters looked somewhat doubtfully at each other.

Sir Arthur reassured them. "You don't have to be so very good to get to heaven," he said.

No, a roomful of American reporters—then or now—would not be the most obvious candidates for halos. What he didn't tell them at the time was that in his view souls may spend a long time giving up their bigotry and selfishness before moving beyond the lower heavens. But he was purposely optimistic; he'd seen too many good people terrorized by the fire-and-brimstone theology of Christian preachers. On any given nineteenth-century Sunday, in both England and America, the message from most pulpits was this: *Yes there is life after death—and most people are going to spend it rotting in hell. Unless you clean up your act big-time, that includes you.* Spiritualists had been hearing a very different message from the next world: God embraced everyone, and not just Catholics or Calvinists or Buddhists. This was a key theme that Doyle proclaimed onstage. "When I said that the average human being, hard-worked and ill cared for, deserved compensation rather than punishment, there were hearty cheers of assent," he wrote. "It was our own man-made theology which draped our future with terrors."

Yet he wondered why so many Christians despised him and wanted him dead.

During his dozen years of missionary work, Conan Doyle said and wrote things about Christianity and the Bible that would have gotten him tarred and feathered in places like Tennessee.

(Even today.) Particularly in *The Vital Message,* he tore into modern Christianity. He called it stupid and decadent; he said the churches were "empty husks"; he said that Jesus fought the theologians of his day, "who then, as now, have been a curse to the world." He said most of the Bible was worse than worthless; "every hard-hearted brute in history . . . has found his inspiration in the Old Testament." It's an old book but not a good book; it "advocates massacre, condones polygamy, accepts slavery, and orders the burning of so-called witches."

The New Testament is inspirational if you focus upon the Gospels and the teachings of Jesus, who was "the sweetest soul that ever trod this planet." The same cannot be said of Saint Paul. "One thing that can safely be said of Paul is that he was either a bachelor or else was a domestic bully with a very submissive wife, or he would never have dared to express his well-known views about women," Doyle wrote. Paul's letters to the early churches could be confusing, Doyle wrote, but they make a little more sense when you realize that the early Christian church was a psychic movement. "When we translate Bible language into the terms of modern psychic religion the correspondence becomes evident," he explained. "It does not take much alteration. Thus for 'Lo, a miracle!' we say 'This is a manifestation.' 'The angel of the Lord' becomes 'a high spirit.' Where we talked of 'a voice from heaven,' we say 'the direct voice.' 'His eyes were opened and he saw a vision' means 'he became clairvoyant.' "

Despite all this, he couldn't understand why the churches didn't greet him with open arms and embrace spiritualism as a powerful ally. (Some ministers did. They were the Christian spiritualists, a subset of the movement. Doyle's friend and first biographer, the Reverend John Lamond, was one of them.) Their common enemy was the worldview of Joseph McCabe—*there is no God, the universe doesn't care about us, and death really does end all.* This was the philosophy known as materialism. Here it is in a nutshell: In Doyle's one work of psychic fiction, the 1926 novel *The Land of Mist,* Professor Challenger's daughter, Enid, says to him before his conversion, "Don't tell me, Daddy, that you with all your complex brain and wonderful self are a thing with no more life hereafter than a broken clock!" Challenger's reply: "Four buckets of water and a bagful of salts."

Doyle's steadfast vision was the unity of all religions of the world, refreshed and revivified by psychic knowledge. "The differences between various sects are a very small thing as compared to the great eternal duel between materialism and the spiritual view of the universe," he wrote. "That is the real fight." In his last years, he refined his thinking: He wanted to see spiritualism merged into Christianity as a practical first step, before Christianity was eventually merged with the world's other religions. He proposed to the Spiritualists' National Union an eighth principle, recognizing Jesus as their leader in the realm of ethics. It was promptly turned down.

IF SPIRITUALISM was its own distinct religion, it wasn't much of one—at least in the sense of being an organized institution. Spiritualists the world over were a disorganized bunch. After touring Australia, Doyle would write, "It would be far better to have no Spiritual churches than some I have seen." As for England, he complained to Lamond after the rejection of the eighth principle, "What is the use of calling me their leader, when they refuse to follow?" In the last days of his life, infighting between the Spiritualists' National Union and the London Spiritualist Alliance scuttled his attempt to stop the police from arresting honest mediums under the old witchcraft and vagrancy laws.

Nor could spiritualists be relied on for earthly funds. In early 1923, Doyle wrote a letter to the publication *Light,* asking readers to contribute to an international memorial for the "piercing of the barrier" that occurred in Hydesville on March 31, 1848, "the greatest date in human history since the great revelation of two thousand years ago." He would take the donations with him on his upcoming second American tour. A month later, he wrote back to say forget it. The response was "so scanty that I cannot bring myself to present it."

American spiritualists were no better, and it was ever thus. The birthplace of the movement had produced a few congregations by the end of the 1850s, but they were meeting in auditoriums, not churches per se. A typical weekday or Sunday service would include music, a prayer, and a lecture. Then they got to the most important part: the receipt of spirit messages. When it was over, they would disband without a blessing. There was no reading of Scripture, no recital of a creed, no ordained minister, and no worship of God in the old God-fearing ways.

And even that was too formal for most believers. No more than one in ten spiritualists became regular members of a congregation, and a permanent umbrella organization, the National Spiritualist Association, wasn't formed until 1893. Spiritualism was a do-it-yourself religion whose adherents were happiest when holding séances at home; most would go anywhere to see a table turned for the fortieth time, complained the editor of *The Spiritual Telegraph,* but they weren't keen on spending time and money to start a church. In 1869, one frustrated organizer summed up the limits of their faith: "So soon as they become satisfied that there is no death, no eternal hell, no angry God to appease, or vindictive or seductive devil to escape from; . . . and they are required to make effort and use time and means to bring these facts before the world, their zeal falls below zero."

This was the cause to which Conan Doyle gave the last years of his life. In 1930, he would publish his final book, *The Edge of the Unknown.* It had a print run of fewer than a thousand copies. By the end of the Roaring Twenties, Arthur Conan Doyle's religious writings had reached the edge of the obscure.

When two young girls claimed to have actually photographed fairies in 1917, Conan Doyle believed their story and even wrote a book about it.
GLENN HILL/SCIENCE & SOCIETY PICTURE LIBRARY

CHAPTER EIGHT
An Embarrassment of Fairies

They would later become some of the most famous photographs of the twentieth century, the subject of furious debate, derisive laughter, and, in the end, scalding ridicule aimed squarely at Sir Arthur Conan Doyle.

The five pictures showed two adolescent girls cavorting with what appeared to be a clutch of semitranslucent, fluttering fairies and a cute little gnome with panpipes. The photographs, Sir Arthur would later write, represented "either the most elaborate and ingenious hoax ever played upon the public, or else . . . an event in human history which may in the future appear to have been epoch-making in its character."

So which was it? Were the pictures evidence of epoch-making genuineness, or were they ordinary, quite embarrassing fakes and a permanent stain on Doyle's reputation?

In long accounts published in *The Strand Magazine* in 1920 and 1921, and later in a short 1922 book called *The Coming of the Fairies,* Conan Doyle came down foursquare on the side of the fairies. Even though he hedged his bets somewhat by writing things such as "If I myself am asked whether I consider the case to be absolutely and finally proved, I should answer that in order to remove the last faint shadow of doubt I should wish to see the result repeated before a disinterested witness," elsewhere he simply came out and said it: He believed that "a strong prima-facie case has been built up" that the photographs were for real.

And so, by extension, were the fairies.

How did all this happen? How did Sir Arthur Conan Doyle, creator of the world's most rigorously rational detective, get so roundly snookered by a couple of adolescent girls in ringlets, one of whom was nine? Or was the story considerably more nuanced than the one that has been handed down through history?

It takes a bit of telling.

THE STORY begins in the summer of 1917, in the bucolic English countryside of western Yorkshire, near the tiny village of Cottingley. Threading through the town was a sylvan stream (known to the locals as a beck), sometimes called Cottingley Beck.

Two cousins, nine-year-old Frances Griffiths (who had grown up in South Africa) and sixteen-year-old Elsie Wright, loved to play in and around the woods and streams behind their family's home in the village. For several years, the girls had been telling Elsie's parents that they sometimes saw and played with fairies in the woods. Though the parents scoffed at this girlish moonshine, the children stuck with their story.

Many years later, when she was in her seventies, Frances wrote of those innocent days, "I was up the beck alone quite a lot after school. It was good to sit quietly on the willow branch and listen to the sound of the water, the odd bee buzzing and an occasional splash as a frog plunged into a deep pool. I suppose I must have been day dreaming one day when I looked across the beck and saw a willow leaf twirling around rapidly, moving as it were, on its own. I did think it odd, as there was no breeze. I had never seen a leaf do that before. . . .

"That was the beginning, although at the time I didn't realise it. The leaf was being held by a little man. The first time I saw the little man—he was about eighteen inches high—he was walking purposefully down the bank on the willow side of the beck, holding a willow leaf in his hand, twiddling it very fast as he crossed the water to the other side. I wasn't unduly surprised—the beck was a wonderful place and I wouldn't have been surprised at anything that happened there."

One day that summer of 1917, Elsie begged to borrow her father's camera. Arthur Wright, who worked as an electrician at a nearby estate, was a bit of an amateur photographer who owned an inexpensive "Midg" quarter-plate box camera and had set up a small darkroom in the house. He lent the girls the camera, and they danced off into the woods. They returned less than an hour later with an exposed photographic plate they asked their father to develop. Elsie, excited, pushed her way into the tiny darkroom, and when images began to appear on the developing plate, she cried, "Francis! The fairies are on the plate! The fairies are on the plate!"

The image showed Elsie staring directly at the camera and around her a dancing chorus line of five cavorting "fairies." Later, the girls returned to the woods with the camera and came back with another exposed plate, which showed "the quaintest goblin imaginable," according to someone who saw it.

It must be said that to the modern eye, jaded by Photoshop and every other kind of digital manipulation, the "fairies" in these century-old photographs look transparently fake. But it's important to remember that in that more innocent age the original images were quite indistinct and sepia toned; only later were they cleaned up and clarified.

Arthur Wright, convinced that the girls had faked the pictures somehow, searched the wastebaskets in Elsie's room and the tall grass down by the beck, to find evidence that the "fairies" had been pictures cut out of magazines. But he found nothing. Frances sent one of the pictures to a friend in South Africa and jotted casually on the back, "Elsie and I are friendly with the beck fairies. Funny, I never used to see them in Africa. It must be too hot for them there."

The girls sent the pictures to a few other friends and family members, without fanfare. In a bright, newsy letter dated November 9, 1918, Frances wrote to another friend in South Africa, mentioning that her dad had just come back from France, that everyone thought the war would be over in a few days, and—oh, yeah—that "I am sending two photos, one of me in a bathing costume in our back yard, Uncle Arthur took that, while the other is me with some fairies up the beck, Elsie took that one. . . . How are Teddy and Dolly?"

It was as if seeing fairies were as ordinary as seeing the sun come up.

Then, in 1919, Elsie's mother attended a lecture on "fairy life," sponsored by the Theosophical Society, in the nearby town of Bradford. (The Theosophical Society, founded in 1875 by the flamboyant Madame Blavatsky, was a quasi-religion that incorporated Buddhist ideas about reincarnation and mystical insight and believed in the existence of diminutive "elementals," or nature spirits, inhabiting the natural world.) Polly Wright had become interested in occult subjects and took along her daughter's curious fairy pictures, which she showed to the lecturer. A few months later, the pictures were displayed at another Theosophical Society meeting, where they came to the attention of a prominent Theosophist and lecturer named Edward Gardner.

Gardner was transfixed by the pictures, partly because they seemed to support the Theosophists' notion that humanity was undergoing a cycle of evolution toward increasingly greater "perfection." Gardner later wrote, "The fact that two young girls had not only been able to see fairies, which others had done, but had actually for the first time ever been able to materialize them at a density sufficient for their images to be recorded on a photographic plate, meant that it was possible that the next cycle of evolution was underway."

MEANWHILE, ABOUT that same time, Sir Arthur Conan Doyle had been asked by *The Strand Magazine* to write a story about fairies for its Christmas 1920 issue. In the course of sleuthing the story, he learned of the existence of the fairy photographs and eventually made contact with Edward Gardner. The two men arranged to meet at a gentlemen's club in London.

Doyle found Gardner to be "quiet, well-balanced and reserved—not in the least of a wild or visionary type." He became convinced that Gardner was "a solid person with a reputation for sanity and character." (As a gentleman of breeding and culture, Conan Doyle often put great store in the personal character and credentials of those who professed to have seen or demonstrated psychic phenomena—an important consideration, certainly, but no substitute for rigorous scientific proof, of which there was often none.)

When Gardner showed Doyle "beautiful enlargements of these two wonderful pictures," they took his breath away. Could these photographs help provide the long-sought proof of the realities of spiritualist belief? Doyle and Gardner agreed that they would do everything possible to test the veracity of the pictures and seek out and interview the girls and their family and that—if the whole thing passed muster—Doyle would "throw [this news] into literary shape."

After his meeting with Gardner, Doyle showed the pictures to a few colleagues whose opinions he valued. Chief among them was the fiercely rational Sir Oliver Lodge. "I can still see his astonished and interested face as he gazed at the pictures which I placed before him in the hall of the Athenaeum Club," Doyle later recalled. But Lodge wasn't buying it. He suggested that photographs of classical dancers had been taken and cutouts of the prints superimposed on a rural British background. Doyle argued that such photographic tricks would be beyond the skills of a couple of country girls. But Lodge remained unmoved. And for good reason. As other critics later pointed out, the fairy dancers were actually less neoclassical than oddly up to date: Some of them had bobbed hair and wore beaded Charleston dresses, like flappers.

As news of the fairy photographs got around, Doyle was surprised to notice that some of the noisiest critics were fellow spiritualists, who argued that the whole debate over the existence or nonexistence of some diminutive, separate race was a distraction from the core beliefs of spiritualism—the existence of the human personality after death. If the fairy pictures were shown to be fake, they worried, it might have a negative impact on other, more important concerns of the movement.

It is clear from the written record Doyle left behind that while he went about dispassionately investigating the pictures, he desperately wanted to believe that they were genuine. It turns out that he had some deeply personal reasons to hope that the little people—what he called "dwellers at the border"—were real.

In his celebrated public life, Conan Doyle seldom spoke of his father. But the ghost of the dreamy, depressed, alcoholic Charles Doyle, with his fanciful drawings of fairies, elves, and brownies, scribbled in the dayrooms of a series of lunatic asylums, never hovered too far away. One sketch, so realistic it almost appears to have been drawn from life, depicted a female cupid dangling a string out of a potted plant, with a tiny elf hanging on to it down below. The caption read, "This bracket and plant are opposite my daily seat." One could imagine Conan Doyle's father, disheveled and with a long black beard, fixedly staring into thin air, into his own fevered imagination, or perhaps even into another world. Though this world had chosen to consider Charles Doyle crazy, dangerous, or simply useless, if his celebrated son could prove, for the first time, that there really *was* a diminutive race of beings that existed on the borderlands, Conan Doyle's investigation would turn into a chivalric quest: to redeem his father's honor.

NOW EDWARD Gardner and Doyle set about subjecting the fairy photographs to expert scrutiny. Gardner took them to a photographic expert at Harrow named Harold Snelling, of whom it was said that "what Snelling doesn't know about faked photographs isn't worth knowing." He had worked for thirty years at the Illingworth photographic studios. After examining the negatives carefully, Snelling said (according to Gardner), "This is the most extraordinary thing I've ever seen! Single exposure! Figures have moved! Why, it's a genuine photograph! Wherever did it come from?" Snelling later sent Gardner a letter stating, "These two negatives are entirely genuine, unfaked photographs of a single exposure, open-air work, showed movement in the fairy figures, and there is no trace whatever of studio work involving card or paper models, dark backgrounds, painted figures, etc. In my opinion, they are both straight untouched pictures."

Then the photographs were taken to Kodak, where three experts concluded that though there was no evidence of a double exposure or any other kind of fakery they could detect, because fairies don't exist, it was obvious there was some kind of flim-flam going on, somewhere. Kodak declined to warrant the genuineness of the images.

It seemed to Doyle, at this point, that the girls and the family needed to be interviewed directly. He himself was preparing to leave on a lecture tour of Australia, so Gardner made the trip to the quaint village of Cottingley. He took with him two dozen unexposed and secretly marked photographic plates, in hopes that he could get the girls to take more fairy pictures.

Mr. Wright, Gardner later reported, "impressed me favourably. . . . He is clear-headed and very intelligent, and gives one the impression of being open and honest." Mr. Wright "simply did not understand the business, but is quite clear and positive that the plate he took out of the Midg camera was the one he put in the same day." Even so, Wright remained unconvinced and later wrote that the whole matter had lowered his opinion of Conan Doyle for being fooled "by our Elsie, and her at the bottom of the class!" Mrs. Wright told Gardner that Elsie had always been a truthful girl and that some people in the village believed in her fairy stories simply because it was Elsie.

When Gardner met Elsie herself, she seemed cheerful and guileless, though a little weary of all the attention. She told him that she had no power at all over the fairies and that the way to " 'tice" them was to sit passively with her mind turned in that direction. Then, when she heard faint stirrings or movements in the grass, she'd beckon, to show they were welcome.

But Gardner also learned that Elsie was a fairly accomplished artist who once did design work for a jeweler and who sometimes liked to draw fairies. But when he asked her to draw a fairy, the pictures were "entirely uninspired, and bore no possible resemblance to those in the photograph," he said. (Of course, it's easy enough to draw a fairy badly, even if you can draw one well.)

Later that year, when Sir Arthur related this whole long story for the Christmas issue of *The Strand Magazine* (using fictitious names to protect the privacy of the family), under the title "Fairies Photographed: An Epoch-Making Event," he seems to have felt that he had investigated the matter thoroughly enough to put it before the public. (Or at least to protect his reputation from ridicule.) Whatever people were to make of it was up to them.

Even so, having satisfied himself that the photographs were very likely genuine, he ventured further and further out onto ice so thin it would later prove acutely embarrassing. In answer to the objections of some photographers, that the shadows on the figures seemed "off," he explained that "ectoplasm, as the etheric protoplasm has been named, has a faint luminosity of its own, which would largely modify shadows." In one picture, depicting a gnome, it's not difficult to see what appears to be a stick pin in the gnome's midriff, but Doyle explained this away by concluding that the point was an umbilicus and that therefore birth in the fairy kingdom might be a similar process to human birth. He went on to respond to questions about the differences between the gnome and the fairies, noting that "most observers of fairy life have reported . . . that there are separate species, varying very much in size, appearance, and locality—the wood fairy, the water fairy, the fairy of the plains, etc."

Though he had opened the *Strand* story with a careful distancing, backing off the claim that the pictures were genuine, the piece ended with what appeared to be Sir Arthur's true position: "The recognition of [fairies'] existence will jolt the material twentieth century mind out of its heavy ruts in the mud, and will make it admit that there is a glamour and mystery to life."

The Christmas issue of the magazine sold out in a couple of days. But the public's response to Doyle's spectacular revelation was hardly what he had hoped. One magazine ran a scornful story with the headline "Poor Sherlock Holmes—Hopelessly Crazy?" Another sharp attack came from Major John Hall-Edwards, a pioneer in the early use of X-rays in medicine (who lost his left arm due to overexposure to radium). Hall-Edwards claimed the photographs could easily have been faked in a variety of ways, that the apparent transparency of the "fairy wings" could have been accomplished by attaching insect wings to cutout pictures, and that "on the evidence I have no hesitation in saying that these photographs could have been 'faked.'"

Other papers took the middle ground. One opined, "It seems at this point that we must either believe in the almost incredible mystery of the fairy or in the almost incredible wonders of faked photographs."

Several Yorkshire newspapers also carried letters from writers who claimed to be unsurprised by the girls' revelations, because they'd seen little people on the moors themselves. One letter writer related a conversation with a notable author, William Riley, who "knows the Yorkshire moors and dales intimately," who, though he had never actually seen fairies there, "asserted that . . . he knew several trustworthy moorland people whose belief in them was unshakeable and who persisted against all contradiction that they themselves had many times seen pixies at certain favored spots."

CONAN DOYLE was still on his lecture tour in Australia when a jubilant letter from Gardner reached him in Melbourne. "The wonderful thing has happened!" he wrote. "I have received from Elsie three more negatives taken a few days back. . . . [They] are the most amazing that any modern eye has ever seen surely!"

Doyle answered back, equally ecstatic, saying that the average busy man, who hadn't kept up with "psychic inquiry," would need to be reminded again and again that "this new order of life is really established and has to be taken into serious account, just as the pigmies of Central Africa."

In a second article for *The Strand,* which appeared in 1921, Conan Doyle included these three new pictures. This story became the basis for his small 1922 book *The Coming of the Fairies,* which also included many first-person accounts of fairies. He also added a long theosophical explanation from Mr. Gardner—what fairies eat, what their wings are made of, their speech and gestures, even their sex lives (they don't have any).

He quoted a famous clairvoyant Theosophist, Bishop Charles Webster Leadbeater, about the great national varieties of fairies: "No contrast could well be more marked than that between the vivacious, rollicking, orange-and-purple or scarlet-and-gold mannikens who dance among the vineyards of Sicily and the almost wistful gray-and-green creatures who move . . . amidst the oaks and furze-covered heaths of Brittany."

He also described inviting a clairvoyant named Geoffrey Hodson to Cottingley Beck to see what he could "see."

Not only did he see fairies, but he described seeing water nymphs, wood elves, goblins, and a brownie. Elsie and Frances, who also went along, were unmoved; they later said they hadn't seen anything at all and concluded Hodson was daft.

Doyle ended his little book by saying that the case for fairies was strong enough "the matter is not one which can be readily dismissed" and that "far from being resented . . . criticism, so long as it is honest and earnest, must be most welcome to those whose only aim is the fearless search for truth."

It's fair to say that many people felt the fearless search for truth led them to believe that Sir Arthur was a credulous old fool. For them, Conan Doyle's reputation, both literary and personal, never recovered from the embarrassment of the Cottingley Fairies incident. But to the very end of his days, no matter what further evidence or counterarguments emerged, Sir Arthur Conan Doyle stuck with his story: The Cottingley Fairies were real.

OVER THE years following Doyle's death in 1930, various newspapers, magazines, and TV crews periodically reinvestigated the fairy story. It appeared that it would never die.

In 1966, when the BBC tracked down Elsie, she made a firm but cagey statement: "I've told you that they're photographs of figments of our imagination, and that's what I'm sticking to." Did she mean that they had photographed "thought forms" or that the pictures were simply made up? Eventually, the two cousins got tired of the publicity; they told reporters they were fed up with talking about the fairies. Finally, in a letter dated February 17, 1983, Elsie came clean. She admitted that the "fairies" had been fakes: She'd drawn them on cardboard, cut them out, and fastened them to the grass with long hat pins. They appeared to be "fluttering" only because of the wind.

In the 1980s, it was discovered that a children's book published in 1914, called *Princess Mary's Gift Book,* contained pictures of fairies that were almost identical to the ones in the Cottingley photographs.

In a 1985 television interview, Elsie added that she and Frances had staged the pictures as a lark, but when the pictures attracted the attention of the famous Sir Arthur Conan Doyle, they were too embarrassed to back out. "Two village kids and a brilliant man like Conan Doyle? Well, we could only keep quiet," she said. In the same interview, Frances added, "I never even thought of it as being a fraud. It was just Elsie and I having a bit of fun and I can't understand to this day why they were taken in. They *wanted* to be taken in!"

Even so, until her death in 1986, Frances maintained that though four of the five photographs had been staged, the girls really *had* seen fairies "down the beck," and the fifth picture was genuine. "It was a wet Saturday afternoon and we were just mooching about with our cameras and Elsie had nothing prepared," she told a TV interviewer. "I saw these fairies building up in the grasses and just aimed the camera and took a photograph." It showed what looked like two translucent fairies beside a kind of grassy cocoon.

Though Sir Arthur had always believed that Frances was telling the truth, most of the world had already moved on—whether she was telling the truth or not.

Conan Doyle and Houdini were respectful friends in private and bitter enemies in public. Their quarrel: whether spiritualism was genuine or fraudulent.
CHRONICLE / ALAMY STOCK PHOTO

CHAPTER NINE
The Strangest Friendship in History

If there had been any doubt about where Sir Arthur stood on the subject of the supernatural, by the time of the Cottingley Fairies incident it was clear to the world whose side he was on. By the early 1920s—in addition to his fast-growing literary fame as the creator of a certain brilliant detective—he had become the world's most famous defender of spiritualism. He was its high priest, its most earnest advocate, its most charming and congenial convert.

"If ever there was a whole-hearted believer, he was one," an acquaintance later wrote of him.

But as Sir Arthur strutted across the world's stage, with his droopy walrus mustache, his tweed coats, and his compelling convictions, there was another man in the popular press whose fame had begun to exceed Conan Doyle's. He was hardly bigger than a boy—five feet five in his stocking feet—a diminutive Hungarian with a huge head, a mop of bushy, center-parted hair, and pale, laser-focused sea-blue eyes. Erich Weisz, one of seven children of a poor rabbi, had emigrated from Budapest to the United States with his family when he was four years old. From a very young age—for some reason—he seemed inexorably drawn to the limelight. He performed publicly for the first time as a nine-year-old trapeze artist calling himself "Erich, the Prince of the Air." Later, he did card tricks and escape acts at circuses and sideshows and briefly ran a Punch-and-Judy show.

When he was twelve, he hopped a freight car and ran away from home but returned a year later and with his brother Theo began to develop magic acts. He was still a teenager when he took on the stage name that would make him famous, after his idol, the nineteenth-century French illusionist Jean Robert-Houdin.

Harry Houdini, or sometimes Harry "Handcuff" Houdini, soon developed an almost supernatural ability to slip free from almost any entanglement. Eventually, at the urging of a promoter, he decided to give up his conjuring and card tricks and focus on his amazing ability to escape from handcuffs, chains, padlocks, straitjackets, and anything else that attempted to bind him. His antics spawned a new word: "escapologist." He began challenging police departments to lock him up in a jail cell, bound by chains or whatever else they could find. Inevitably, incredibly, he would escape. In 1906, J. H. Harris, the warden of the United States Gaol in Washington, D.C., signed the following statement:

> This is to certify that Mr. Harry Houdini, at the United States Gaol to-day, was stripped stark naked, thoroughly searched, and locked up in Cell No. 2 of the South Wing—the cell in which Charles J. Guiteau, the assassinator of President Garfield, was confined during his incarceration. . . . Mr. Houdini, in about two minutes, managed to escape from that cell, and then broke into the cell in which his clothing was locked up. He then proceeded to release from their cells all the prisoners on the ground floor. . . . Mr. Houdini accomplished all of the above mentioned facts, in addition to putting on all his clothing, in twenty-one minutes.

Houdini took this act on a tour of the jails of Europe, and when he returned to America in triumph, he bought a brownstone in Harlem and bought his beloved mother a dress that had once belonged to Queen Victoria.

Houdini was extraordinarily attached to his mother, who lived with the magician and his new wife, Bess, in the Harlem brownstone. He loved to put his head on his mother's chest to feel her heart beating; he would often only wear clothes that she had picked out for him. When she died in 1913, Houdini's devotion to her did not seem to diminish in the slightest. In fact, one acquaintance later observed, Houdini's "love for his dead mother seemed to be the ruling passion of his life." He was also unnaturally attached to Bess, who was his accomplice in various magic acts. Once, in a public hearing, when he was accused of sometimes being viciously vindictive against his enemies, he turned to Bess and asked plaintively, "I have always been a good boy, have I not?"

Now Houdini began enthralling the world with escapes from ever more incredible and dangerous restraints. He developed a famous act in which he was tied up and locked into an oversized milk can filled with water—the ads read, "Failure Means a Drowning Death!"—bound with chains and locks, and escaped. He was dangled from cranes, in a straitjacket, over the streets of Manhattan and escaped. He was padlocked into steel boxes dunked into the freezing-cold East River and escaped. Three times, he was buried alive, without a casket, under six feet of dirt; he almost died trying to escape. But escape he did.

It was as if Houdini had become the avatar of limitless human possibility—a soaring, indomitable spirit who could break free from any chains, even the chains of mortality. As if, for all the people watching, wrapped in their own personal manacles of bad marriages, crushing debt, or health worries, he was demonstrating that they could break free.

In one of his most famous escapes, London's *Daily Mirror* challenged him to escape from handcuffs that a locksmith claimed had taken him five years to perfect. Four thousand people showed up at the Hippodrome theater in London and waited, breathlessly, for more than two hours after Houdini disappeared into his "ghost house" (an onstage cabinet) to attempt the escape. Several times he emerged from the cabinet, still bound, once to complain that his hands were turning blue, another to snatch a kiss from Bess. (Some later suggested that she'd passed a tiny handcuff key from her mouth to his.) But eventually, Houdini strode onto the stage, a free man. It was, he later said, his most difficult escape; he was so overcome afterward that he broke down and wept and was carried off on the shoulders of the triumphant crowd.

Houdini's preparations for these stunts were legendary. He taught himself to hold his breath for more than three full minutes. He sat in ice-cold baths, surrounded by the gentle ting-tinging of ice cubes, to inure himself to pain. A lithe, compact, powerful man, he made a fateful boast that his stomach muscles were so strong he could withstand a direct blow from anyone.

No illusion seemed too incredible for him. He vanished a full-grown elephant from the stage. In his famous "needle trick," he swallowed five packages of needles and twenty yards of thread, then coughed them up—with the needles threaded. He started challenging the public to devise traps that could hold him, and he escaped from them all—even the belly of a whale and an enormous barrel filled with beer.

In 1913, Houdini introduced the Chinese Water Torture Cell, an act in which he was locked upside down in a glass-and-steel box filled with water so that the audience could actually watch him wriggle free. To escape, he had to hold his breath for more than three minutes while frantically wriggling free from all manner of restraints. By then, he had become the highest-paid act in American vaudeville and—to this day—a household name. Ninety years after his death, he is almost universally recognized simply by his last name.

Houdini's onstage marvels were so remarkable that there were spiritualists who came to believe that he must be harnessing some kind of psychic power, whether he admitted it (or even knew it) himself. At least during his early days, Houdini himself appeared to encourage this notion, claiming in ads that he was able to "dematerialize" while chained inside a locked box and then "rematerialize" once he'd floated free.

What was not widely known was that Houdini had a great

personal interest in the claims of spiritualism and a vast research library in his Harlem brownstone spanning the arcana not only of magic but also of spiritualism, "soul return," and the occult. One friend called this enormous library a "fearful and wonderful thing." His reasons for this obsession were personal: He longed to make contact "across the veil" with his beloved mother. After her death, he began visiting mediums across the United States and Europe in hopes of making contact.

But as the years went by, without success, Houdini became increasingly scornful of the so-called trance mediums he had visited, maintaining that any of the spooky phenomena they seemed to manifest could be replicated by any decent magician, using un-supernatural tricks. Toward the end of his life, demonstrating how "fraud mediums" engineered their effects became part of Houdini's most popular stage act.

But at the same time, in private, he remained an earnest if unconvinced seeker.

In the early spring of 1920, having followed Conan Doyle's celebrated career as a spiritualist in the newspapers—though the two men had never met—Houdini sent Doyle a copy of his first book. *The Unmasking of Robert-Houdin* was the story of his own deep study of, and later disenchantment with, his idol. (Houdini came to believe that many of Robert-Houdin's famous illusions had been pirated from other magicians.)

In the book, Houdini also discussed the intriguing case of the Davenport brothers, a pair of famous illusionists who claimed that their phenomena were accomplished by means of supernatural power. In their most famous act, the brothers were tied up and placed in a box filled with musical instruments; after the cabinet was closed, the instruments could be heard merrily playing. When the box was opened, the brothers were still tied up as they had been at the beginning.

Houdini maintained that the Davenports had wowed their audiences with mere stage magic. In the letter he sent to Doyle with the book, he also suggested that many spiritualists had later confessed to fraud.

On March 15, 1920, Sir Arthur wrote back to Houdini from

his East Sussex home, Windlesham Manor: "I have always wondered whether the Davenport brothers were ever *really* exposed. As to Spiritualist 'Confessions,' they are all nonsense. Every famous medium is said to have 'confessed,' and it is an old trick of the opposition." At the end of his brief, breezy letter, Doyle added, "Some of our people think that you yourself have some psychic power, but I feel it is art and practice."

Houdini wrote back promptly and cheerily, tucking in a photograph of himself with Ira Davenport, whom he had met just before Davenport's death in 1911. (In his usual meticulous way, Houdini had studied the Davenports' case so thoroughly that Davenport allegedly told him, "Houdini, you know more about myself than I do!")

"I envy you the privilege of having met Ira Davenport," Doyle wrote back cordially. "How people could imagine those men were conjurers is beyond me." And thus began a long and fascinating epistolary relationship, followed by a series of personal meetings, described as "one of the strangest friendships in history," in a 1933 book by Hereward Carrington and Bernard Ernst, who knew both these extraordinary men well and had access to their personal letters and diaries.

Nowadays, these two remarkable men might be known as "frenemies," but one extraordinary thing that emerges from their letters is clear evidence that even when they bitterly disagreed, they held each other in high esteem. Both men were gentlemen, through and through. In one letter to Houdini's wife, Bess, Doyle wrote that Houdini "was a great master of his profession and, in some ways, the most remarkable man I have ever known." Elsewhere, in his book *The Edge of the Unknown,* Doyle writes, "In a long life which has touched every side of humanity, Houdini is far and away the most curious and intriguing character whom I have ever encountered."

In his private letters, Houdini always reciprocated with a respectful doff of the hat, addressing the author as "My dear Sir Arthur." In his 1924 book *A Magician Among the Spirits,* Houdini writes that Doyle's name "comes automatically to the mind of the average human to-day at the mention of Spiritualism. . . . There is no doubt that Sir Arthur is sincere in his belief and it is this sincerity which has been one of the fundamentals of our friendship."

After their initial contact, the letters became increasingly chummy and lighthearted. Trying to set up a face-to-face meeting with Houdini while he was in New York, Doyle wrote, "Until Thursday is over I shall be in a turmoil. Then, when I can breathe, I hope to see you—your normal self, not in a tank or hanging by one toe from a skyscraper." Elsewhere he wrote, "All good wishes to you, my dear Houdini. Do drop these dangerous stunts."

But the primary subject of most of these letters was spiritualism and the truth or falsity of the claims offered by the many mediums, table tippers, psychics, and mind readers currently practicing in the public square. In general, Doyle frankly admitted that there were plenty of fakes—with a caveat. "A retinue of rogues has been attracted to Spiritualism by the fact that séances have been largely held in the dark, when the object has been to produce physical phenomena," he wrote. "This has served as a screen for villainy. When such a fraud has been discovered it has naturally come before the police courts and been reported in the papers, while the successful work of the honest mediums gets no public notice." But Doyle also took this claim one step further, adding (incorrectly), "I am sure no medium has ever deceived me."

The character of the two men emerges in the letters and writings that chronicled their friendship. Doyle observed that "a prevailing feature of [Houdini's] character was a vanity which was so obvious and childish that it became more amusing than offensive. I can remember, for example, that when he introduced his brother to me, he did it by saying, 'This is the brother of the great Houdini.' This without any twinkle of humor and in a perfectly natural manner."

For his part, Houdini complained that though he never doubted Doyle's sincerity, "he has refused to discuss [psychic phenomena] in any other voice except that of Spiritualism and in all our talks quoted only those who favored it in every way, and if one does not follow him sheep-like during his investigations then he is blotted out forever so far as Sir Arthur is concerned."

Sometimes Doyle's comments were more revelatory of himself than of Houdini. At one point, he wrote to the magician, "I see that you know a great deal about the negative side of Spiritualism—I hope more on the positive side will come your way. But it wants to be approached not in the spirit of a detective approaching a subject, but in that of a humble, religious soul, yearning for help and comfort." Which, arguably, was precisely why there was so much fraud afoot: People "yearning for help and comfort" were practically begging to be taken advantage of.

Dr. Walter Franklin Prince, a serious psychic investigator of the day, who knew both men and their writings, observed, "Houdini shows his bias especially by the selection, for the most part, of mediums and phenomena long regarded, by most careful researchers in America and England, as either spurious or very dubious, and by silence concerning psychics and phenomena generally treated with respect by such persons. Doyle shows his bias by the ingenuity of his defense of some of the most doubtful characters of the past and by his oversight of unpleasant particulars."

Though both men were public evangelists for their own point of view, Prince once said that "the fervor with which [Houdini] carried on his anti-Spiritualistic propaganda, not publicly only but in private conversation, was to me so striking, that I once told him that the preaching zeal of his father [the rabbi] had descended on him."

As their friendship deepened, Sir Arthur appears to have grown ever more convinced that Houdini must have been making use of some sort of "supernormal" power to accomplish his amazing stage tricks—even if he didn't know it. Responding to critics who scoffed at this notion, Doyle wrote, "It is said, 'How absurd for Doyle to attribute possible psychic powers to a man who himself denies them!' Is it not perfectly evident that if he did not deny them his occupation would have been gone forever? What would his brother magicians have to say to a man who admitted that half his tricks were done by what they would regard as illicit powers?"

Because of this, he reasoned, Houdini would be doubly motivated to denigrate any apparent proof of the claims of spiritualism.

This lingering dispute came to a head one May afternoon in 1922, when Sir Arthur was in New York on his lecture tour. Houdini and Bess invited the Doyles to come for lunch at Houdini's brownstone, on West 113th Street, in Harlem. Outside the front door the two famous men posed for what would later become a famous press photograph, with the rumpled, bearlike Sir Arthur towering a full head above Houdini.

Afterward, Houdini led his guests on a tour of his house, filled with trophies, photographs, playbills, and awards celebrating his remarkable career. Despite the vainglorious decoration, Lady Jean commented that it was "the most home-like home" she had ever seen.

After a congenial lunch, Houdini and Doyle repaired to the upstairs library. Houdini's lawyer, Bernard Ernst, joined them there. The conversation had by then turned—once again—to certain types of "psychic phenomena" that Doyle fervently believed demonstrated the truth of spiritualist claims. In particular, he talked about the "spirit hands" that certain mediums seemed able to produce in séance. Doyle maintained that these rubbery, somewhat misshapen appendages were created out of the mysterious, moist substance known as "ectoplasm," which appeared to emanate from the mouths, noses, and other orifices of mediums. Doyle was convinced that the study of this mysterious substance would someday constitute a new branch of science, called plasmology.

But Houdini would have none of it. In an effort to convince Doyle that spirit hands, spirit photography, table tipping, and all the rest of it were no more than ordinary bunk, produced by simple sleight of hand, he decided to give Doyle a demonstration.

First, "Houdini produced what appeared to be an ordinary slate, some eighteen inches long by fifteen inches high," Ernst later recalled in his 1933 book, *The Story of a Strange Friendship.* In the upper corners two holes had been bored, through which long wires had been passed, with hooks on the ends. Houdini passed the slate to Sir Arthur, who examined it, and then Houdini hung the slate from hooks in the ceiling so that it was suspended in the middle of the room at about eye level, clearly visible on both sides.

Next Houdini invited Sir Arthur to examine four cork balls, sitting in a saucer, and to select one at random. Doyle picked one, and Houdini then sliced it clean through with a sharp knife, to show there was nothing inside but cork. Then Conan Doyle randomly selected another of the four balls, which Houdini placed into a large inkwell filled with white ink. With a tablespoon, he stirred the ball around to make sure it was completely coated with ink.

Then Houdini invited Doyle to go out of the house, in any direction he pleased, to make sure he was not being observed, and write a phrase or message on a scrap of paper, put it into his pocket, and return to the house. Doyle did so, walking three blocks from the house, turning left, and then (covering the paper as an extra precaution) jotting something on the sheet. He pocketed it and returned to the house, where Houdini and Ernst were waiting in the library.

Houdini then told his guest to fish the cork ball, soaked in white ink, out of the inkwell and hold it up to the slate, which was still hanging in the middle of the room. When Doyle did this, the white ball appeared to attach to the slate, as if it were magnetized, and then it began to move across the slate, spelling out words as it went. Once finished, the ball abruptly dropped to the floor.

With a theatrical flourish, Houdini asked Sir Arthur to read the words.

Mene, mene, tekel, upharsin, Doyle read out, in evident shock.

This ancient prophecy of doom was the exact phrase he had written on the scrap of paper.

In the biblical story from which the phrase is taken, the vain king Belshazzar and his host of lords are drinking wine from golden cups pillaged from the temple in Jerusalem when suddenly the king sees a disembodied human hand writing an inscrutable message on a wall. The king calls for Daniel, interpreter of dreams and riddles, who translates the message to mean that Belshazzar's days are numbered and his reign will soon end. That very night, the king is killed.

But if Houdini's intention was to convince Doyle that almost any kind of psychic phenomena could be faked, it was a spectacular failure. The *mene, mene, tekel, upharsin* episode only cemented Doyle's conviction that Houdini was somehow enlisting the help of the great beyond to pull off his stunts. Ernst, too, was shocked by the incident. He later wrote that he thought the trick was similar to a telepathy act Houdini had once performed onstage but had stopped doing because it was "too spooky."

Houdini himself later observed that "Sir Arthur thinks that I have great mediumistic powers and that some of my feats are done with the aid of spirits. But everything I do is accomplished by material means . . . no matter how baffling it is to the layman."

Baffling indeed.

A MONTH after this memorable incident, in June 1922, Sir Arthur and Lady Jean joined Bess and Harry Houdini at the Ambassador Hotel, in Atlantic City, for the weekend. After a bracing swim in the ocean, Houdini joined Doyle on the beach, where he was sitting in a deck chair with his bare feet in the sand, incongruously dressed in a neat dark suit. Before too long, Doyle brought up the subject of spirit photography, his new favorite subject. From under his chair, he pulled out a picture of a coffin with ghostly "spirit faces" floating around it and eagerly showed it to Houdini (who feigned interest but secretly rolled his eyes).

After a short while, Doyle excused himself to go up to the

hotel room for his usual afternoon nap. But a few minutes later, a small boy came scampering down the beach with the illustrious author in tow; Lady Doyle had dispatched the boy and her husband to fetch Houdini. Doyle brought the news that Lady Jean "might have a message coming through" for Houdini and would be willing to give him a private sitting and perhaps even make contact with his beloved mother. (From here forward, most of the particulars of this story are in dispute. According to Doyle's later recollection, it was Houdini who requested the séance, not the other way around. Doyle later wrote, "The method in which Houdini tried to explain away, minimize and contort our attempt at consolation, which was given entirely at his own urgent request and against my wife's desire, has left a deplorable shadow in my mind which made some alteration in my feelings towards him.")

At this point, someone snapped a photograph of the two famous men—both wearing straw hats and smiling gaily, Houdini wearing a rumpled white suit, Doyle still wearing his dark one. Then Doyle turned to Bess and asked if she would mind if he and Houdini could be alone with Lady Jean. "Smilingly, my good little wife said, 'Certainly not, go right ahead, Sir Arthur; I will leave Houdini in your charge,'" Houdini later recalled.

Now, according to Houdini's later account, his wife "cued" him—that is, communicated a secret message using a code they'd developed for his stage act, something they were able to do in the presence of others, while appearing to be merely chatting or doing nothing but "the most innocent things." The primary thing Bess communicated, Houdini claimed, was that the night before she had told Lady Doyle about the great love Houdini had for his mother, including his love of laying his head on her breast to hear her heartbeat. (Never mind how improbable it seems that this message could have been conveyed in code.)

Houdini and Doyle walked up the beach to the Doyles' hotel suite, where Lady Doyle met them. The shades were drawn, and the three of them sat down at a table on which lay a couple of pencils and a writing pad. (Lady Jean's apparent psychic talents involved "automatic writing"—the ability to slip into a trance state and "channel" messages by writing on paper.) They put their hands on the table, and Sir Arthur started the séance with a devout prayer.

"I excluded all earthly thoughts and gave my whole soul to the séance," Houdini recalled. "I was *willing* to believe, even *wanted* to believe. It was weird to me and with a beating heart I waited, hoping that I might feel once more the presence of my beloved Mother."

In a few moments, Lady Doyle appeared to be "seized by a Spirit." Her hands began to shake, and her voice trembled as she called out, asking for a message to come through her. "Sir Arthur tried to quiet her, asked her to restrain herself, but her hand thumped on the table, her whole body shook and at last, making a cross at the head of the page, started writing," Houdini recalled.

Then she began furiously writing—fifteen pages in all—with Sir Arthur tearing off each sheet of the pad as she finished and handing them to Houdini without even reading them. Doyle later described what he saw: "It was a singular scene, my wife with her hand flying wildly while she scribbled at a furious rate, I sitting opposite and tearing sheet after sheet from the block as it was filled up, and tossing each across to Houdini, while he sat silent, looking grimmer and paler every moment."

The scrawled message began, "Oh, my darling, thank God, thank God, at last I'm through—I've tried, oh, so often now I am happy. . . . [N]ever had a Mother such a son—tell him not to grieve—soon he'll get all the evidence he is so anxious for. . . . I am so happy in this life—it is so full and joyous—my only shadow has been that my beloved hasn't known how often I have been with him all the while."

Conan Doyle interrupted at one point to ask Houdini if he would like to speak to the spirit directly, requesting proof that it was indeed Houdini's mother who was speaking. Doyle suggested that Houdini ask the question, mentally, "Can my mother read my mind?" and Houdini dutifully did so. Lady Jean began scribbling furiously: "I *always* read my beloved son's mind—his dear mind—there is so much I want to say to him—but I am almost overwhelmed by this joy of talking to him once more. . . . God bless you, too, Sir Arthur, for what you are doing for us—for us, over here—who so need to get in touch with our beloved ones on the earth plane—if only the world knew this great truth. . . . [A] happiness awaits him that he has never dreamed of."

Once Lady Jean had finished (according to Doyle's account), Houdini picked up one of the pencils on the table and mused aloud, "I wonder if I could do anything at this." Then he wrote one word on the page. Afterward, Doyle recalled, "he looked up at me and I was amazed, for I saw in his eyes that look, impossible to imitate, which comes to the medium who is under influence."

Houdini had written the name "Powell" on the page.

And when he saw this, Sir Arthur instantly jumped up excitedly. An old spiritualist friend of his, an editor at the *Financial News* of London, had died a week earlier in England. "The Spirits have directed you in writing the name of my dear fighting partner in spiritualism, Dr. Ellis Powell," Doyle crowed. "I am the person he is most likely to signal to, and here is his name coming through your hands. Truly Saul is among the Prophets. You are a medium!"

According to Doyle's account, Houdini "seemed to be disconcerted by my remark. He muttered something about a man called 'Powell' down in Texas, but he failed to invent any reason why that particular man should come back at that particular moment. Then, gathering up his papers, he hurried from the room."

When the two men met again two days later, Houdini told him that he had been "walking on air ever since" the séance.

But Houdini's take on all of this, which later appeared in print, was entirely different from Doyle's account. First of all, he later wrote, though he had hoped and wished for a feeling of his mother's presence, "there wasn't even a semblance of it." Anyone who had ever deeply loved his mother would know the feeling of her presence, he said. But he felt nothing at all.

There were also a couple of other problems with this

"séance," he pointed out. For one thing, the day of the séance, June 17, was his mother's birthday—"my most holy holiday"—and though Lady Jean did not know this, if it really *had* been his mother "coming through," she would have mentioned this. But she didn't. (Weirdly enough, Houdini got the date wrong—the reading actually took place on Sunday the eighteenth, not Saturday the seventeenth. For all his meticulous attention to detail in his stage acts, he was surprisingly careless about details in his writing.) Also, Lady Jean—or whomever she was allegedly channeling—made the sign of the cross at the top of the page. But Houdini's mother was Jewish, not Christian. Doyle later brushed this off; his wife *always* made the sign of the cross when she did automatic writing, he said, to ward off malicious spirits.

The other problem was a bigger one. The entire message was written in English, but Houdini's mother, though she had lived in the United States for more than fifty years, did not speak English. She only spoke Hungarian.

The other problem was that name, "Powell."

Houdini claimed that he'd written the name, entirely of his own volition, because he'd thought of a magician friend named Frederick Eugene Powell, with whom he'd recently had a good bit of business correspondence. It was simply a coincidence that the name matched that of a recently deceased friend of Doyle's. But Doyle would have none of it. A few days later, he sent Houdini a letter in which he protested that "no, the Powell explanation won't do." The "coincidence" was too improbable. Besides, the evening after the séance, Doyle had gone to a medium, who told him, "There is a man here. He wants to say he is sorry he had to speak so abruptly this afternoon."

Also, he added, the fact that Houdini's mother spoke in English was immaterial, because in the spirit world language does not matter. Houdini, in a letter of reply, reiterated his skepticism but closed in his usual gentlemanly way by saying, "Trusting you will accept my letter in the same honest, good faith feeling as it has been written."

Nevertheless, a couple of months later Houdini felt it necessary to file an official disclaimer, witnessed by a notary, maintaining that he had not made contact with his mother during the séance and that "in case of my death, no one will claim that the spirit of Sir Arthur Conan Doyle's friend Ellis Powell guided my hand."

This "strangest friendship," while still starchily polite, had turned increasingly icy. And it was about to get worse.

Cunning fraud or the genuine article? "Margery" became one of the most celebrated, and controversial, mediums of the spiritualist era. Oddly, this picture was taken by Houdini himself.

CHAPTER TEN
Sex, Lies, and Séances

On the steamy summer night of August 25, 1924, shortly before 10:00 p.m., in a small upstairs room in an imposing brick house in Boston's tony Beacon Hill, five distinguished middle-aged gentlemen, in starched shirts and ties, sat down at a low table in semidarkness and formed a circle, holding hands. Included in the circle was a sixth person, a fetching thirty-six-year-old woman with keen, saucy eyes and a blond flapper's bob, who was seated inside a large wooden cabinet with only her head and arms exposed. She was so comely that some said she was "too attractive for her own good." Other séance goers were warned, only half jokingly, "not to fall in love with the medium."

Each of her small hands firmly grasped one of the men's hands to her left and right, which carried an erotic charge, because inside the box, the men all knew, the young woman was wearing nothing more than a flimsy dress, silk stockings, and bedroom slippers. (It was widely rumored that she sometimes gave séances in the nude, ostensibly to demonstrate that she wasn't hiding anything under her clothes; tonight she was only barely clothed for the same reason.)

The young woman's name was Mina Crandon, a former Canadian farm girl who was quickly becoming one of the most celebrated, and most unlikely, trance mediums of the spiritualist era. She was, after all, only modestly interested in the claims of spiritualism and had only become involved in all this a few years earlier when she quite unexpectedly discovered she seemed to be a "channel" for transmissions from the spirit world. That is, *supposedly.* To the vast throngs of disbelievers, she became known as "the blond witch of Lime Street."

To the throngs of enthralled believers, she became known as "Margery the Medium" (a pseudonym bestowed by her friend J. Malcolm Bird, in a failed attempt to protect her privacy).

Tonight's séance circle was an august group. Holding Margery's right hand in the semidarkness was Dr. Daniel Frost Comstock, a theoretical physicist and engineer at MIT (who had helped develop an early color film process for movies). Next to him sat Dr. Walter Franklin Prince, a stern, intellectually rigorous psychic investigator who held a Ph.D. from Yale and was the chief research officer of the American Society for Psychical Research. To his right sat Dr. L. R. G. Crandon, Margery's husband, a prominent Beacon Hill physician and devoted spiritualist. Next to him sat Orson Munn, owner of *Scientific American* magazine, whose offer of a cash prize to anyone who could produce psychic phenomena to the satisfaction of a committee of judges was the reason for tonight's séance.

Holding Margery's left hand, and thus completing the circle, was none other than Harry Houdini. Houdini had been invited to join this séance partly because of his unsurpassed knowledge of the ways in which the human mind can be tricked into believing that something is true when it is not. In fact, the cabinet in which Margery now sat had been designed and built by Houdini himself in order to circumvent the sort of trickery and sleight of hand that had made him famous. Once the cabinet was completed, Houdini—in his usual vain and imperious way—had announced that the cabinet was "fraud-proof."

But the distinguished gentlemen in the room were not holding hands out of camaraderie. In fact, mistrust hung in the air like a suffocating mist. They were holding hands to provide a "control," that is, to prevent anyone else from either faking psychic phenomena or, conversely, attempting to prevent genuine psychic phenomena from occurring. This was an attempt to create scientifically rigorous conditions under which it would be possible to judge whether "supernormal" phenomena—something outside the known laws of science—had actually taken place, even in the presence of bitter unbelievers.

In the center of the circle, on the table, sat a contraption called a bell box. It was a small wooden box with a bell inside, attached to a dry cell battery. It measured fourteen inches long by six inches wide and five deep. The top of the box was a hinged lid held open by a spring. If the lid were depressed far enough, two small metal contacts would connect and complete a circuit, and the bell would ring. Because Margery was apparently prevented from physically touching the bell box, tonight's test was to see if she could ring the bell by means of some unfathomable, "supernormal" power.

This was an improvement over the setup used in earlier séances, in which the bell box was simply set on the floor not too far from Margery's feet. In one of those séances, when Houdini was seated next to her, the magician claimed he'd felt her moving her foot in order to ring the bell—which prompted him to insist that he build her a "fraud-proof" cabinet, which later became known as a "Houdini box" or a "Margery box." The cabinet was about the size of a rolltop writing desk, with hand holes on the sides and a hole for her head on top. Its dimensions were four feet deep, five feet wide, and six feet high. It weighed about 140 pounds.

In a small adjoining room sat a female stenographer, taking notes under a very dim red light. According to her real-time notes, it was 9:45 p.m. when the lights in the séance room were lowered to near darkness. It was standard procedure to either completely darken the séance room or light it only with dim red light, because spiritualists claimed full light could prevent phenomena from occurring or might actually harm the medium. Skeptics, of course, claimed this whole business about dim light was utter hogwash and merely a convenient cover for all manner of fakery.

Nevertheless, once the lights were lowered, the séance sitters sank into an awkward and uncomfortable silence, clasping each other's sweaty palms without speaking. Eight minutes of silence went by.

Then, suddenly, a bright, cheery whistle rang out into the room.

"Leave everything to me!" a young man's voice called out. "Be of good cheer!"

The voice seemed to originate from Margery's general location. It did not appear to be Margery's voice, or if it was, it was cleverly disguised as the voice of a robust and mischievous young man. (In earlier séances, the voice still sounded even if Margery was asleep and snoring or her mouth was full of water. The voice also sometimes seemed to come from elsewhere in the room, even the ceiling.)

In fact, the voice itself claimed to be that of one Walter Stinson, Margery's beloved older brother, who had died in a railroad accident years before, at the age of twenty-eight. Hamlin Garland, the noted novelist and spiritualist who had attended several previous séances with Margery, described Walter's usual entrance as "a loud merry whistle, like that of a boy signaling his fellows; and a moment later a curious guttural voice was heard that might have come from deep in a man's throat." It was the voice of "a vigorous, humorous, rough-and-ready man of twenty-five or thirty, with such intonation as a Canadian youth . . . would use." His tone and comments tended to be sarcastic and irreverent; he referred to his sister as "the kid."

In previous séances, Walter had taken particular aim at Houdini, for whom he seemed to harbor a delicious disdain. He was profoundly suspicious of Houdini's motives and delighted in mocking him, at one point singing out,

> *Harry Houdini, he sure is a sheeny,*
> *A man with a crook in his shoe.*
> *Says he "As to Walter,*
> *I'll lead him to the slaughter."*
> *"But," says Walter, "perhaps I'll get* you!*"*

At another point, Walter snarled, "You Munn and Houdini think you're pretty smart, don't you? Straighten up there!" He was, he claimed, no "little sunbeam" or "gladiola" but "a full-grown man who wears an 11½ shoe on a supernormal foot."

At other times, Walter seemed to have access to private information obtained in unfathomable ways. "Very interesting conversation you men had on the train," he said to Houdini in one séance. "I was there. I can always be where my interests lie." Houdini's own interests, Walter made clear, were to prevent any kind of psychic phenomena from occurring, because according to his own account, in his book *A Magician Among the Spirits,* he was a wounded seeker who had turned into an angry professional debunker.

"I have said many times that I am willing to believe, *want* to believe, *will* believe, if the Spiritualists can show me any substantiated proof," Houdini had written, but "none of the evidence offered has been able to stand up under the fierce rays of investigation."

A healthy skepticism was fair, and there was no shortage of fake psychics and table tippers in the public square. But in the face of phenomena that were entirely unexplainable, Walter argued, Houdini was willing to take his skepticism one step further and cheat to keep it from happening. In fact, in a séance two days earlier, Walter had predicted that Houdini would do something to prevent Margery from ringing the bell box, possibly by slipping a die between the box and the hinged lid. "Search his pockets . . . you'll find the other die," he'd said.

If this was indeed the disembodied voice of Margery's brother, the voice was entirely in character, because in life Walter Stinson had been willful, rebellious, and filled with reckless joy, with tousled blond hair and broad shoulders. He was strong enough to stand up to his father, a grim and disapproving fundamentalist. But he was also kind enough that he once gave away his expensive overcoat to a tramp. Mina and Walter had been very close. They shared a casual interest in the shadow world of the occult, partly because they had a cousin named Henry, crippled by a childhood accident, who was a "dowser"—able to find water by means of a forked stick. All the wells on the Stinson farm had been dug with the help of Henry's magic stick. Mina and Walter were both amused and puzzled by Henry's seeming inexplicable abilities. Walter was intrigued enough that he once came back from town with wild tales of a "spook show," or séance, that he had attended.

When Walter was killed after a railcar fell on him, Mina had been heartbroken. She left home shortly afterward, got married, and had a son, but the marriage was an unhappy one, and she divorced soon afterward. When she went to the hospital for an operation, she charmed the doctor who treated her, a tall Boston surgeon named Le Roi Crandon. After all, those who knew her, especially men, stumbled over superlatives for her. She was "deep and frivolous, superficial and solemn," one observer wrote, "an elusive beauty, a delicate and mischievous loveliness."

Several years later (in 1918), with the coming of the world war, Mina volunteered to drive ambulances for a navy hospital. There she crossed paths once again with Dr. Crandon (now a lieutenant commander of a medical unit), who was by then also divorced. Shortly afterward, a somewhat unlikely relationship blossomed between the thirty-year-old Canadian farm girl with sensuous eyes and a throwaway laugh and the forty-four-year-old doctor, who had developed a deep interest in the claims of spiritualism. The newlyweds moved into Dr. Crandon's four-story brick house at 10 Lime Street in Boston.

Dr. Crandon had first developed an interest in spiritualism after reading Sir Oliver Lodge's famous 1916 book, *Raymond,* about the son Lodge had lost in World War I. Eventually, Dr. Crandon declared his conviction that he was at least "intellectually convinced" of the reality of some psychic phenomena. As time went on, Dr. Crandon became ever more deeply involved in the spiritualist movement, becoming a close friend and colleague of Sir Arthur Conan Doyle's. Mina, who at first had no particular interest in spiritualism beyond her cousin's crazy dowsing stick, lightheartedly went along with her husband's hobby.

One day, on a lark, after a day of horseback riding, Mina and a friend stopped in to see a local Boston psychic. Still dressed in their riding clothes, both women were taken aback when the clairvoyant described an invisible presence in the room—a laughing young man with broad shoulders and blond hair. Mina was immediately convinced it must be Walter. At the conclusion of the sitting, the medium gravely told Mina that she had been chosen for "The Work."

One evening shortly afterward, in May 1923, Mina, Dr. Crandon, and four friends sat down for a séance in a small fourth-floor room once used as a den, in their home at 10 Lime Street. They made a circle with linked hands around a Crawford table (named after a well-known psychic researcher and built without nails according to the latest occult instructions). But nothing happened. "They were all so solemn about it that I couldn't help laughing," Mina recalled later. "They reproved me severely, and my husband informed me gravely that 'This is a serious matter.'" That's when the table began, ever so slightly, to move. Then it moved some more. And then it rose up on two legs and fell to the floor with a resounding crash.

Someone suggested that the séance sitters take turns leaving the room to see who in the group was the "medium," channeling this alarming phenomenon. One by one, the sitters left the room, but the table kept moving. Finally, Mina got up and left, and the table immediately stopped moving. When she reentered the room, the others cheered.

Mina, of all people, a medium? She seemed the most improbable candidate in Boston. She didn't even really "believe." But over the next weeks, months, and years, Mina Crandon, as "Margery," became one of the best-known, and most-studied, psychics in the world.

The phenomena that appeared to manifest during her séances, attested to by others who were present, were startling. As one writer observed, Margery "was able to produce an extraordinary spectrum of spiritistic phenomena that are very difficult to explain." Once the table tipped up on two legs and played a tune on the piano. Another time, according to the record, the table followed a guest "out through the corridor into the bedroom . . .

then, on request for more, the table started downstairs after him, when we stopped it to save the wall plaster."

In later séances, there seemed to be all manner of psychic high jinks. There was ghostly "psychic music," of bells and harmonicas, from no discernible source. Then there were the rapping sounds, allegedly from a total of forty-four different discarnate entities in the first year. The messages Margery seemed to be transmitting didn't come through only in English; she also communicated, according to one observer, in "good French, bad German, ideographic Chinese, in Swedish, Dutch, and Greek." Then, finally, came the actual voice of "Walter," merry and impudent, which frequently accompanied the phenomena. Walter's widely reported antics would eventually become known to much of the English-speaking world.

One famous psychic investigator from Europe came to a séance and, when he heard the voice of Walter, held his hands over Mina's mouth and nose.

"Now, Doctor, isn't that convincing?" the voice said.

"How do I know you don't talk through your ears?" the skeptical investigator asked.

Mina later gleefully retold this story, to show "what amazing things people are willing to believe in order to avoid believing the things they don't want to believe."

THE SUSPICION and mistrust that had begun to poison the otherwise cordial private relations between Sir Arthur and Houdini had also begun to poison the national debate on the subject of spiritualism. While the "new revelation" could now claim millions of adherents across the Western world, its detractors—whether drawn from the worlds of religion, science, or elsewhere—seemed to grow ever more bitterly vocal. The huge popular success of Sir Arthur's second American lecture tour, in the late winter and early spring of 1923, only seemed to ratchet up the volume of the quarrel.

Partially in response to all this, the sober and serious-minded *Scientific American* magazine chose to enter the fray, in an effort to introduce objective evidence that might conclusively prove or disprove the truth or falsity of spirit voices, spirit photographs, communications from the dead, and all other strange manifestations that had so divided the nation. In the December 1922 issue, Orson Munn instructed his editors to run the following notice:

> **ANNOUNCING**
> **$5000 FOR PSYCHIC PHENOMENA**
>
> As a contribution toward psychic research, the SCIENTIFIC AMERICAN pledges the sum of $5000 to be awarded for conclusive psychic manifestations.
>
> On the basis of existing data we are unable to reach a definite conclusion as to the validity of psychic claims. In the effort to clear the confusion, and to present our readers with firsthand and authenticated information regarding this most baffling of all studies, we are making this offer.
>
> The SCIENTIFIC AMERICAN will pay $2500 to the first person who produces a psychic photograph under its test conditions and to the full satisfaction of the eminent men who will act as judges.
>
> The SCIENTIFIC AMERICAN will pay $2500 to the first person who produces a visible psychic manifestation of other character, under these conditions and to the full satisfaction of these judges. Purely mental phenomena like telepathy, or purely audible ones like rappings, will not be eligible for this award. The contest does not revolve about the psychological or religious aspects of the phenomena, but has to do only with genuineness and objective reality.

The magazine then named an esteemed five-person committee, which included eminent people from both sides of the debate, to officiate. There was Dr. William McDougall, a psychologist at Harvard; Dr. Daniel Frost Comstock; Dr. Walter Franklin Prince (SPR); Dr. Hereward Carrington, another psychic investigator and spiritualist; and Houdini.

J. Malcolm Bird, a member of the *Scientific American* staff, served as secretary; though he was not on the committee itself, his role would become increasingly influential, and controversial, with the passage of time. Among other things, it was widely rumored that he was having an affair with Margery. Also, though Dr. L. R. G. Crandon was not seated on the official *Scientific American* committee, as time went on, he became a regular participant, with many of the sittings being held in his house on Lime Street in Boston.

Though this collection of résumés appeared impressive on paper, the rules of engagement would later be bitterly challenged. By mutual agreement, anyone could be voted off the committee, for any reason, and as time went on, the composition of the committee changed. Also, it was agreed that the committee would assent to the genuineness of any phenomena only if the vote was unanimous, or if four of the five board members were in agreement. (Thus, it was later argued, a stalemate was virtually certain.) The business of the committee was to carry on through 1923 and 1924, with periodic public updates on the august committee's findings.

No one could have been more keenly interested in the committee's creation, makeup, and progress than Sir Arthur Conan Doyle. As the world's foremost spokesman for the spiritualist cause, his great walrus-whiskered Scottish visage hung over the proceedings like an enormous spirit photograph. However, he was not physically present in Boston for any of the sittings during 1923 and 1924 (being either off on another world-girdling lecture tour or fast at work on a new book, at Windlesham, in East Sussex). Nevertheless, Doyle was kept in close touch on the goings-on through an unrelenting barrage of letters from his dear spiritualist colleague Le Roi Crandon, his man on the ground in Boston.

Like Doyle, Dr. Crandon was not someone who shrank from a fight. In fact, both men clearly relished the intellectual battle between the spiritualist camp and those they disdainfully referred to as "materialists"—those who believed in a dead, soulless, strictly rational world, stripped of radiance and mystery. The *Scientific American* séances were not so much principled inquiry into the two camps' differences as a bitter dogfight. As Crandon's and Doyle's letters flew back and forth across the Atlantic, it was clear that the animosity between the spiritualists and their detractors was ratcheting up almost daily.

"We continue to sit for the *Scientific American* Committee every night," Dr. Crandon wrote in one letter. "Every night I insist on their living up to their agreement and giving me signed copies of their notes. This was an agreement made in advance between them and me and if they ever make any announcements not consistent with these notes you can readily see I have the material to crucify them. We are not wasting any time in compliments or politeness. It is war to the finish and they know I shall not hesitate to treat them surgically if necessary."

When Houdini published his book *A Magician Among the Spirits* while the *Scientific American* sittings were still in progress, Crandon and Doyle nearly exploded. The book laid out Houdini's experiences with all manner of phony trance mediums and so-called psychics and explained that any of their tricks could be reproduced by ordinary magic. He described how he would sometimes attend séances wearing a fake beard or mustache, and after he'd gathered enough evidence to incriminate the phony medium, he would throw off his disguise and shout, "I am Houdini! And you are a fraud!"

What was especially galling to spiritualists about Houdini's book was that the frontispiece bore a photograph of the conjurer posing with Sir Arthur, in apparent good-natured companionship, but the text made Doyle out to be a kindly but gullible true believer. On the first page of his copy of Houdini's book, Doyle later scrawled, "A malicious book, full of every sort of misrepresentation."

In one letter, Crandon complained that Houdini "has collected every lie and innuendo that has ever been raised against psychic science. He has an advantage over the rest of us in writing this book because he is not in any way held back by the ability or intent to tell the truth." In other letters to Doyle, Crandon jacked up the ill will: "My only regret is that this low-minded Jew has any claims on the word 'American.'" Elsewhere he referred to the magician's "general nastiness" (without mentioning his own).

Both men were disappointed by Houdini's selection to serve on the committee in the first place, because it was by now widely known that Houdini had an ax to grind. Doyle wrote to him directly to complain: "I see that you are on the Scientific American Committee, but how can it be called an Impartial Committee when you have committed yourself to such statements as that some Spiritualists pass away before they realize how they have been deluded, etc.? . . . What I wanted was five good clear-headed men who can push it without any prejudice at all."

Nevertheless, the *Scientific American* committee saved a seat for Houdini in the séance circle (though it was many months before the magician actually participated, due to his hectic performance schedule). As the committee got fully under way during the winter of 1923, it began to appear that Houdini's doubts might actually be well-founded. A series of mediums gave sittings for the committee, but all failed, were judged "inconclusive," or were shown to be out-and-out frauds.

One early "medium" was a man from Wilkes-Barre, Pennsylvania, named George Valentine, who tried to rig the test by arranging to have an electric light go off when he stood up from his chair, which in turn switched on a phosphorous button in an adjoining room to create "spirit photographs." Another woman, Mrs. Elizabeth Tomson, of Chicago, refused to participate at all unless she strictly controlled the situation (she was not allowed to). Then a young Italian lad named Nino Pecoraro, who could not read or write, impressed the committee with two séances in which he made a bell ring and a bugle toot, among other "rattlings, shrieks and high-pitched sound effects." Houdini was not present for these sittings, but when he showed up for a third sitting—and personally tied up Pecoraro with rope, chains, and padlocks—the boy was unable to produce anything but a few muffled thumps and complaints (in the voice of the medium he was supposedly channeling) that he felt uncomfortable.

It was Sir Arthur, someone who by now claimed to have attended more séances than perhaps anyone else in the world, who first suggested Mina Crandon, his fellow physician's comely young wife, as a study subject. After discussing the matter with her husband, "Margery" agreed to sit for the committee, on one stipulation. If she won the five-thousand-dollar prize, she told them, she would not accept the money personally but donate it to psychic research.

In all, the *Scientific American* committee had more than ninety sittings with Margery. The phenomena witnessed in the first several dozen sittings were so remarkable that Bird and Carrington seemed almost ready to hand over the prize money. *The New York Times* reported the development under an eye-catching headline:

"Margery" Passes All Psychic Tests
Scientists Find No Trickery
Scores of Séances with Boston Medium

But Houdini was aghast when he heard about all this. The reports in the magazine written by Bird, he wrote in his book, "were such as to lead an ordinary layman to believe that the magazine had found a medium who had successfully passed all its crucial tests and to all intents and purposes was 'genuine.'" But in fact, these reports were "the worse piffle I ever read," he wrote. It was all nonsense, a trick that he vowed to expose.

Alarmed that the *Scientific American* committee might actually award the prize before he had a chance to debunk Margery—and even though he had so far not attended a single one of her séances with the committee—Houdini now cut short his harried performance schedule to come to Boston to participate in the séances and presumably put a stop to this nonsense.

Malcolm Bird, in a 1925 book he published about the Margery mediumship, claimed that Houdini had been difficult from the very start. Unlike the others selected to sit on the committee, Houdini "regarded himself as the hub about which the committee would revolve, the one member whose abilities were of moment." (Odd for a man who showed up for only five of the more than ninety sittings.) He had no respect for the credentials or honesty of his peers, asking at one point, "Who is this man, McDougall, anyway? I've never heard of him."

Houdini's whole attitude, according to Bird, was one that made any kind of objective judgment impossible. Houdini was now fifty years old, and his physically demanding escape tricks were increasingly difficult to perform. More and more, he was leaning on his exposure of mediums as a primary source of income. Therefore, Bird wrote, "in building up a new stage personality as exposer of mediums . . . he must behave toward all mediums as he has toward Margery. He must assume in advance that the phenomena are fraudulent, must at all cost make them so appear."

By now the distrust and suspicion among the committee members had distilled into a dark and lethal venom.

In a July 30, 1924, letter to Doyle marked "confidential," Dr. Crandon reported that "at this moment it looks as if Mr. Munn, seeing that there was apparently grave danger of having to grant the award and give the prize, came on with Houdini to block it at any price."

SUCH WAS the atmosphere that steamy night of August 25, 1924, when Houdini and the four other men joined hands with Margery, lowered the lights, and prepared to see what might happen next. After eight minutes of silence, there was a wrenching, grating sound that came from the vicinity of the cabinet containing Margery.

"She's forced open the cabinet with her shoulders!" Houdini cried out. "She's pushed out the front, and bent some brass staples!"

This "precipitated a long row" in the darkness, according to the notes by the stenographer (who referred to Margery as "Psyche"). Responding to Houdini's accusation, the stenographer coolly observed that Houdini "did not state . . . that there had been the slightest strain of muscles of Psyche's hands or forearm and he did not state why he had made a fraud-proof cabinet which could be forced open by the Psychic."

Once the hubbub died down, the group sat in watchful silence until 10:35, when, according to the real-time notes, Dr. Crandon angrily spoke up.

"Houdini, do you have a white flashlight hidden on you?" he demanded.

"No!" Houdini snapped back, in evident surprise.

A few minutes later, at 10:43, it was Walter's turn to accost the magician.

"Houdini, have you got the mark just right?" he jeered. "You think you're smart, don't you? How much are they paying you to stop these phenomena?"

"It's costing me $2500 a week to be here, from loss of contracts," Houdini said.

"Where are these contracts? You didn't have a job for this week."

Suddenly Dr. Comstock broke in. "What do you mean by this, Walter? This is not psychic research!"

"Comstock, take the box out in the white light, and examine it," Walter said, "and you will see what I mean!"

The distinguished Dr. Comstock scooped up the bell box from the table and took it into the fully lit hall outside the séance room. He could clearly see that the eraser from the end of an ordinary pencil had been wedged between the top of the box and the hinged lid, making it very difficult to lower the lid and cause the bell to ring. (Comstock later calculated that with the eraser in place it would not be impossible to ring the bell, but it would have taken about four times the amount of force to ring it than if it had not been there.)

The female stenographer noted drily that "it is unknown who put [the eraser] there." Though the bell box had been examined at the beginning of the evening's sittings, it had not been examined at the beginning of this particular sitting.

No one directly accused Houdini of putting it there, but he denied having done it anyway. Everyone else denied doing it also (including those seated in the back of the room but outside the séance circle). In the judgment of at least seven people who were present, the stenographer noted, the "evidence pointed wholly toward Houdini, who was the last person to examine and test the bell-box." At least according to the note taker, "It seems apparent . . . that the committee, unofficially at least, does not intend to allow any further phenomena to take place."

Walter, jolly and jubilant, seemed to be unbowed by all this.

"Tomorrow have the kid sit in the box, have every opening closed, except for the neck, and let these fellows declare themselves satisfied, and then we'll see!" he sang out.

And with that, Walter jauntily signed off for the night.

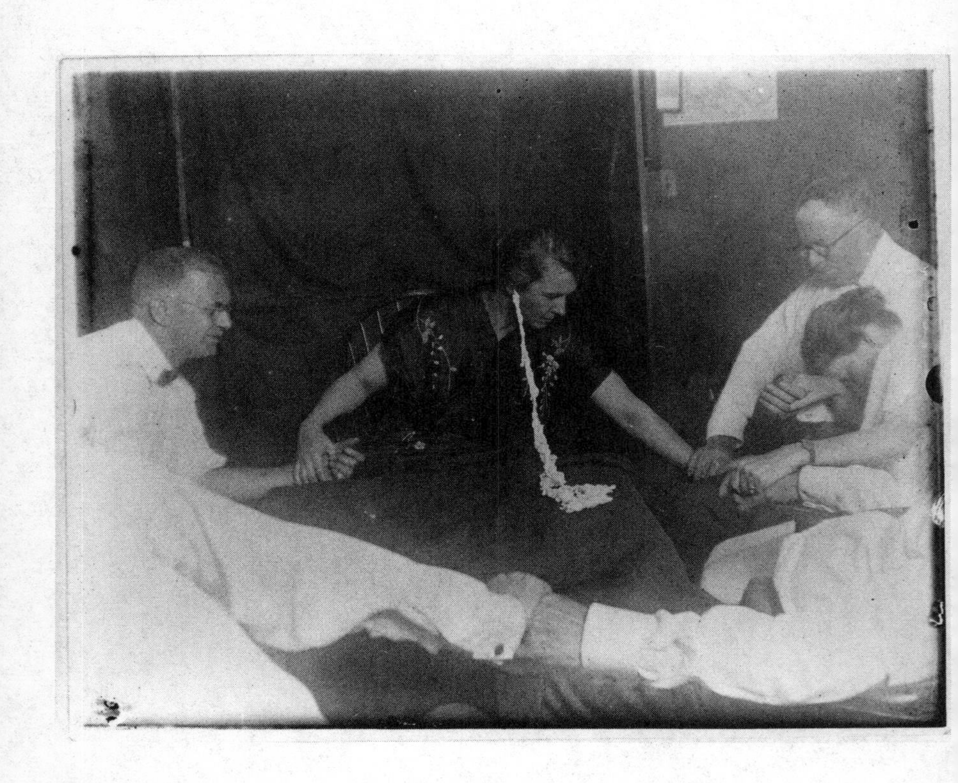

During séances an eerie putty-like substance called "ectoplasm" emerged out of Margery's ear. The spirit of her brother Walter said he used it to speak—and whistle.
COURTESY LIBRARY OF CONGRESS

CHAPTER ELEVEN
Houdini Cheats . . . Again

Walter often seemed to be the smartest, funniest, most vividly alive personality in the séance room. But who or what was he? A bit of mischievous ventriloquism concocted by Margery (even with a mouthful of water)? A two-player con game engineered by Margery and her husband, Dr. Crandon, a frequent participant in the sittings and a bitter partisan warrior in the fight against the "materialists"? Or was he what he claimed to be—an actual discarnate spirit whose high-spirited high jinks demonstrated the survival of human personality after death?

Those who followed the progress of the *Scientific American* séances in the spiritualist press, and sometimes even in popular newspapers, were roundly entertained by Walter's irreverent antics and witticisms. In fact, as time went on, Walter began developing a fan base akin to that of his now-famous sister "Margery." He bounced around the séance room, laughing and cajoling, mocking, taunting, and rhyming with sardonic glee, like an irreverent flapper-era rapper. After one especially lively session, Mrs. Margaret Cameron Lewis, who had extensive experience in the psychic world, remarked that she had "never heard anything to equal the voice of Walter."

During another session, Walter was asked whether he was happy when he first "went over" to the other side. "No, I slept six years and was homesick and lonesome," he replied. "I admit I would have preferred to finish out my earth life as other people do," adding, "Within the next five years the reality of psychic phenomena and the truth of spirit return will be established."

At other times, Walter's mood grew more somber. When his and Mina's mother died, he sent out a remarkably deft poem:

IN MAJESTY DEATH COMES

In majesty death comes:
He walks alone.
Comes here as your friend.
Why weep? You'd have it so.
He knows you know 'tis not the end.

As with a perfect day:
The sun has set.
With gracious hand he gives you perfect peace.
They answer his great call:
They find release.

Ah! Majesty, we worship at thy throne.
Thy will be done: the power,
We do believe.
God, give us strength
To know and feel and not to grieve.

At the same time, Walter seemed to engineer the production of eerie phenomena that were increasingly difficult to dismiss. Yet the *Scientific American* committee always found some way to equivocate or deny them. Like Dr. Crandon, Walter grew increasingly short-tempered at the intransigence of Drs. Prince, Comstock, and McDougall, who seemed unwilling to accept even the most flagrant demonstrations of unexplainable phenomena. Walter also objected to the fact that old Dr. Prince was almost completely deaf, so how could he possibly pass judgment on voice phenomena or the ringing of a bell? In one séance, Walter remarked that there was no need to consider the *Scientific American* committee "intellectually dishonest," but simply "tell them to go to hell."

Then he proceeded to give a demonstration of what he could

do with the bell box. He instructed a Mr. Patten, who was visiting from Chicago, to pick up the box while it was ringing and allow all the other sitters to feel around it, especially the area between the box and Margery, to make sure she had no contact with it at all. Then another visitor was instructed to put the bell box on top of his head, and it rang off and on, according to commands. Then he instructed another sitter to pick up the box while it was ringing, carry it over to one window and then to another, then turn his body in a complete circle while it was still ringing. Then the visitor returned to the table, whereupon—when someone asked Walter to stop the box from ringing—it stopped. When Mr. Patten asked Walter to ring the bell two longs and three shorts, he did that too, after which the bell box was examined and no tricks or anomalies were found.

In another session with Margery, attended by Dr. Crandon and two others, Walter seemed acutely aware of the larger controversy surrounding the *Scientific American* committee's work. He said he thought bad publicity from Orson Munn's efforts to block phenomena might actually do "the cause" more good than a mere five-thousand-dollar award. Then he seemed to counsel the sitters on strategy. "They are trying a smart game on you," he said. "Every move must be made after deliberation. Consult only a baloney—I mean, 'attorney'—if necessary. Not that lawsuit is the only way to get them, but reproduce all the correspondence and crucify them before honest opinion of the world for their unfair dealing."

He closed his comments by jeering at the naysayers: "Now I am going to put a nail in your coffin!"

Then he instructed a séance sitter named Mr. Adler to "control" Margery by holding her two hands with his two hands and her two feet with his two feet. He instructed Mr. Cross to control Dr. Crandon in the same way. Then the bell box rang out loudly, twenty times in a row.

"What do you want me to do now?" Walter asked.

"Seven short rings and one long one," someone said.

The bell rang seven short rings, one long.

"This is what I can do for Dr. Prince or anybody you want it done for," Walter said. "Let the doubter examine the chair and the cabinet and the Psyche and the contact apparatus and then let him be alone in the room with the foot and hand control of Psyche and let the door be guarded by a friend of his, the room having been searched, and I will ring the bell. That way we can make converts as far as they will line up!"

To Dr. McDougall, in particular, the phenomena that the committee had witnessed were enough to push a rational man to the brink of belief but not quite over the edge. In a letter to Dr. Crandon, McDougall clarified his intellectual conundrum, distinguishing between three stages of conviction:

> 1. One observes a physical phenomenon which one cannot explain, but believes one can suggest possible explanations.
> 2. One observes a physical phenomenon which one cannot explain and for the explanation of which one cannot conceive a physical or normal explanation, but one is not in a position to assert that such an explanation is impossible.
> 3. One observes physical phenomenon and is convinced that any normal or physical explanation is impossible and therefore believes that it is supernormally produced.

McDougall went on, "In regard to the bell-box, I am in the second stage as above defined. . . . I agree that the bell-box phenomena are very impressive but I cannot say outright that they have yet convinced me of their supernormal nature."

Hence, the committee as a whole still officially remained unconvinced.

ON AUGUST 26, 1924 (the night after the séance in which Houdini appeared to jam a pencil eraser under the hinged lid of the bell box to stop it from ringing), the séance sitters reconvened in the same upstairs room in Dr. Comstock's Beacon Hill home. In the smallish room, the atmosphere among the sitters was stiff and uncomfortable, leavened only a little by a few forced pleasantries. As the men took their places around the table with the bell box sitting in the center, Houdini's Cockney helper, Jim Collins, assisted the magician as he moved the Houdini box into position beside the séance table.

Before the sitting, the lighthearted Margery was thoroughly searched by a young female stenographer, though the medium (as usual) was wearing only a thin dress, a slip, and stockings. Then Houdini and Orson Munn helped Margery up over the high edge of the box and into a seated position inside. Once she was seated, Collins closed the top over her head and locked her in with eight padlocks, in melodramatic Houdini fashion.

Afterward, Collins left the room, and the door was locked behind him. The other doors leading to the corridor outside the séance room were also locked. Once again, the men linked hands in a circle around the table, with Houdini taking hold of Margery's left hand, followed by Dr. Comstock, Mr. Munn, Dr. Crandon, with Dr. Prince completing the circle by holding the medium's right hand.

This time, by prior agreement, the séance would consist of two parts. In the first, Margery would sit in the box as she had the night before, with her head and arms protruding. In the second, the arm holes would be covered with wooden plates, screwed into place, so that only her head protruded from the box. (Though Houdini professed to disbelieve the existence of "Walter," he had taken up Walter's challenge anyway.) According to tonight's agreement, Mr. Munn was also to loudly dictate the events of the séance so that the stenographer, seated in a small adjoining alcove, could take notes under a very dim red light. Other sitters also later made notes of the séance and entered them into the official record. (These form the basis of this account. Unfortunately, many of the notes are unsigned, making it difficult to determine who is speaking.) These carefully negotiated protocols were important, because an enormous audience of interested parties, from both sides of the debate and on both sides of the Atlantic, was watching with rapt interest. (Houdini referred to the Crandons as "messiahs to a half million or more Americans.")

"Prince, hold her right hand firmly all the time," Houdini said to Dr. Prince as they prepared for the sitting. "I want to put my hand inside the left arm-hole of the box for a minute."

Then, according to the notes jotted by an unidentified sitter, "Houdini at about this time felt up along her left forearm and followed up her arm to see what position her elbow was in, and while doing so, his right hand and part of his forearm were partly in the box."

Given that Houdini was the world's greatest master of sleight of hand, with an enormous chip on his shoulder, this seemingly casual incident was significant indeed.

"Why don't you search me again?" Margery asked at this point.

"Oh, no, that won't be necessary," Houdini said, offhandedly. "I'm not a physician."

"Why don't you search the box?" she repeated.

Once again, Houdini demurred.

Then everyone sat in the darkness, in uneasy silence, waiting for something to happen. After two minutes, a low whistle rang out into the room. It was Walter, the smart-aleck spook. When he spoke, one observer noted that it was "as loudly and clearly as [he] ever has during the past fourteen months."

But tonight his voice was brimming with rage and sarcasm.

"What did you do that *for, Houdini?"* Walter howled. *"You god damn son of a bitch! You cad, you! There's a ruler in this cabinet, you unspeakable cad! You won't live forever, Houdini—you've got to die. I put a curse on you now that will follow you every day until you die!"*

After a moment, Houdini responded, seemingly flustered and surprised.

"Oh, this is terrible!" he said. "I don't know anything about any ruler! Why should I do a thing like that?"

According to the real-time notes of someone else who was present, he then cried, somewhat inexplicably, "My dear sainted mother *was* married to my father!" And, moments later, "I am not well. . . . I'm not myself."

But Walter's voice was still shaking with rage.

"You get the hell out of here or I will, and don't you ever come back!"

Despite the atmosphere of generalized suspicion in the room, this enraged outburst came as a shock. Dr. Comstock tried to restore order.

"Walter," he said calmly, "if you will reflect for a minute you will see that this box has been in this room where there are tools and workmen, and it is indeed possible that someone may have left or locked a ruler in it."

It was true that there had been some minor repairs going on in the house, and Walter conceded the point.

"That is possible," he said, a little more quietly. "I apologize to Houdini. You may cut all the nasty words out of the records, but leave all the rest."

At that point, with general consent, the lights were turned back on. Houdini, according to Dr. Crandon, was in a position of prostration, with his face in his hands. Collins was called in, the box was opened, Margery stood up, and Houdini climbed into the box. On the floor, he found a carpenter's ruler, folded up into four six-inch lengths, so that the extended length would have been two feet long. Because the bell box was only about eighteen inches from Margery's face, it was conceivable that she could have unfolded the ruler and with her hands or mouth extended it to ring the bell. No one seemed to recognize the ruler, and no one took the blame for putting it there.

Finally, Houdini said to Margery, "I'm willing to forget this, if you are."

But what had just happened was very difficult for anyone to forget. And what was it that had just happened? One of the note takers observed that "if Walter had not discovered the ruler and [Margery] had gone into the second part of the sitting with her hands in, although the box was boarded up, and the bell had rung, of course, an examination of the box would have been demanded at the end of the ringing. If then, that ruler had been found, it would be quite apparent that bending one quarter of it at right angles, and holding that short end in her hands, and protruding that long end out through the neck hole, she would have had a firm instrument over eighteen inches long with which to reach the contact bell." On the other hand, "Houdini's defense is probably . . . that the ruler was a plant by Psyche to prove him to be crooked."

The finger of suspicion seemed to point both ways.

The unnamed note taker went on to say that "it seems to the

writer, however, that the fact that Houdini's right hand was in the box for a few seconds just before the light went out, combined with the ingenuity of the ruler device, suggests the trickery of an expert, such as Houdini is."

In his signed notes, Dr. Crandon expressed no doubt at all about what had just happened. "The presumption, which amounts to a practical certainty, is that the ruler was placed there by Houdini. . . . Since the first apparent 'plant' [the eraser forced into the bell box the previous night] was such to make manifestations more difficult, and the second 'plant' could only have been placed to discredit the medium, it seems to be reasonable to conclude that the committee-man who placed the 'plants' is not interested in Psychic Research, but only in either preventing phenomena, or in discrediting the medium."

Eventually, after the hubbub died down, the sitters decided to carry on with the second stage of the séance, in which Margery's hand holes would be boarded up. Once this was done, and the lights lowered, the participants sat for more than an hour, waiting for something to occur.

The only one who spoke was Walter.

"A great chance I have to do anything with all you and myself in this state of mind," he remarked, finally. "I admit I lost my temper."

It was 11:52 when Walter said "goodnight" and the lights came on again.

Afterward, someone suggested that Margery be photographed sitting in the box, for the historical record. Since Margery had already gotten out of the cabinet and left the room, apparently exhausted, someone else suggested it was just as well to let somebody else sit in the box. At this point, Houdini spoke up.

"Oh, no—that box is sacred," he said. "No one else should ever sit in it. I would rather sink it to the bottom of the sea." On the other hand, archival photographs show Houdini himself sitting in the box.

In the ensuing discussion of this rather odd request, someone else pointed out, suspiciously, that the night after the séance in which the eraser "plant" was discovered, Houdini had ordered

Collins to move the box into the service elevator of Comstock's building, take it to the basement, and nail it back into its packing case. "Why should he be fearful of leaving that box in the supposedly friendly apartment of a fellow committee-man, Dr. Comstock?" one note taker asked. Also, earlier that day, before the ruler incident, one of Dr. Comstock's employees had quietly walked into the room where Houdini and Collins were working on the box. Houdini angrily accused the man of "sneaking around" and later complained to Dr. Comstock about it. "Why was Houdini so suspicious of a committee-man's helper, if the box were on the level?" the note taker wondered.

TWO NIGHTS after this disputed, interrupted sitting, another séance was held, this time at Dr. Crandon's residence at 10 Lime Street. There were five sitters this time, including Dr. Crandon, but without Houdini, who had left town. Margery sat at the séance table, no longer confined to the box. Walter came through almost immediately, with his usual jaunty whistle. He was in fine fettle tonight, convinced that he had discredited Houdini in the eyes of the committee.

"If Houdini says anything false on the stage, I'll finish him!" Walter exulted. "No telling that he might be a raging Spiritualist in a week. You know his father lived with his mother for a couple of years before they were married, and then Houdini came along and they had to get married. But now Houdini is going—he's slipping fast!"

Walter even suggested a couple of sensational headlines, including this:

GHOST-HUNTER BOXES PSYCHE—GETS BOXED

Walter told the sitters that the Houdini box was a trick one, just as they suspected, and that it would all come out eventually.

Houdini, for his part, seemed so rattled by the ruler incident that several days later he added the following oath to the historical record: "I wish it here recorded that I demanded Collins to take a sacred oath on the life of his mother that he did not put the ruler in the cage and knew positively nothing about it. I also pledge my sacred word of honor as a man that the first I knew of the ruler in the cage was when I was so informed by Walter."

Houdini's oath would seem to put an end to the matter. But many years later, in 1959, long after Houdini's death, the author William L. Gresham published a book called *Houdini: The Man Who Walked Through Walls,* in which he claimed to have interviewed the now-elderly Collins about the ruler incident. When asked about it, Gresham writes, "Collins smiled wryly. 'I chucked it in the box meself. The Boss told me to do it. 'E wanted to fix her good.' "

Then Gresham interjected, "But he swore on his mother's grave . . ."

"Sure—that was after 'e told me to do it. By that time 'e 'ad it all figgered out in 'is mind that 'e 'adn't done it. There's one thing you got to remember about Mister 'Oudini in his last years. For 'im the truth was bloody well what 'e wanted it to be."

IN LATER séances, Margery announced that Walter was now ready to establish his identity in a new, even more convincing way: by leaving his fingerprint on a block of soft dental wax, called Kerr wax. He instructed that two pans of water, one warm and one cold, be added to the séance room. A ball of Kerr wax would be added to the warm dish, in order to keep it soft; once he announced that his prints had been made in the soft wax, it was to be transferred to the cold dish in order to harden it.

And when the lights came up after the very next séance, lo and behold, there were "two beautiful indentations" in the wax, according to Dr. Crandon. The doctor hired a Boston detective named John "Sherlock" Fife to authenticate the prints, and he did so. But when Houdini got wind of this, he checked into Fife's background and concluded the man had seriously exaggerated his credentials. "He just materialized out of nowhere. . . . Ha! *That's* a good trick," Houdini wrote. Later Dr. Crandon enlisted the help of a better fingerprint expert, from the U.S. Navy, to authenticate the prints.

Over the course of six months, a series of thumbprints appeared in the wax after Margery séances. Dr. Crandon wrote exultantly to Doyle, summarizing these findings:

> 1. The Walter finger-print . . . is always the same.
> 2. It is never that of a sitter.
> 3. One of the thirteen is a mirror-print of the other twelve.
> 4. These prints are made in dental wax and have, therefore, three dimensions. The mirror-print (as distinct from positive and negative) cannot be made in a three-dimensional world. The best way to understand it is to say that the man behind the mirror has pushed his thumb through into our world. . . .
> 5. Now comes the unexpected observation: The Navy finger-print expert whom we have, went over the prints last night of Psyche, Walter and Walter's mother. He found approximately a 45% resemblance in characteristics in all three thumbs which is precisely what ought to be the case in relationships of this degree.
>
> *Do you realize what this means? It means that we have proved that there is in the séance room a person who is not one of us. That it is always the same person and that that person's thumbprints have an average percentage of resemblance which a brother should have to a mother and a sister. This entity or person declares himself in a voice proven to be mechanically independent of the normal anatomy and physiology of the medium, to be Walter, her brother discarnate.*

Nevertheless, a couple of years later the skeptics got some ammunition to shoot down this latest evidence. In 1932, a report appeared in the bulletin of the Boston Society for Psychic Research claiming that Margery had gotten the fingerprints not from Walter but from her dentist, Dr. Frederick Caldwell (who had originally suggested the idea of using dental wax for digital impressions). According to the report, by one E. E. Dudley, Dr. Caldwell's right and left thumbprints were virtually identical to those Walter had been claiming were his own since 1926.

Dudley claimed there were no fewer than twenty-four correspondences between the prints.

But this startling claim—clear evidence of fraud—resulted in a furious exchange of counterclaims. William Button, president of the American Society for Psychical Research, now claimed that it was Dudley who was the fraudster, having substituted Dr. Caldwell's prints for Walter's, either inadvertently or because of deep-seated resentments toward the Crandons. And a new analysis found that the match between the two sets of prints was actually questionable anyway.

Still later, the medium's son, John Rand, gave a different version of events. He floated the story that Conan Doyle and Crandon had visited a Boston funeral home late at night to steal fingerprints from a dead body in the morgue. One problem with this story (in addition to the oddball image of two distinguished doctors creeping around a midnight morgue): Doyle was never in Boston during the period the prints appeared in the wax.

But despite all the evidence that had been presented, the *Scientific American* committee refused to budge from its position that at least so far nothing that had occurred constituted incontrovertible proof of the reality of psychic phenomena. Though they could not catch Margery or the Crandons in some ruse to concoct the voice of Walter, or figure out how the bell box was rung with no one physically touching it, they remained firmly in Houdini's corner: "None of the evidence offered has been able to stand up under the fierce rays of investigation."

And Orson Munn—the owner of the *Scientific American*—never had to write a check for five thousand dollars.

OVER THE months that followed the disputed séances, Sir Arthur exchanged a series of letters with Dr. Crandon, brimming with anger and frustration over the continued intransigence of several members of the committee. In one letter, dated November 22, 1924, Dr. Crandon noted that in the sittings of both July 23 and July 24, Houdini had gotten "positive results [of psychic phenomena] and signed his name to them." Then, later, he claimed to have witnessed no such thing and accused Margery of fraud.

"After [the committee member] McDougall, last week, had seen everything done by the bell-box which he had asked for and all in good red light, he was asked by Dr. Elwood Worcester to sign that he had seen psychic phenomena. He replied: 'If I were to do that, I should have to recast and deny the philosophy of a lifetime!' Can you imagine a more hopeless statement?

"Dr. Worcester threw up his hands. McDougall's philosophy is something inviolable and immutable like Gibraltar, forsooth! I give up. Prince is worse, and Comstock is sick in a nervous way, so I think the Siam [*Scientific American*] Committee is over."

Doyle wrote back in agreement. "It [is] difficult to say which is the more annoying. Houdini the conjurer, with his preposterous and ignorant theories of fraud, or such 'scientific' sitters as Professor McDougall of Harvard, who, after 50 sittings and signing as many papers at the end of each sitting to endorse the wonders recorded, was still unable to give any definite judgment, and contented himself with vague innuendoes."

BUT BY now, the science-minded readership of *Scientific American* had begun expressing general discontent at the early reports from the psychic investigation committee that had appeared in the magazine's pages. Most of them had been penned by J. Malcolm Bird, and they made it sound as though the committee seemed willing to at least entertain the possibility that Margery's mediumship might in fact be genuine. Uneasy with this development, the magazine's editors urged the committee to wrap things up.

In November 1924, the magazine published the considered judgments of the five committeemen.

The statement of Dr. Walter Franklin Prince, the committee's chairman, ran first. After first apologizing for only having attended six of the more than ninety sittings, he concluded, "I am compelled to render an opinion that thus far the experiments have not scientifically and conclusively proved the existence of supernormal powers."

Hereward Carrington's statement was next: "I am convinced that no snap judgment is of any value in a case such as this; nor will preventing the phenomena demonstrate their non-existence. The present case is peculiarly difficult, for many reasons; but I am convinced that genuine phenomena have occurred here, and that a prolonged series of sittings, undertaken in an impartial spirit, would demonstrate this." This statement was remarkable in that it was a nod of assent—and one of the first—from someone with truly sterling credentials.

Dr. McDougall remained, on the whole, unconvinced, even though on one occasion (the séance of May 12) he had said, in the face of some eerie phenomenon, "If that happens again, I shall leave this house an altered man!" but when it promptly happened again, he did not seem changed in any way.

After attending forty sittings, Dr. Comstock was still on the fence: "My conclusion . . . is that rigid proof has not yet been furnished but that the case at present is interesting and should be investigated further."

Houdini's conclusion, not surprisingly, contained no such waffling: "My decision is, that everything which took place at the séances which I attended was a deliberate and conscious fraud, and that if the lady possesses any psychic power, at no time was the same proven in any of the . . . séances."

Mr. Munn tried to close the book on the whole matter, telling his readers, "The famous Margery case is over so far as the *Scientific American* Psychic Investigation is concerned." In summing it all up, the magazine's editors concluded that the psychic investigations committee was "unable to reach a final and unanimous decision with regard to the mediumship of 'Margery.'"

Isn't it rather odd? All these famous men had gathered around the séance table—Houdini, Dr. Comstock, Dr. McDougall—to denounce spiritualism or cast a cold eye on it at the very least. They were there, basically, to disprove the very idea that the living can communicate with the dead. And yet, night after night, there they were, talking to a ghost: Walter. They talked about him; they talked to him. Recall what happened after Walter discovered the ruler in Houdini's box and flew into a rage: Dr. Comstock addressed Walter and got him to calm down.

Would Comstock have bothered, if he really thought "Walter" was some trick?

Detailed notes of these séances were made every night—Dr. Crandon made sure of that. He also made sure that the sitters signed the notes to verify their accuracy. At the end of every evening, they all agreed that Walter had said this and done that. Even Houdini agreed. Here's just one example. On possibly the first time he sat for a séance with Margery, on July 23, 1924, the notes begin, "During first part of sitting nothing observed except Walter's whistle and whisperings. Next, Houdini was touched several times on inside of right leg. He did not announce it, but Walter did so for him, specifying the place touched. Houdini . . . confirmed what Walter said."

But how did Walter whistle? And how did he speak? Was it Margery talking? Was he using Margery's voice?

After the failure of the *Scientific American* committee to agree on genuine phenomena, Dr. Crandon attempted to answer these questions. He asked his colleagues at Harvard Medical School to test his wife. One of them, Dr. Mark Wiley Richardson, devised an apparatus he called a "voice-cut-out machine," a three-foot-high glass U-tube with a luminous cork floating in each arm and two flexible metal hoses with mouthpieces. Each mouthpiece had to be held between the teeth and the tongue positioned over three holes to keep the corks in disequilibrium. It was an ingenious way to keep Margery from talking or whistling, and yet Walter could be heard doing both. Walter's was an independent voice.

Yes, there were controls: This was done in a locked room at a house other than 10 Lime Street, and Dr. Richardson held Margery's hands the whole while. Under these conditions, wrote Dr. Crandon, "the Walter voice talks and whistles freely, will whistle any tune requested, if he knows it, and takes apparent delight in pronouncing words which contain many labial, dental and lingual sounds."

So how did Walter talk? Usually through the ectoplasm, he explained. Out of Margery's right ear would emerge a blob, the size of a large potato; it was cold, gray, and clammy and settled on her shoulder. That, Walter said, was the machine by which his independent voice talked. The ectoplasm vanished in the light, hence the need for darkness in séances. The many photographs of ectoplasm were taken with flash photography and fast shutter speeds, a technology just emerging in the 1920s.

With this and other experiments, the Crandons kept trying to prove the genuineness of psychic phenomena. But their enemies would keep going to extreme lengths to prove fakery.

Conan Doyle with Lady Jean and their children arriving in New York to begin a lecture tour.
COURTESY LIBRARY OF CONGRESS

CHAPTER TWELVE
"We Have Just Begun to Fight!"

Not long after the inconclusive results of the *Scientific American* séances were announced, a bound pamphlet with a bright pink cover began circulating among the many people who had followed the case, believers and disbelievers alike. The pamphlet was emblazoned with the headline, "HOUDINI Exposes the Tricks Used by the Boston Medium 'Margery,'" with Houdini's name in the biggest, boldest type.

Written by the magician himself, the pamphlet purported to show exactly how Margery had accomplished her frauds, which Houdini referred to as "the 'slickest' ruse I have ever encountered."

When Sir Arthur, Dr. Crandon, and their colleagues got wind of Houdini's "exposé," they were furious. According to the agreed-upon terms of the *Scientific American* sittings, Houdini had signed statements agreeing that the "controls" were adequate during all the séances he participated in. Yet his very public pamphlet claimed that Bird's early reports on the Margery mediumship were "tommy-rot" and "fulsome, gushing reports of nothing." It was all fraud, he claimed, probably engineered by the Crandons working together, possibly with the collusion of Malcolm Bird, though only a clever magician like himself could detect it.

Without mentioning his own apparent dishonesty, Houdini claimed in the pamphlet that he'd caught Margery cheating. In the first of the five séances Houdini attended, he said, the bell box had been placed on the floor between his feet, with Margery's left foot making contact with his right foot as a form of control. (The pamphlet included a diagram of the placement of their feet.) In order to prepare himself for that night's task, Houdini explained that he had worn a silk rubber bandage around his leg, just below the knee, all that day. By the time of the séance, that leg had grown "swollen and painfully tender," enabling him to detect the slightest movement of Margery's foot.

Houdini claimed that during the séance he detected the medium surreptitiously sliding her foot past his in order to ring the bell. Later, when the table tipped, he said he could feel her ducking her head to do it and that when a megaphone flew through the air, supposedly tossed by Walter, it would have been quite simple for her to toss it with her head. It was as a result of these tricks, he said, that he later designed the so-called Houdini box to circumvent them.

But other people who attended the séances had an entirely different story to tell. Malcolm Bird, in a 1925 book, called Houdini's pamphlet "scurrilous," calling his motives and methods into question. As someone who helped to set up and coordinate the séances from the beginning, Bird recalled that all the other committeemen were cooperative and respectful of each other. But Houdini was different. From the very start, he was arrogant, rude, and temperamental, Bird said.

He seemed to have nothing but scorn for the other members. He was not willing to assume the personal honesty and competence of his colleagues or impartially consider evidence, which was the whole point of the investigation, Bird said. Instead, Houdini "regarded a major part of his duties to be the protection of himself and the *Scientific American* against possible collusion between committee members and fraudulent mediums." Primarily, though, he needed to protect his own reputation as the world's most famous fraud buster and flatly said so. He had agreed to serve on the committee under certain stringent conditions, he said, including having the right to reject any other proposed member, because "while an ordinary investigator . . . could make a mistake and later correct himself without damage to his standing, I was in a different position, for due to the peculiar nature of my work my reputation was at stake and I could not run the risk of having it injured."

In other words, Bird observed, Houdini was under professional and financial pressure to make sure no phenomena witnessed during the séances were judged genuine, no matter how convincing. He "stacked" the committee and its rules to make sure of this. In Bird's view, in other words, Houdini had "abandoned all pretense at judicial consideration. All that had been reported from prior sittings was, in his eye, necessarily the result of mediumistic fraud. The phenomena must be invalid because they couldn't possibly be valid."

And that was that.

In his pamphlet, as mentioned above, Houdini included a diagram showing the position of Margery's and Houdini's feet, with the bell box on the floor nearby, to show how she had secretly rung the bell. But in his book, Bird ran Houdini's diagram side by side with an actual photograph of their two feet, taken immediately after the séance ended. The photograph showed that Margery's foot was clearly blocked by Houdini's foot and too far away from the bell box to ring it. Bird claimed that Houdini hadn't run the photograph in his pamphlet, but instead substituted a diagram, because the photograph clearly contradicted his claim.

Bird also recalled that after the very first séance Houdini had announced to the others, "Well, gentlemen, I've got her. All fraud—every bit of it. One more sitting and I will be ready to expose everything. But one thing puzzles me—I don't see how she did that megaphone trick." (At one point in the séance, Walter had asked, "Which direction should I throw the megaphone?" and when someone suggested toward Houdini, it flew in his direction and landed on the floor nearby.)

Bird and the others told Houdini that they, too, had considered how this phenomenon might have been faked. The megaphone couldn't have been in her lap (too easy to be found with an exploring hand) and couldn't have been on her shoulder (Houdini had explored that, he said). "Then an expression of relieved triumph spread over his face," Bird wrote. "Though admitting that he had made no search there, he stated as fact that the megaphone had been on her head during the critical moments. The reasoning here is simple. The megaphone *can't* be in the air; it *must* be somewhere; it is nowhere else; it *must* be on her head. Ergo, it *is* on her head."

By means of this kind of circular, self-serving logic, according to Bird, Houdini was able to dismiss anything that happened in the sittings and preserve his reputation not only as the world's greatest escape artist but also as the preeminent debunker of spiritualistic nonsense.

IN THEIR private correspondence during this period, Sir Arthur and Dr. Crandon seethed with indignation. Both men were fighters, by nature and inclination. "We are too supine and must fight back!" Doyle wrote to Crandon. "We have just begun to fight!" Crandon fired back. For Sir Arthur, the matter was even more personal than it was for Crandon, because the accusations in Houdini's inflammatory pamphlet came from a man he still considered a friend. (Perhaps the most remarkable thing about this highly public squabble was that in their private letters to each other Doyle and Houdini continued to treat each other with what appeared to be genuine courtesy and respect.)

It wasn't as if Doyle and his colleagues had any shortage of material against Houdini, if they chose to fight back. After all, what had happened in the *Scientific American* séances appeared to be very suspicious, if not incriminating. But Crandon, a bit more circumspect, counseled caution in the way they chose to proceed.

"The case against Houdini is, of course, circumstantial and deductive, the sort of thing which convicts most murderers, the sort of thing of which Sherlock Holmes is the master!" Dr. Crandon counseled Sir Arthur, implying that he might consider enlisting the help of the world's canniest sleuth against the world's noisiest enemy of spiritualism. However, Houdini "would be only too glad to tempt us into a mud-slinging contest, but at that he might easily beat us, because of his experience. We remain, however, steadfast in psychic research and there will be no mud-slinging except a publication of the official notes [of the *Scientific American* séances] with all the details."

Doyle tried to hold his tongue, as Dr. Crandon had advised, but it was difficult. Eventually, his rage boiled over.

On the morning of January 26, 1926, the front page of the *Boston Herald* carried a long letter from Sir Arthur Conan Doyle—a double-barreled blast from the man Crandon called "the great leader of this present movement." Doyle criticized the committee's findings, its flawed methods, its members, the general reluctance of people to admit it when the mystery has plainly shown its face, but most particularly the methods and motives of the Hungarian magician Erich Weisz, known to the world as Harry "Handcuff" Houdini.

"It is Christmas morning and I sit at a table which is heaped with documents and photographs. They are the dossier of the Crandon case," Sir Arthur began, that gray winter day, sitting at a writing desk in a hotel in Switzerland, where he and his family were vacationing for the holidays. "Perhaps one should not work on Christmas day, yet surely there is no day so holy that one may not use it for the fight for truth, the exposure of evil and the defense of the honor of a most estimable lady."

He was, he said, deeply offended as a gentleman that Mina Crandon, this "charming lady," and her eminent husband, the physician, had been so gracious as to host many of these out-of-town American guests over a period of many months; had declined any payments at all, if Margery won the prize; and had even continued the sittings after Houdini had publicly accused her of fraud. Yet after she was publicly accused, the American gentlemen of the committee had not stood up for her, thus permitting "this attack upon the reputation of a lady who had entrusted herself to their hands."

The committee itself, he complained, might have sounded imposing on paper, but it had significant practical limitations, including "an entire lack of harmony and confidence." Nobody seemed to trust or even respect anybody else. And "as every Spiritualist knows, harmony is the first essential for psychic success." It was a testament to Mrs. Crandon's psychic powers that she got the results she did "with such a hopeless crowd," he said. Psychic phenomena were fickle and ephemeral, like dappled moonlight; they couldn't be forced, especially in an atmosphere of deep suspicion. In short, the whole committee was "a farce."

It was Doyle's considered opinion that the committee's efforts were also poisoned by the fact that Houdini and Dr. Prince seemed to have formed a cabal against Dr. Carrington and Mr. Bird, the secretary. They had invented "the monstrous theory that their own secretary was helping to produce the results which they could not explain away." It did not matter that the phenomena occurred even when Bird was not there or that there was not a "tittle of proof" of these charges.

Walter, Doyle said, "was a vigorous and virile personality, whose whispered voice could be heard throughout the room, often at some distance from the medium, and continued equally loud when the medium's mouth was filled with water." This alone should have qualified as a "fairly well-marked psychic phenomenon," but because the committee could not award the prize without a unanimous or four-out-of-five vote, even after more than sixty separate psychic manifestations, in more than ninety sittings, witnessed by 140 respected people—ministers, doctors, lawyers, "men and women of education and of all creeds"—they could not reach a positive conclusion.

In essence, Sir Arthur said, the committee was set up to fail.

There was also Walter, and of course the ringing of the bell box, when Margery and her husband were both under strict controls. "When I say that this was done not once, nor a hundred times, but more likely a thousand times, that it was done when out of all possible reach of the medium, that it was done in the darkness, in the red light, and in subdued daylight, and finally that it was done in Dr. Prince's lap, while . . . he waved his arms all round it, one realizes how invincible was the prejudice which the Crandons had to overcome."

One observer, Joseph De Wyckoff, whom Doyle said was "a rather strict critic," made the following sworn statement after observing one of the sittings: "In good effective light playing directly upon the contact box I have known the electric bell to ring to my order long and short rings when the medium was at a clear distance of several feet and I controlled her hands and feet, all the other sitters at the time plainly visible." This statement, Sir Arthur maintained, "utterly demolishes all the theories afterwards put forward by Houdini."

Another practical problem was spotty attendance. Both Carrington and Bird attended nearly all the séances, but Houdini and Prince missed most of the sittings, so that convincing phenomena were produced when only a partial committee was present, and therefore they didn't count. One other practical problem: Dr. Prince's deafness. He could barely hear Walter, the star of the show, so how could he possibly render judgment?

Then Doyle laid out his most damning charge—that Houdini had actually tried to jinx the results on two separate occasions, explaining the evidence for these two "plants," once the eraser and once the ruler, in detail. Doyle added that based on a letter Houdini had written to the editor of the spiritualist journal *Light* even before the sittings began, it was apparent to him that Houdini meant to block the phenomena however possible, no matter what happened. Houdini was concerned about protecting his own reputation and could not possibly be party to an investigation that suggested psychic phenomena might be genuine. Hence, Houdini's willingness to make sure that nothing happened in the Margery séances, even if it involved fraud.

Unfortunately for Houdini, Doyle added, there was one "dramatic factor" Houdini hadn't counted on—the wiseass discarnate Walter, haughty and self-assured, who called out the famous magician in front of the committee. Houdini claimed to have "exposed" Margery, but it was Walter who exposed Houdini.

"Far from exposing anyone," Doyle concluded, Houdini left Boston "a very discredited man so far as psychic research is concerned."

THE *SCIENTIFIC American* séances, intended to conclusively prove or disprove the reality of psychic phenomena and thus put the metaphysical quarrel to rest, seemed to have done no such thing. Angry squabbles continued to rattle through the spiritualist and scientific press for months and even years afterward (these events occurred, after all, almost a century ago). People looked at the evidence, aired their opinions, and then reached for their foregone conclusions.

Some leading investigators came down foursquare on the side of the genuineness of Margery's mediumship. Eric Dingwall, the research officer of the SPR, produced a report based on séances with Margery during January and February 1925. "I have never on any occasion detected anything that could be called fraud or deceit," he wrote. "It is the most beautiful case of teleplasmic telekinesis with which I am acquainted. We can freely touch the teleplasm. The materialized hands are joined by cords to the medium's body; they seize objects and move them. . . . I held the medium's hands; I saw [teleplasmic] figures and felt them in good light. The 'control' is irreproachable."

Meanwhile, as the Margery séances continued, weird phenomena were witnessed by many—whether they were "real," faked, or something in between. A tambourine and a ukulele appeared to dance in the air. A Victrola started and stopped on command without being touched. A rose was picked up from the table and dropped in a séance sitter's lap. Cold, clammy, putty-like "ectoplasm" appeared to emerge from Margery's nose, mouth, and ears, one of the most alarming and repulsive phenomena of the spiritualist era. People felt someone or something touch them on their legs, hands, and faces. On two occasions, Walter's voice and Margery's voice actually overlapped.

Strange lights danced around the room. In one case, a "nebulous luminosity about two feet high and eight inches wide appeared above the table. . . . This was visible to all." It appeared to take on the shape of a human face, then dissolved. There was table tipping, mysterious voices, and strange perfumes wafting through the air. On one occasion, a photographer came to take a picture of the bell box for publication. He exposed a single photographic plate, in a sunlit room. Twice while he was doing this, Margery passed through the room, doing her household duties. On exposure, the box was almost completely obscured by two blobs of diffuse white light, on one edge of which some people said they saw a vague human face. When Walter was asked about this in séance, he said, "I was waiting for you to ask that. This house is haunted. There are lots of us around."

But for every believer there was a disbeliever.

One summer day in 1926, a thirty-year-old Joseph Banks Rhine and his wife arrived for a sitting with Margery. J. B. Rhine, then a young professor at Duke, would later become the father of modern "parapsychology" (he coined the word), subjecting "psi" (psychic) phenomena to the rigors of scientific inquiry. Rhine was unimpressed with Margery. Among other things, he believed he saw her kick a megaphone during the séance, to give the impression it was levitating. In fact, Rhine concluded that the whole show was "premeditated and brazen trickery" and that other, unpublished reports he knew about were sufficient "to place the question of any particle of genuineness in the realm of utter absurdity."

He suspected that Dr. Crandon was Margery's confederate and that Malcolm Bird might also be in on the con (because, after three years of working with her, Bird had not seemed to detect the fraud Rhine had noticed in one sitting). Rhine was especially suspicious of the Crandons' hospitality. "Many find the Crandons such charming hosts that they find it difficult to think of them as fraudulent. This field is a dangerous place in which to be appreciative. Flies are caught with molasses. It is evidently of very great advantage to a medium, especially if fraudulent, to be personally attractive; it aids in the 'fly-catching business.'" Rhine was aghast when Margery actually kissed one of the male séance sitters. "Could this man be expected to detect trickery in her?" the Rhines asked.

The Rhines also offered something else: a theory of motivation, because many had wondered, if the Crandons really were faking the whole thing, what they had to gain from such a dangerous, years-long fraud. Mrs. Crandon knew of her husband's "morbid fear of death and intense interest in psychic affairs," the Rhines suggested, and started the table-tipping stunt to please him and save their relationship. He responded to this apparently genuine phenomenon with such enthusiasm that she soon found herself "in deep water" and unable to stop. Later, "he gradually found out she was deceiving him, but had already begun to enjoy the notoriety it gave him, the groups of admiring society it brought to his home to hear him lecture and to be entertained, the interest and fame aroused in this country and Europe, etc." Due to his "loss of position and prestige suffered in recent years," he "continued to play the game—and was pleased to be hailed in many quarters as a 'martyr to the cause of science.'" (The Rhines tacked on a scurrilous, unexplained charge to this explanation, pointing out that both Mina and her husband had previously been married, adding, "We refrain from publication of other pertinent and explanatory material for reasons which must be evident to the reader . . . [but] the raw facts must be dragged out into naked publicity for such as they.")

It was an unsupported accusation more fitting for the *National Enquirer* than a peer-reviewed scientific journal.

When Sir Arthur read the Rhines' report of the Margery séance, published in the *Journal of Abnormal and Social Psychology,* he took out ads in the Boston newspapers. Surrounded by a black border, the notices read simply, "J. B. Rhine Is an Ass."

Yet another somber academic study of the Margery mediumship began in March 1926, led by a Princeton psychology professor named Henry Clay McComas, along with a psychiatrist, Dr. Knight Dunlap, and a physicist, Robert W. Wood. For the first sitting, everyone gathered in the Lime Street house with the Crandons for an evening of food, drink, and merriment. Dunlap woke up in his hotel room at 2:00 the next afternoon suffering from what he later called an "ideological hangover," having been "completely won over by the couple's extraordinary personal charm." Ultimately, the McComas investigation concluded that "Mrs. Crandon's mediumship is a clever and entertaining performance, but unworthy of any serious consideration."

Later, more serious charges were leveled against Margery.

In 1933, Walter Franklin Prince wrote an article for the *Scientific American* claiming that Malcolm Bird intended to publish a confession in the journal of the American Society for Psychical

Research admitting that he had been part of a fraud arranged to humiliate Houdini during the *Scientific American* séances of 1924. According to Prince, Bird wrote that Margery "sought a private interview with me and tried to get me to agree, in the event the phenomena did not occur, that I would ring the bell-box myself, or produce something else that might pass as activity by Walter. . . . It seems to me of paramount importance, in that it shows her, fully conscious and fully normal, in a situation where she thought she might have to choose between fraud and a blank séance; and she was willing to choose fraud."

But none of this deterred Margery's defenders. In a letter to Sir Oliver Lodge, Dr. Crandon wrote confidently that Margery "will turn out to be the most extraordinary mediumship in modern history."

When Dr. Crandon died in 1939, after falling down the stairs, Mina seemed to slip into a disordered haze of alcohol and depression. She seemed lost, at sea. One of her lifelong friends, a psychoanalyst named Nandor Fodor, later observed that "physical mediums, in the course of years, find themselves so much drained of vital energies that they almost invariably become chronic alcoholics or dope addicts," a melancholy pattern that began with Maggie and Kate Fox.

But Dr. Fodor, like many others, had come to a mixed conclusion about the remarkable mediumship of "Margery." So many people had witnessed the phenomena she produced, and she had been studied by so many investigators, her mediumship was very difficult to discount entirely. Fodor felt that many of the phenomena were easier to explain as evidence of supernormal powers than as evidence of fraud. But there were other things, like the controversy over the thumbprints in wax, the ringing of the bell box, even the whole persona of Walter, that he had questions about.

Now Margery seemed to be slipping away fast and was soon confined to bed most of the time. One day Dr. Fodor came to sit with his once-celebrated, once-beautiful friend, now a diminished old gray lady in a big feather bed. Gently but persistently, he began to ask her pointed questions. Everyone was in agreement that many of the phenomena were genuine, he said, but what about the rest of it? Had she succumbed to the temptation to fake phenomena? If so, how did she do it?

Mina Crandon listened quietly to his questions, then muttered something he couldn't understand. He asked her to repeat herself.

"Sure," she said, more loudly. "I said you could go to hell. All you 'psychic researchers' can go to hell." Then she chuckled softly, with something like that old twinkle in her eye. "Why don't you guess? You'll all be guessing . . . for the rest of your lives."

Houdini's shows debunking the methods of phony mediums became wildly popular. And as he got older, they were also easier than his trademark escapes.
PHOTO RESEARCHERS, INC. / ALAMY STOCK PHOTO

CHAPTER THIRTEEN
A Death Foretold

The Greatest Necromancer of the Age—if Not of All Time!" the garish posters read, announcing Houdini's latest multi-city, blockbuster, death-deriding tour. It was September 1926, and Houdini was to begin the tour in Boston, crisscrossing the United States and Canada for the next five months. The tour was billed as "3 Shows in One!" because it was to consist of Houdini's mind-boggling magic tricks, followed by his even more mind-boggling escape acts, followed by his new favorite crowd-pleaser, the exposure of phony mediums. Some of the posters read, "Do the Spirits Return? Houdini Says No . . . and He Can Prove It!"

Houdini's escape acts, ironically, seemed to taunt death, such as his classic "Buried Alive," in which he was placed in a glass-fronted coffin and then covered in a ton of sand. He also planned to perform the hugely popular Chinese Water Torture Cell escape, in which he would be suspended by the ankles, upside down, and then lowered into an enormous glass-sided, water-filled fish tank, and then locked in place. A curtain would then be drawn across the tank, and as an orchestra played the popular tune "Asleep in the Deep"—"Crawl into this hole I've made! Transform these feelings of fear!"—Houdini would somehow wriggle free, release himself from bondage, break out of the tank, and then burst onstage, soaking wet but triumphant, as the hall roared with awestruck applause, the audience members' own personal shackles released.

But it was his final act, in which he demonstrated how fake mediums and soothsayers accomplished their nefarious tricks and then exposed some of them in person, that had by now become as popular as his other wonders. The popularity of these exposures was clear evidence that by 1926 small-time swindlers and hustlers had joined the spiritualist bandwagon in droves, and more than a few of the people in Houdini's audiences had been snookered by their desperation to believe.

In the weeks prior to Houdini's scheduled arrival, a small cadre of assistants would pay undercover visits to the most well-known mediums and fortune-tellers in towns and cities on his tour and attempt to catch them red-handed in some act of deceit. Then, a day or so before Houdini arrived, he would openly provoke these purveyors of moonshine in the local papers:

HOUDINI CHALLENGES LOCAL SOOTHSAYERS! WARNING TO ALL ORGANIZATIONS OF SPIRITUALISTS!

"I hereby dare the following individuals to come to the theater tonight to try and take some of my money!"

If the mediums had the temerity to show up in person, he would lambast them mercilessly from onstage, to the boisterous delight of the audience.

In one case, Houdini sent a female accomplice, Rose Mackenberg, to visit an Indianapolis medium named Charles Gunsolas before Houdini's stage act arrived in town. Gunsolas charged Mackenberg twenty-five dollars to be introduced to his supposed eight-hundred-year-old Hindu guide. He also gently suggested that things might go better if she met the guide in the nude, while he acted as a kind of spiritualist chaperone, watching from the shadows. (Mackenberg demurred.) When Houdini arrived in Indianapolis later, Gunsolas was foolish enough to show up for the performance. Houdini confronted him from onstage, excoriating him for a full forty minutes while, one after another, Mackenberg and Houdini's other incognito accomplices told of being fleeced in various ways for the medium's phony and often licentious "services." Gunsolas slunk out of the theater "amid the boos and catcalls of those previously counting themselves among his clients." He also abruptly announced that he was retiring from the business. Outside the theater, skirmishes broke out, as if this were a flat-out war between those who believed and those who did not.

Which, in many ways, it was.

Sometimes Houdini could not resist going out on these fraud-busting raids in person, wearing a blond wig and glasses and calling himself "F. Raud."

Now, on the national stage, egged on by the aggrieved masses, Houdini began issuing ever more strident attacks against the spiritualist cause. He called spiritualism "a systematic evil . . . the greatest self-imposed calamity in human history!" He referred to its "armies of sadly deluded followers." And sometimes he even went further, aiming his bitter diatribe squarely at his old friend Sir Arthur. "Men like McDougall and Conan Doyle are menaces to mankind!" he railed during one performance.

The U.S. Congress seemed to agree.

Earlier that year, Houdini had testified before a joint Senate and House subcommittee that was soliciting evidence before drafting an anti-fortune-telling bill. The proposed legislation would have levied a fine or six months' imprisonment for "those claiming to predict the future [or] unite the separated for reward or compensation." The various panelists had made it known, in their public statements and editorials, that they were at war with "hocus-pocus magicians, rain-makers, card sharps [and] pseudo-mediums," referring to them as "itinerant hustlers" and "un-American occultists."

Houdini testified over the course of three days. The atmosphere in the august gallery, reporters noted, was more like a circus than a congressional hearing, with Houdini at one point waving ten thousand dollars in cash toward the audience, offering it as a reward for any medium who could reveal what his childhood nickname had been. (None could.) Rose Mackenberg also testified, making headlines when she said that a spiritualist fortune-teller from Washington, D.C., named Jane Coates had told her many senators had come in secret, seeking her occult services, and that "I know for a fact that there have been Spiritual séances held at the White House with President Coolidge."

On the last day of the hearings, as Houdini was leaving the Capitol after his testimony, a spiritualist medium named Madame Marcia, who had angrily testified that the bill would violate her freedom of religion, screamed out a strange prophecy.

"When November comes around, you won't be here!" she howled at the departing Houdini.

"How's that?" he yelled back.

"You'll be dead!"

The same prophecy had come from none other than Walter, Margery's discarnate brother. Toward the contentious end of the *Scientific American* séances, Walter had snapped at Houdini one day, "You won't live 'til Halloween!"

And the prediction was heard in Sir Arthur's family séances in England. On April 12, 1925, their spirit guide, Pheneas, announced to the home circle, "Houdini is doomed, doomed, doomed."

In some ways, Houdini's angry public denunciations of spiritualism were like letters from a jilted lover—all the more angry because he was still in love. In his private letters and confidences, Houdini revealed that he still held out hope that communication across the veil of death was actually possible. Despite all his disappointments, and all his years of trying, he still believed it might be possible to make contact with his "sainted" mother. Once, during an interview with the *Chicago Tribune,* he suddenly stopped and said in a low voice, "My mother is here." Elsewhere he wrote of his "strong sense of communion with worlds unseen." In 1925, while publicly denouncing Margery, he wrote to a man in Boston, "As you know, I am not a skeptic and mediums who are genuine need have no fear." When his older brother Bill died of tuberculosis in the winter of 1925, Houdini had locked himself in the attic for forty-eight hours, clearing his mind to receive a message from beyond. Bill and other family members, including his mother, had agreed to send a coded message or cipher from the other side after their deaths. And even though he told Sir Arthur he never used psychic power to accomplish any of his astounding stage acts, elsewhere Houdini confided that there were "many cases where [he had] escaped from quite a tight spot" by offering a prayer to his late father, Rabbi Weisz.

UNFORTUNATELY, HOUDINI'S "3 Shows in One!" tour did not get off to the sort of start he'd hoped for. In early October, Bess, who was traveling with the show, grew quite feverish and ill. Houdini attended to his sick wife with such solicitude that he barely slept for three days. Then, on the night of October 11, perhaps thrown off his game by anxiety and lack of sleep, he was performing the Chinese Water Torture Cell act when he managed to break his left ankle while hanging in the device that held him upside down. When he finally emerged from behind the curtain, he was soaking wet and victorious but also limping and clearly in pain. A doctor took a look at the ankle and recommended that he be immediately taken to the hospital to have it set in a cast. But Houdini, with his characteristic disdain for pain or even any mortal limits, insisted on finishing out the show. Later that night, after the performance, he had his left foot set in a cast, but against medical advice he insisted on continuing his tour.

So it was that Houdini arrived in Montreal on October 18 in a somewhat fragile state, still tired and limping from his broken ankle. The next afternoon he regaled over a thousand students from McGill University, telling them that they needed to ignore pain and fear, "and then the miraculous is possible." Afterward, he appeared to shove a long sewing needle through his cheek, just to prove the point.

After several nights of performances in Montreal, Houdini was relaxing on a couch backstage when two McGill students, Sam Smilovitz and Jacques Price, stopped by for a visit. It was the morning of October 22, a Friday. Houdini, as usual, was congenial and generous with his time, confessing to the boys that his ankle was still painful and that he'd gotten through the last week "through force of will." As they chatted, Smilovitz began doing a freehand sketch of the famous magician. After a short while, another student, J. Gordon Whitehead, entered the small backstage dressing room. Whitehead, a thirty-year-old postgraduate researcher at McGill, was an amateur boxer, and according to Smilovitz he was "powerfully built."

According to Price's later recollection, Whitehead began asking about Houdini's strength, and the magician boasted that the muscles in his forearms, back, and shoulders were extremely powerful, asking the boys to feel them. Then Whitehead asked if it was true, as had been widely rumored, that Houdini was able to withstand any blow to his stomach. Houdini remarked "rather unenthusiastically" that his stomach muscles were also quite strong and was in the process of getting up off the couch, apparently to demonstrate this, when, quite abruptly, Whitehead lunged forward and delivered a series of "hammer-like blows" to Houdini's stomach. Houdini seemed to be unprepared for this.

"*Hey there!*" Price yelled. *"You must be crazy! What are you doing?"* But Whitehead delivered another blow to Houdini's abdomen with all his strength.

After the fourth or fifth punch, Houdini held out his hand and said, with amazing equanimity, "That will do!" He was not doubled over in pain; in fact, afterward he took a few minutes to look at Smilovitz's sketch and said, "You make me look a little tired in this picture." Then he added, "The truth is, I don't feel so well." After a short while, the three students left, and Houdini cordially thanked them for visiting.

Three hours later, when his assistant Julia Sawyer stopped in to see Houdini in his dressing room, he was clearly steeling his nerves against pain. Nevertheless, Houdini insisted on performing his show that night. During the intermission, he collapsed on a backstage couch in a cold sweat. After two more nights of performances in Montreal, he caught a night train to Detroit, but as soon as he arrived there, he finally sought medical attention. A doctor diagnosed appendicitis and recommended that he immediately enter a hospital to have the burst appendix removed. But Houdini once again insisted on pushing forward with the show. At intermission, he spiked a fever of 104 and collapsed, twice, in a cold sweat. After the show was over that night, he was at last taken to the hospital, where doctors opened him up and discovered that infection had spread through his abdominal cavity (peritonitis). After the operation, he seemed to improve, but then, over the next several days, his condition dramatically worsened.

On October 29, Houdini confided to Bess, "Be prepared, if anything happens." This admonition was not just a warning to his wife in the event of his death but an apparent veiled reference to their secret message. As he had done with his brother Bill and other family members, Houdini had arranged with Bess to attempt to communicate a secret cipher from the other side, should his current illness take him there.

On October 31, Houdini confided to his brother Theodore, "I'm tired of fighting, Dash. I guess this thing is going to get me." At 1:26 that day, Harry "Handcuff" Houdini died, still conscious to the end, with his beloved Bess's arms wrapped around him.

It was Halloween.

Houdini had managed to escape Walter's prediction for two years, but it finally caught up with him. And according to some people, Houdini knew the predictions would come true. He was expecting his own death.

"I know for a fact that Houdini knew, although perhaps he did not know that he knew, that he was going to die." This remarkable sentence tops off a three-page letter written to "My dear Sir Arthur" on December 27, 1926, two months after Houdini's passing. The writer is Fulton Oursler, a magician and novelist who was friends with both Doyle and Houdini, whom he'd met fifteen years earlier. The letter paints a vivid scene of Houdini's final days. "My experience with him for the last three or four months of his life was most peculiar," Oursler wrote Doyle. "Upon at least three occasions, and I believe five or six, he called me on the telephone at my house, waking me at seven o'clock in the morning, which is the middle of the night to me, and he was in a quarrelsome mood. He would talk for an hour, for two hours, telling me how important he was, telling me what a great career he was making. In his voice there was a feminine, almost hysterical note of rebellion as if his hands were beating against an immutable destiny."

THE DEATH of Houdini was news around the world. When he was buried in a Jewish cemetery in Queens, New York, on November 4, 1926, two thousand people attended his funeral. He was buried in the same metal coffin in which he'd duplicated the feat of the magician Rahman Bey, who was sealed inside, underwater, for more than an hour. (Houdini, who carried the coffin with him on tour, later duplicated the trick but beat Bey by half an hour.) According to Houdini's instructions, he was buried with his head resting on a packet of his mother's letters.

No doubt there were some who expected the great escapologist to rise from his own coffin, like Christ unbound. Houdini was, after all, not just a gifted magician but someone who had seemed to make the impossible possible, to demonstrate that the human spirit was transcendent, eternal, and unstoppable—even though he and Sir Arthur still disagreed about whether that transcendent spirit would return to earth.

Condolences poured in from around the world. When he was contacted by a reporter from *The New York Times* for some comment on the death of the man who called him a menace to mankind, Sir Arthur responded with his usual graciousness and generosity of spirit: "I greatly admired him, and cannot understand how the end came for one so youthful. We were great friends. . . . We agreed upon everything except spiritualism."

Bess Houdini received more than three thousand telegrams. But though her grief, like Houdini's life, was extravagantly public, she suffered in privacy. "The world will never know what I have lost," she wrote. Later, while going through her husband's papers, she came across a letter he had written to her, a handwritten note that seemed to float like a paper boat across the river of death:

> *Sweetheart, when you read this I shall be dead. Dear Heart, do not grieve; I shall be at rest by the side of my beloved parents, and wait for you always—remember! I loved only two women in my life: my mother and my wife. Yours, in Life, Death and Ever After.*

A month after Houdini's death, Bess wrote to Sir Arthur. She offered to give him a number of books on occult subjects out of Houdini's private collection, knowing that he more than anyone would likely appreciate them. But Doyle declined.

"I thank you for your kind letter and your offer of books," Doyle wrote back. "At the same time it might place me in a delicate position if I were to accept them. I shall probably sooner or later have to write about this remarkable man, and I must do so freely and without any sense of obligation."

Doyle went on to say, "I have never concealed my belief that some of his 'tricks' were of psychic origin. On one occasion he told my wife that you yourself did not know how he did *some* of them." Then, surmising that Houdini might suffer pangs of remorse after awakening on the other side only to discover that the claims of spiritualism were true, Doyle confided to Bess, "I am sure that, with his strength of character (and possibly his desire to make reparation), he will come back. I shall be very glad, if you get a message, if you will tell me."

Bess had confided to Sir Arthur that she and her husband had agreed on a secret message that he was to send her once he reached the distant shores of death. Houdini also told her that he would try to send the same message to Sir Arthur (though he did not tell Doyle what the message was). Though the cipher itself was secret, the fact that Houdini had made such a pact with his wife was about as public as the morning headlines. In fact, all over the world, psychics and mediums began trying their luck at cracking the "Houdini code," and "it was a poor month when there was no newspaper mention of Houdini and his code," one observer wrote.

In her private correspondence with Sir Arthur, Bess continued to insist that Houdini did not make use of so-called supernormal power to accomplish his tricks but still held out the hope that they might exist. "If, as you believe, he had psychic power, I give you my word he never knew it," Bess wrote in a letter dated December 16, 1926. Even so, Bess wrote, "as I told Lady Doyle often—he would get a difficult lock, I stood by the cabinet and would hear him say, 'This is beyond me,' and after many minutes, when the audience became restless, I nervously would say, 'Harry, if there is anything in this belief in Spiritism—why don't you call on them to assist you?' And, before too many minutes passed, Houdini had mastered the lock."

At the same time, her husband never stopped longing for his departed mother. "Often, in the night, I would awaken and hear him say, 'Mama, are you here?' and how sadly he would fall back on his pillow and sigh with disappointment," Bess told Sir Arthur. "He did so pray to hear that sentence from his beloved mother, but as the world did not know of the secret buried in his heart . . . he hoped, and never, despite what was printed, gave up hope of hearing that one word—'forgive.'

"Two days before he went to his beloved mother, he called me to his bedside. . . . He held my hand to his heart and repeated our solemn vow of our compact. 'Mother has not reached me, dear. I never had that one precious word, but you, my dear, must be prepared if anything happens, dear, you must be prepared. When you hear those words you will know it is Houdini speaking. The same message will go through to Sir Arthur, but in that formation only. Never, despite anything, will I come through otherwise'; and with his dying kiss (although we did not know it then) I vowed to wait for that, and only that, message."

In her despairing search for some message from her lost love, in January 1927 Bess offered a ten-thousand-dollar reward to any medium who could conclusively prove that he or she had made contact with her husband. She was deluged by "messages from beyond" from supposed psychics, none of them close to the secret cipher she longed to hear. "Tell my friends I still live" . . . "Tussle with death was agony" . . . "Praise to thee, whose power dominates all creatures" . . . And so on. All bogus. Some mediums even came to the door of Bess's house on Payson Avenue in New York, bearing strange religious and talismanic gifts, as if that were an adequate substitute for direct contact with her husband.

Though she had not yet heard what she longed to hear, she told Sir Arthur in one letter, "Please believe me when I say that I have taken an oath to tell the world when I do hear from him—also if a message directly to you, with our code, comes through. . . . Surely our beloved God will let him bring me the message for which I wait, and not the silly messages I get from the various people who claim to hear from him."

In his return letter, Sir Arthur both praised and castigated his departed friend. Houdini, he agreed, was "a loving husband, a good friend, a man full of sweet impulses." And "so far as his work was confined to really fake mediums, we were all in sympathy. But he got far past that. It was a general wild attack upon all that we hold dear. . . . [Y]ou can understand that, to those of us who had personal experience, a hundred times over, in the matter, it was annoying to be placed in the position of either being a fool or a knave."

Over the next several years, this remarkable correspondence continued, as chronicled in a 1933 book by two contemporaries of both Houdini's and Doyle's, Hereward Carrington and Bernard Ernst. "The most important thing upon earth," Sir Arthur wrote to Bess in one letter, "is to *prove* immortality." And he earnestly wished that it might be the great Houdini himself who was the one to prove it.

One day during the autumn of 1927, Bess wrote to Sir Arthur

to tell him of a curious occurrence: A mirror in her home had suddenly shattered, for no apparent reason. She wondered whether this might be some manifestation from Houdini—an attempt to make contact, perhaps. Sir Arthur wrote back,

> I think the mirror incident shows every sign of being a message. After all, such things don't happen elsewhere. No mirror has ever broken in this house. Why should yours do so? And it is just the sort of energetic thing one could expect from him, if for some reason he could not get his message. Supposing our view of the future is true, is it not possible that the Powers might for a time forbid him to use those gifts which he was foremost in his lifetime in denying? But you will get your test. I feel convinced of that.

On the other hand, was Conan Doyle—a true believer if ever there was one—simply trying to put a positive spin on slender evidence in order to produce the answer he wanted? Meanwhile, Sir Arthur continued to visit medium after medium, hoping to get a direct transmission of Houdini's secret code, for his own satisfaction, Bess Houdini's comfort, and the smug satisfaction of showing the world that he was right.

After her husband's death, those who knew Bess best began to notice that she seemed to be coming unraveled. Her house was a mess. She began drinking heavily, and her appearance grew increasingly disheveled. At Christmastime, in 1928, she apparently took an overdose of sleeping pills and nearly died. A reporter who came to visit later wrote that she was "nearly delirious" and kept asking for her husband.

Meanwhile, the ten thousand dollars offered to anyone who could contact Houdini remained unclaimed. Then, on January 8, 1929, Bess received a quartet of interesting visitors at her home in New York. One was Arthur Ford, a well-known medium and a pastor at the First Spiritualist Church in New York City, along with one of Bess's old friends, Minnie Chester, and a couple of reporters. Bess did not look her best when she appeared at the front door, with her head bandaged from a recent fall.

But she was eager to see them because the previous year, on February 8, 1928, Ford had conducted a séance in which his "guide," named Fletcher, appeared to make contact with a woman who claimed to be "the mother of Harry Weiss, known as Houdini." According to Ford's later account, the woman said that "for many years, my son waited for one word which I was to send back. Conditions have now developed in the family which make it necessary for me to get my code word through before he can give his wife the code he arranged with her. If the family acts upon my code word he will be free and able to speak for himself. Mine is the word 'FORGIVE'!"

When Ford later conveyed this message to Bess, she wrote back that "this is the first message which I have received among thousands which has an appearance of truth." (She did point out that the entity claiming to be Houdini's mother referred to her son as "Harry," though his birth name was Erich, an odd mistake for a doting mother to make.)

Now, on this frigid January night in 1929, Ford and his visitors told Bess they wished to conduct a séance to see if Fletcher, Ford's spirit guide, could make contact with Houdini's spirit directly. Ford explained that over the course of several months, in a series of séances, an entity claiming to be Houdini had laid out a coded message, using a system Houdini and Bess had once used in a stage act they'd done together. Bess told Ford she was willing, so candles were lit, the lights were lowered, and the five of them joined hands around a séance table. Ford, wearing a blindfold, seemed to fall into a trance and began to speak in the strange, quavering voice of Fletcher.

"Hello, Bess, sweetheart," the voice intoned earnestly. "I came to impress you that this is of great importance, greater than you ever dreamed. I desire you to bring this message before the world." He then recited the ten-word code that Houdini and Bess had agreed upon before his death: *Rosabelle . . . answer . . . tell . . . pray . . . answer . . . look . . . tell . . . answer . . . answer . . . tell.*

Then the voice continued, apparently speaking to Bess: "Now take off your wedding ring and show them what Rosabelle means."

Bess, startled and near tears, took off her ring. Along the inside rim of her wide gold ring were inscribed the words to an old song. Then Bess began softly singing it, in a barely audible voice:

Rosabelle, sweet Rosabelle
I love you more than I can tell.
O'er me you cast a spell,
I love you, my sweet Rosabelle.

The song, she explained when she was through, was one she and Houdini had sung as part of their stage act thirty-five years earlier. Houdini had had the ring engraved with the lyrics as a remembrance of their youthful, long-lasting love. Ford, supposedly as Houdini, explained that the ten words were actually a complex code that spelled out the word "Believe."

"My words to you before death were 'Rosabelle, believe,'" he said. "Is that correct?"

Bess, in astonishment, nodded her assent. It was.

"Then tell the whole world that Harry Houdini still lives!" the entranced Ford shouted in triumph. *"There is no death! That is my message to the world!"*

Later that same evening, someone (apparently not Bess, because the handwriting was not hers) wrote out in neat, somewhat childish-looking block letters the following note:

> REGARDLESS OF ANY STATEMENTS MADE TO THE CONTRARY, I WISH TO DECLARE THAT THE MESSAGE, IN ITS ENTIRETY, AND IN THE AGREED UPON SEQUENCE, GIVEN TO ME BY ARTHUR FORD, IS THE CORRECT MESSAGE ARRANGED BETWEEN MR. HOUDINI AND MYSELF.

It was signed by Beatrice Houdini. The statement was witnessed and signed by John Stafford, associate editor of *Scientific American;* H. R. Zander, a reporter for the United Press; and Minnie Chester.

This news flashed across the wires, appearing in the next morning's newspapers around the country. Conan Doyle was exultant. "This might become *the* classic case of after-death return," he was quoted as saying.

But almost as soon as the word was out, the doubts, recriminations, and accusations began.

It was pointed out that the "secret" code, "Rosabelle, believe," had already appeared in print, in a book published the previous year called *Houdini: His Life-Story,* by Harold Kellock. It was also pointed out that Houdini's mother's code word, "forgive," had also appeared in print previously, in an article in the *Brooklyn Eagle* on March 13, 1927.

Two days after the séance, a sleazy tabloid called the *New York Evening Graphic* ran a story headlined "Houdini Message a Big Hoax!" The story claimed that Bess and Ford had arranged the séance to promote a lecture they were supposed to do together. Bess published an angry letter denying it. She did not know how other people might have gotten the code, but if they did, it was not from her. "If anyone claims I gave the code, I can only repeat they lie. Why should I want to cheat myself? I do not need publicity. I have no intention of going on stage or, as some paper said, on a lecture tour. . . . I have gotten the message I have been waiting for from my husband, how, if not by spiritual aid, I do not know." But by three years later, Bess had changed her tune. She asked her friend (and lawyer) Bernard Ernst to issue a statement, saying that "for three years she had sought to penetrate beyond the grave and communicate with her husband, but had now renounced faith in such a possibility: she denied that any of the mediums presented the clue by which she was to recognize a legitimate message."

It's not clear what caused her to change her mind, but when she died in 1943, it appears that she did not believe she had ever heard from Houdini.

For his part, Arthur Ford continued to claim that he'd cracked the Houdini code. He later wrote that he might have had some help from Houdini, who "may have been paying his respects to the fact that my act had been performed not while handcuffed but while sound asleep."

As to the general public, people seemed to believe what they already believed. As Blake once wrote,

Both read the Bible day and night,
But thou read'st black where I read white.

In the 1920s Conan Doyle toured the world promoting spiritualism with slide shows of spirit photographs. Though they could be easily faked, he nonetheless believed that many images were the genuine work of "a wise invisible Intelligence."
COURTESY OF THE ARCHIVES OF TONY OURSLER

CHAPTER FOURTEEN
The Lion in Winter

By 1927, Sir Arthur Conan Doyle was sixty-eight years old, and by all rights he was a man brimming with success, prosperity, and the contentment of what he called his "golden autumn." He was arguably the best-known writer in the world. His lectures and public appearances drew devotees by the thousands. He had a sweet, devoted marriage to a woman who deeply shared his passions and belief in spiritualism. He was financially secure. (In 1928, he calculated his and Lady Jean's net worth at around 110,000 pounds sterling, or more than $9 million in today's dollars.) Though he had lost Kingsley, he had four surviving children from his two marriages—Mary, Jean, Denis, and Adrian—and he lived like a country squire in his rambling estate, Windlesham, in Crowborough. (He had spent so much money on maintaining the place that in his despairing moments he sometimes called it "Swindlesham.")

He also maintained a charming thatched-roof country house in Bignell Wood, surrounded by beech forest, which he had purchased as a love gift to Jean in 1925. He moved easily among the brightest and the best, describing in his memoirs his encounters with the likes of Theodore Roosevelt, Rudyard Kipling, George Bernard Shaw, Winston Churchill, and British royalty of all kinds.

Yet he was not content. He was a man on fire, a man who could not allow himself to rest. He had, after all, a despairing world to convert to his point of view. Because, above all else,

Sir Arthur Conan Doyle in his later years had become the world's greatest defender, most passionate crusader, and most affable advocate of spiritualism. His great goal was to offer scientific *proof* of immortality—not the mere faith of the world's dusty and outdated religions—and the great hope that those who have passed on were not truly gone at all. He considered himself a warrior in a righteous war, a war against the stuffy old dead religions, against the bloodless rationalists and materialists, those who did not believe in magic or elementals or the glorious transcendence of the human soul.

Sir Arthur's productivity had always been prodigious, but for a man approaching seventy it was astonishing. According to John Dickson Carr, an early biographer, who had access to the great mounds of private papers he left at his home, Doyle sometimes wrote forty or more letters a day and at least once as many as three hundred. In his lifetime, he wrote fifteen hundred letters to his mother, "The Ma'am," alone. According to those who knew him, despite his worldwide fame, Doyle felt compelled to respond to inquiries from everyone from Guglielmo Marconi to the ordinary bloke who thought he'd seen a ghost, hadn't even told his wife about it, and just wanted to talk.

Yet now he seemed even more driven to spread the "gospel" of spiritualism, and he never seemed to stop writing, in careful, close-cropped, graceful longhand, on stationery from hotels and restaurants and shipping lines when he was traveling, or on Windlesham letterhead when he was at home, or anything else that was close at hand when the urge struck. By the end of his life, he would author 22 novels, 23 nonfiction books, 204 stories, 14 plays, and even an operetta. (In his younger days, he told The Ma'am, he could dash off two or three Holmes stories a week.) But it was the 13 books he wrote about spiritualist and paranormal matters, especially the two-volume *History of Spiritualism,* published in 1926, that he considered his life's work, the thing he would be remembered for, his contribution to mankind.

Sherlock Holmes? A mere trifle. By comparison with his work as a spiritualist missionary, Holmes seemed to him little more than an indulgence. Besides, he was sick of him. "I couldn't revive him if I would," he told one reporter, "for I have had such an overdose of him that I feel towards him as I do towards *pâté de foie gras,* of which I once ate too much, so that the name of it gives me a sickly feeling to this day."

As part of his great spiritualist calling, Sir Arthur would regularly depart from the Crowborough train station on another far-flung lecture tour, often with his wife and children in tow, drawing huge crowds wherever he went—to South Africa, America, Scandinavia, Australia. By 1923, he had traveled more than fifty thousand miles and addressed nearly a quarter of a million people. According to his booking agent, Lee Keedick, he broke all previous attendance records for a lecture series. Doyle, ever humble, did not believe this had anything to do with his own personal renown. "Me? These crowds have nothing to do with me," he said once. "I tell you because it is the subject, not the man; and it is the subject which counts. They must disprove our facts or else admit them."

Of course, not everyone was enamored of Doyle's facts or his spiritualist message. "Wherever I go, there are two great types of critics," he said, pithily summing things up. "One is the materialistic gentleman who insists on his right to eternal nothingness. The other is the gentleman with such a deep respect for the Bible that he has never looked into it."

His devotion to spiritualism now began to engulf the popular novels from which he had grown rich and famous. In 1926, he'd published *The Land of Mist,* the third in his Professor Challenger series, in which the great, roaring, spade-bearded scientist, the ferocious rationalist and debunker, becomes an improbable convert to spiritualism. The book did not go over terribly well. People complained that it was a thinly veiled spiritualist tract and that Doyle was preaching. Which he was.

"Thank God that book is done!" Doyle wrote to Herbert Greenhough Smith, editor of *The Strand Magazine,* where it was serialized. "It was to me so important that I feared I might pass away before it was finished."

When the book did not sell well, Smith implored Doyle to shift back to stories that were more plot, less preaching. And, above all, what about Holmes? Doyle wrote back, "I wish I could do as you wish but, as you know, my life is devoted to one end and at present I can't see any literature which would be of any use to you above the horizon. I can only write what comes to me."

(During the heyday of his literary career, Conan Doyle's earnings were almost without parallel. In 1901, *The Strand Magazine* offered him 4,795 pounds—about $623,000 in current dollars—to serialize *The Hound of the Baskervilles*. The following year *Collier's* magazine offered him the equivalent of $1.3 million just for the serial rights to thirteen Sherlock Holmes stories. The fact that Doyle chose to turn his back on all this loot, and instead begin self-publishing small books about spiritualism, is convincing evidence of how serious he was about his new convictions.)

Meanwhile, Doyle opened a little "psychic bookshop" and spiritualist museum in Victoria Street, in the shadow of Westminster Abbey. He created a small center for spiritualist literature and began distributing it throughout the world. He spent thousands of pounds of his own money to keep the enterprise running. "I am in a position to do it," he told a reporter for *The New York Times*. "I might play with a steam yacht or own race horses. I prefer to do this."

His daughter Mary, from his first marriage, took over the day-to-day affairs of running the shop. But though she was an earnest believer, as he was, she sometimes wondered about his unflagging devotion to the cause, as if he were forever handing out fiery pamphlets on the street corner.

"Why do you go on hammering at proof after proof after proof?" she asked him one day. "We know these things are true. Why do you try to prove it by so many examples?"

"You have never been a rationalist," he replied.

IT WAS in 1927 that Doyle self-published, through his own Psychic Press and Bookshop, a short book called *Pheneas Speaks*. It purported to be a transcript of observations, advice, and predictions from a spirit channeled by Lady Jean between July 1921 and November 1926. In his preface, Doyle wrote, "We would beg the most orthodox reader to bear in mind that God is still in touch with mankind, and that there is as much reason that he should send messages and instructions to a suffering and distracted world as ever there was in days of old."

Pheneas, the messenger, had first appeared one night when Doyle, his wife, and their young children, Denis, Adrian, and Jean, were gathered for a "home circle" séance at Windlesham. In those days, strange as it might seem now, this was a common, cozy practice in the Doyle family. Lady Doyle was almost immediately seized by a new spirit, who called himself Pheneas. This night, and on many that followed, the transmissions from Pheneas came through Lady Jean in a form that Doyle described as "semi-trance inspirational talking." Jean would sit down in a comfortable chair, cross herself, and begin talking in a low, gruff male voice, without ever fully losing consciousness, though "her hold upon her own organism was slight." Her eyes would close and remain so "until the power left her."

Pheneas offered advice on politics and world affairs, helped Doyle make contact with Kingsley, his brother Innes, and others who had passed on, and gave him practical advice about the homely details of life. Doyle and Lady Jean would routinely ask Pheneas's advice about their travel plans, once scotching a trip to Scandinavia on his warning. And it was Pheneas who originally advised Doyle to buy the country house at Bignell Wood. (Pheneas also explained, when the house was partially burned, that "bad psychic energy" had built up in it and it had to be cleansed with fire.)

When asked to describe the world "up there," Pheneas waxed rhapsodic: "It is lovely. I never saw any home on earth to compare to ours. The whole scheme of home life is so much more radiant. Flowers cover my home. Such roses. Beyond is wonderful scenery and other sweet homes, full of dear sweet, bright people, full of laughter, from the mere fact of living in such wonderful surroundings."

Typical of Pheneas's other transmissions, it was a description filled with flowers but few checkable facts or evidentiary details. In one communication, Pheneas said he had brought Kingsley to speak to his father. Kingsley addressed his father directly, but then Doyle asked, searching for some proof of this spirit's identity, "Why do you not call me what you did in life?"

"Kingsley" he answered, "I do in my heart still, but somehow it is so difficult to get any names through, especially what we feel in our hearts." In other words, attempting to squeeze any hard evidence out of the spirit world was going to be exceedingly difficult.

If Conan Doyle had been worried about being attacked by his enemies when the book came out, he was right. H. G. Wells, in a scathing review in the *Sunday Express,* called the book "a platitudinous bore." But he didn't stop there. "This Pheneas, I venture to think, is an imposter, wrought of self-deception, as pathetic as a rag doll some lonely child has made for its own comfort. . . . We are told of floods of spiritual light. . . . Wonderful prophecies are spoken of. Where are they?"

But not all of Pheneas's prophecies were wonderful. In fact, as the years went by, the premonitions and warnings offered by Pheneas turned into an impending tidal wave of darkness. The picture he painted of the coming days was so dire that Sir Arthur chose not to include any of it in the published book but instead shared these warnings only with an inner circle of true believers.

Very soon, Pheneas warned, the world would be plunged into a horrific natural cataclysm akin to Armageddon. "A great light shall shine into the souls of men through a great external force," he said one night. "It will come very soon. The world will be staggered. It is the only thing which can arouse the lethargy of the human race. Such a shock! It is like Sodom and Gomorrah."

In a private note to his spiritualist colleagues, marked "confidential," Doyle summed up Pheneas's warnings: There would be "a period of terrific natural convulsions during which a large portion of the human race would perish. Earthquakes of great severity, enormous tidal waves would seem to be the agents." In general, Pheneas warned "that the crisis will come in an instant. That the general destruction and utter dislocation of civilized life will be beyond belief. . . . That the total period of the upheavals will be roughly three years. That the chief centres of disturbance will be in the Eastern Mediterranean basin where not less than five countries will entirely disappear."

During this whole period of fiery desolation, there was to be a "complete rending of the veil so that spirit and matter will be face to face for a time." A great number of spiritualists would pass over to the spirit world without having to pass through death. Others of the "Elect" would stay on earth for a few years "to establish a new order." In fact, the coming events sounded not unlike those predicted in Revelation.

In March 1927, Doyle sent a confidential memo to Oliver Lodge summarizing eighty-seven of these warnings. This was all, of course, highly incendiary material, and in private Doyle warned against letting too much of it get out into the public square. He advised other spiritualists in his inner circle that "these various forecasts of the immediate future of the world should be used with the utmost discretion. We have above all to avoid sensationalism and undignified newspaper stunts. . . . We want no hysterical developments, nor do we wish to commit the spiritualistic movement to a prophecy which may not materialize."

Nevertheless, he added, "it is impossible in my opinion not to take them seriously, for they represent in themselves a psychic phenomenon for which I know no parallel."

Though he warned his spiritualist colleagues to be wary of spreading this electrifying message too carelessly, the word leaked out anyhow. And it was not always received with the sort of seriousness Sir Arthur might have wished for. Harry Price, the famous psychic investigator and medium buster at the Society for Psychical Research, openly scoffed at Pheneas's predictions: "The cataclysmic disaster of cosmic magnitude with which Doyle has been trying to make our flesh creep for the past two years still hangs fire and the dawn of 1927 finds us sleeping serenely in our beds, giving little heed to the devastating seismic catastrophe with which—says Sir Arthur—we are threatened by evil spirits on both sides of the veil. . . . We are now promised a new Armageddon for 1928!"

Even Sir Arthur began to have his doubts about the timetable of these supposed events. Pheneas kept using words like "soon" or "very soon," but what did that mean? When, exactly, was all this supposed to happen? In a year? Five years? Fifty? Five hundred?

"I have moments of doubt," Doyle wrote to a friend, "when I wonder if we have not been victims of some extraordinary prank played upon the human race from the other side. . . . I have literally broken my heart in the attempt to give our Spiritual knowledge to the world and to give them something living, instead of the dead and dusty stuff which is served out to them in the name of religion."

At the same time, Doyle pointed to upheavals around the world in recent times. There had been earthquakes in various places that seemed to correspond to Pheneas's warnings. In Russia, the Bolsheviks had upended an empire. Meanwhile, on October 24, 1929, later known as Black Thursday, the Dow Jones Industrial Average would lose a quarter of its value in a single day. In almost an instant, the gay exuberance of the 1920s would pop, like a champagne bubble. And in the coming weeks and months, the Great Depression would rumble across the industrialized world, leaving desolation in its wake. And in Germany, a little man with an absurd little mustache was preparing to drag the world into the bloodiest war in human history.

No: It wasn't exactly what Pheneas predicted (or even close, actually). But the old lion was not about to back away from the fight. And he refused to kowtow to H. G. Wells or anybody else about his convictions.

IT WAS about this time that a series of events began unfolding that would become one of the most remarkable and complex cases demonstrating what Doyle had always wished for—*proof* of life after death. Investigated in great detail in a 1979 book by the journalist John G. Fuller called *The Airmen Who Would Not Die,* the case drew Sir Arthur into its web of intrigue very early and kept him there for the rest of his life.

At that time, in the spring of 1928, the world was thrilled by the exploits of the daring young men (and some women) who took to the air to break ever-more-dangerous records in the new world of aviation. Only twenty-four years after the invention of heavier-than-air flight, by two bicycle mechanics from Dayton, Ohio, in 1903, an obscure twenty-five-year-old postal service pilot named Charles Lindbergh, equipped with four sandwiches and a thermos of water, flew alone across the Atlantic from New York to Paris. The year was 1927, and "Lucky Lindy" became an instant international hero. Not surprisingly, daring young pilots in Europe quickly began scheming how they could match Lindbergh's feat by flying across the North Atlantic in the opposite direction. The great challenge was that a pilot would face brutal and unpredictable headwinds, making the east-to-west crossing far more difficult. In fact, in the previous year seven men and one woman had lost their lives attempting an east-to-west transatlantic crossing.

Some felt that these crazy-dangerous attempts in tiny planes would soon be eclipsed by the enormous, gas-filled dirigibles now being built by the Germans and the Americans. In fact, the world's largest and most luxurious dirigible, the R101, more than seven hundred feet long and with glorious accommodations akin to a lavish steamship, including seven-course meals and a dance floor, was already being built at the Royal Airship Works in Cardington, in the British Midlands. Its maiden voyage was to be a flight from London to India—the outer reaches of the British Empire—in five or six days, traveling at a mile a minute.

But the hope of glory was heady, and in 1928 a daring British pilot named Captain Raymond Hinchliffe decided to throw his hat in the ring and attempt an east-to-west transatlantic crossing. He was one of the most experienced pilots of his day, having shot down seven German planes during World War I, though he still bore one unforgettable mark of combat: He'd lost his left eye to a German machine gunner and wore a black eye patch.

He was an old-fashioned hero, devoted to his young wife, Emilie, and their two small girls, fluent in four languages, and an Olympic athlete.

As it happened, there was someone else who dearly wished to become the first European to cross the Atlantic: the stunning, stylish, and obscenely rich thirty-four-year-old Elsie Mackay, who was heir to her father's shipping fortune and considered one of the wealthiest, and best-dressed, women in England. She was also an accomplished actress and a pilot in her own right. In secrecy, Hinchliffe and Mackay struck a deal. Despite his reservations, and with his wife's consent, Captain Hinchliffe agreed to take Mackay on as co-pilot, in exchange for which Mackay would pay him a considerable sum, including a generous insurance payment for his wife and two small children should the risky venture fail and they crash into the North Atlantic.

Just after dawn on March 13, 1928, with driving snow blowing in off the heath, Captain Hinchliffe and Elsie Mackay were driven to the Cranwell Aerodrome, near Grantham. They had their picture taken beside the alarmingly tiny plane, the *Endeavour,* in their leather flying suits, smiling but nervous. Though it was no secret that Hinchliffe was going to attempt an Atlantic crossing—it was reported in *The Times* of London that afternoon—it had been decided that Elsie's participation would be kept secret. She slipped into the cockpit at the last minute, seen only by the small crew gathered around the plane on the freezing runway. If they succeeded, she would become the first woman to cross the Atlantic in either direction—and give the world a big surprise to boot. Then they took off, and the plane quickly disappeared into the brightening dawn, like a brave little bee.

Like Lindbergh in the *Spirit of St. Louis,* Hinchliffe did not carry a wireless radio, so the only thing his wife, Emilie, could do was to wait at home with her two children and one of her husband's pilot friends, Gordon Sinclair, and hope for news that her husband had made the crossing safely. But the weather news quickly darkened; a North Atlantic gale, laden with rain and sleet, was rapidly moving across the little plane's path. At 1:30 that first afternoon, a lighthouse keeper in County Cork, Ireland, reported seeing the *Endeavour* pass over, a tiny dot moving into the teeth of an incoming storm. But after that, there was nothing but silence. That day passed, and the next, and the next, with no news. Emilie Hinchliffe, not a religious woman, began to pray. But gradually, after the days turned to weeks, all hope seemed to be lost.

Meanwhile, about the end of March, a gentle elderly lady named Mrs. Beatrice Earl (a pseudonym later used by Emilie Hinchliffe in retelling the story) came back from a meeting of the London Spiritualist Alliance, filled with wonder and with questions. At the meeting, a well-known trance medium named Eileen Garrett had slipped into a trance state and channeled the weird, Oriental-sounding voice of a spirit "control" called Uvani. This spirit had seemingly made contact with Mrs. Earl's son, whom she had lost in the war, passing on precise and accurate details about his life.

On the night of March 31, drawn on by her sorrow and curiosity, Mrs. Earl got out her Ouija board, put her fingers on the tablet, and watched as it moved aimlessly around the alphabet. Then, suddenly, the tablet seemed to move deliberately to a series of letters and stop on each one in turn.

It spelled out this message:

CAN YOU HELP A MAN WHO WAS DROWNED

Startled, Mrs. Earl asked aloud, "Who are you?"

I WAS DROWNED WITH ELSIE MACKAY

Like everyone else, she'd read about the heiress's disappearance at sea and wondered if that was what this was about.

"How did it happen?" she asked.

FOG STORMS WINDS WENT DOWN FROM GREAT HEIGHT

Then the board seemed to continue of its own accord:

OFF LEEWARD ISLANDS TELL MY WIFE I WANT TO
SPEAK TO HER AM IN GREAT DISTRESS

And that was all. After this last anxious message, the tablet stopped moving. Not knowing what to make of all this, if anything, Mrs. Earl put the board away until April 11, when she tried again. The messages came through right away.

HINCHLIFFE TELL MY WIFE I WANT TO SPEAK TO HER

"Where shall I find her?"

PURLEY IF LETTER DOES NOT REACH APPLY
DRUMMONDS HIGH STR CROYDON PLEASE FIND OUT
WHAT I SAY IS QUITE CORRECT

Mrs. Earl knew that Purley was a suburb next to the town of Croydon, where the big aerodrome was. That was the busiest airport in London and where Lindbergh had landed after his flight from Paris. It was all so curious and distressing, but she still did not know what to make of any of it. The next night, when she tried the board again, more messages came through:

HINCHLIFFE PLEASE LET MY WIFE KNOW I IMPLORE
YOU
TAKE THE RISK MY LIFE WAS ALL RISKS I MUST SPEAK
TO HER I WISH I HAD NOT BEEN OVERPERSUADED TO
COME

Ultimately, Mrs. Earl put down her usual British reserve and decided to write to two people. One was Hinchliffe's wife, Emilie, whom she wrote to care of Edridges, Martin & Drummonds, her lawyers, whose offices were on High Street in Croydon. The other was Sir Arthur Conan Doyle, whom she knew slightly because he was president of the London Spiritualist Alliance, where she'd heard Eileen Garrett.

She wrote to Emilie,

> Will you excuse a perfect stranger writing to you? I am supposing you are the wife of Mr. Hinchliffe, the airman, lost the other day. I get writing, and I had a communication from him the other day that they came down into the sea off the Leeward Islands, at night, etc. His great anxiety is to communicate with you. Of course you may not believe the possibility of communication, but he has been so urgent, three times, that I must direct to you and risk it.

The grieving Emilie, not knowing what to make of this letter, showed it to some of her friends. They pointed out that the reference to "Leeward Islands" was crazy, because the only islands known by this name were in the West Indies, hundreds of miles off her husband's course. She concluded it was what it appeared to be: nonsense. Meanwhile, Mrs. Earl went back to the Ouija board. It spelled out this message:

> THANK YOU FOR WHAT YOU HAVE DONE MY WIFE STILL HOPES I AM ALIVE GLAD YOU HAVE TOLD DOYLE

When Doyle got Mrs. Earl's letter, he, too, was intrigued but bothered by the reference to "Leeward Islands." But then he wondered, could this be a reference to the leeward side (the side sheltered from the wind) of some *other* islands? Checking his map, he noticed that the Azores would qualify: They were on Hinchliffe's route, they were reachable, and they might have become his target if he and Elsie Mackay were foundering in a storm.

Believing that the transmission might be genuine, Doyle contacted Mrs. Earl and made an appointment for her to have a séance with Eileen Garrett, probably the most respected deep-trance medium in England. Because Mrs. Earl already knew Eileen Garrett, she was comfortable with this arrangement. So it was that on April 18, 1928, a sweet little elderly lady from Surrey sat down with Eileen Garrett as she slipped into trance and her "control," Uvani, came through. And a spirit claiming to be the airman Hinchliffe told a harrowing tale of how the *Endeavour* encountered a terrific storm at sea and was swept four or five hundred miles south. When the plane went down and he drowned, he did not suffer, he said. "It happened too quickly." After reviewing a transcript of this séance, Sir Arthur wrote directly to Emilie Hinchliffe, expressing his "deep sympathy" and laying out a series of specific details that made him believe the transmissions might be genuine.

Sir Arthur Conan Doyle's reputation as a serious student of the paranormal, as well as a kindhearted Edwardian gentleman, preceded him. The same day she got Doyle's letter, Emilie Hinchliffe wrote to Mrs. Earl, and they arranged to meet and to go to see Eileen Garrett for a séance. Emilie Hinchliffe, who was extraordinarily adept at shorthand, was able to take real-time notes of all of it. Afterward, the two of them went to have tea with Conan Doyle, who was as kindly and gracious as his reputation suggested.

And over the next weeks and months, through a series of remarkable sessions with Eileen Garrett, Emilie Hinchliffe recorded a catalog of the sorts of specific, verifiable details that were often so hard to come by in most séances (including those given by Pheneas).

Some examples of things Uvani communicated that were true: He described the interior of their house perfectly. He mentioned that Emilie had not one but two wedding rings. That he had a portrait of baby Joan with him when he crashed. That he had a small scar on his throat. He asked if she had the watch he gave her, the one with his name on it. He said she could find an important document hidden *behind* a certain drawer in a certain writing desk, and she later found it there.

He also implored Emilie not to worry about money, though she did. The insurance policy that Elsie Mackay had set up for Hinchliffe's family was now in limbo because her wealthy but difficult father, Lord Inchcape, had refused to honor his daughter's arrangement. The matter had even made it into the newspapers. But Hinchliffe claimed that the money would come through, on

July 25. On that day, Winston Churchill announced in the House of Commons that Lord Inchcape had honored the insurance policy taken out by Elsie Mackay.

And, in agonizing detail, Hinchliffe also retold the story of his own death at sea. How the *Endeavour*'s left strut broke in the storm, the plane began losing altitude, he altered the plane's course to the south, desperately trying to find someplace to land, perhaps in the Azores, but by 3:00 a.m. he had lost all hope. Elsie was "terrified, out of all limits," and at one point tried to take over the plane. He took a swig from his flask—"he says his wife knows the flask he means," Uvani said—and when the plane crashed in the water, he broke free from the wreckage. He made a "superhuman effort" to swim to shore, a few miles away, but did not make it, he said. He said the name of the island where he crashed, in the Azores, was "Carvo" (the correct spelling is Corvo).

Eventually, in a Ouija board message to Beatrice Earl, he said,

MY BODY HAS WASHED NEAR JAMAICA

Yet there he was, continuing to speak from a world that was, he said, in many ways like the world of the living. Eventually, Emilie Hinchliffe became a convert to spiritualism and began giving lectures about her experiences in the séance room. She shared the sense of peace and reassurance she had gained from these transmissions from her lost husband, conveyed through Uvani.

But not all the news from Uvani was good.

By October 1929, the British newspapers had begun to crow about the upcoming maiden flight, to India, of the empire's greatest dirigible, the R101—a floating luxury hotel that moved through the air like a great fish, almost silent and perfectly splendid. But Hinchliffe, coming through Uvani, had begun to give vent to his anxieties. "I do not think these dirigibles are able to face climatic conditions. . . . R101's maiden flight may be all right. . . . But there certainly is a great risk. . . . There *will* be an accident. I have seen Leslie Hamilton [a pilot friend of Hinchliffe's, killed in an attempted Atlantic crossing in 1927] and he agrees with me."

AMONG THE many other spiritualist matters that crossed his desk, the matter of the airman Hinchliffe, and the warnings about R101, were of enormous concern and interest to Sir Arthur. But he was a busy man. In the winter of 1928–29, Doyle embarked on another spiritualist lecture tour, this time to South Africa, Rhodesia, and Kenya, accompanied by Lady Doyle and the three children. His lectures included the story of the Cottingley Fairies, explaining later, "I took the line that I was prepared to consider any explanation of these results, save only one which attacked the character of the children." (More than likely a mistake, as any parent knows.)

Though Doyle found the spiritualist movement alive and thriving in South Africa, not all of his audiences were appreciative or respectful. Especially in areas where the strict Dutch Reformed Church held sway, Doyle's belief that spiritualists were true Christians, and that Jesus was in essence a medium who stood between two worlds, was met with stony silence or open hostility. He gave a lecture in Cape Town to an audience of nearly two thousand, and afterward, during the question period, someone called out mockingly, "If the other world is so pleasant, why don't you all commit suicide?" Someone else asked, about relationships in the afterlife, "*Must* I have the same husband?"

Despite their somewhat mixed reception in Africa, when Doyle returned to England, he told the press brightly, "We come back stronger in health, more earnest in our beliefs, more eager to fight once more in the greatest of all causes, the regeneration of religion and of that direct and practical spiritual element which is the one and only antidote to scientific materialism."

By autumn, he was off again on another lecture series, this time to Scandinavia and the Low Countries. Doyle remained sweetly cheerful and phenomenally busy, as always. He published a collection of essays on spiritualism, *The Edge of the Unknown,* much of which had earlier been published in newspapers but had been extensively revised. In May, he turned seventy. That summer, he appeared in his garden at Windlesham in a short Movietone newsreel, chatting about Sherlock Holmes and the "psychic matter." Sitting at a little table in the garden, with his dog, looking like a beloved, nattily dressed, though slightly daft, uncle, Doyle gently chided the naysayers. "When I talk about this subject, I am not talking about what I think, or what I believe; I'm talking about what I *know,*" he said. "I suppose I've sat with more mediums, good, bad, and indifferent, than anyone," and with all the wonders he had seen over forty-one years of psychic research, "there were usually six or eight or ten other witnesses, all of whom have seen the same thing. . . . [T]his is not the foolish thing as it is often represented, but a great philosophy and as I think the basis of all religious improvement."

But now the old boxer, whaling-ship doctor, and cricketer was beginning to show his age. He wrote to Bernard Ernst, "I have broken down badly and have developed Angina Pectoris. So there is just a chance that I may talk it all over with Houdini himself before very long." But he added, "I view the prospect with perfect equanimity. That is one thing that psychic knowledge does. It removes all fear of the future."

The spring of 1930 rolled around, and one morning Doyle wandered out into the garden, just after the snow cover had melted and the first flowers appeared. As he did every spring, he picked a single snowdrop flower—*Galanthus,* the pendulous, three-petaled harbinger of the coming sun—and brought it indoors for Jean.

But there was no getting around it. His health was failing. Breathing was difficult. His feet hurt. He grew exhausted easily. Now seventy-one, he'd begun to have heart trouble. Sometimes the boys would have to drive into nearby Tunbridge Wells to get bottled oxygen for their father. At two in the morning on July 7, 1930, Denis and Adrian—who loved fast cars—blasted into town on an emergency run to get oxygen, because their father was having trouble breathing. They brought it back to the house, and shortly after seven that morning Doyle asked to be lifted out of his bed so he could have a better look at the world. He was clearly sinking quickly. The boys helped him into a big basketlike armchair by the window, where he could look out over Crowborough Common. He said to Lady Jean, with a serene smile, "You are wonderful." And shortly thereafter, with his wife and three children gathered around him, Sir Arthur Conan Doyle went to greet whatever lies on the other side.

SEVERAL DAYS later, on July 11, 1930, the family had a private burial, and the old warrior was laid to rest in a flower-lined grave in the garden at Windlesham, under a copper beech tree beside the little summerhouse where he loved to write. About three hundred people were there, mainly spiritualists and literary friends—an "intimate" gathering for a man who was by now beloved by the world. There was a short service by a spiritualist pastor, which dwelled not upon mourning but upon the coming wonders of Summerland, the spiritualist conception of the paradise that awaits us.

"We know that it is only the natural body that we are committing to the ground," said the Reverend C. Thomas. "The etheric body . . . is the exact duplicate, and lives on, and is able when the psychic conditions are attuned to the spiritual, even to show itself to earthly eyes. . . . Sir Arthur will continue to carry on the work of telling the world the truth."

In its obituary of July 8, 1930, *The New York Times* described Doyle as "creator of Sherlock Holmes and a noted spiritist." In fact, the paper noted, Sherlock Holmes was probably better known than his author, and countless visitors to Baker Street in London were bitterly disappointed to discover that Holmes was not a real person.

In the latter part of his life, the *Times* opined, Sir Arthur "presented an heroic and at the same time somewhat tragic figure. For the past few years he had devoted virtually all his time to the propagation of spiritism, and was recognized as one of the great leaders of the world in that belief. Because of his association with this crusade which he himself characterized as an unpopular one, he gradually lost some of his old-time literary friends who saw no virtue in spiritism and were inclined to look upon him as an eccentric."

Nevertheless, Sir Arthur was quoted as saying, "I pledge my honor that spiritism is true, and I know that spiritism is infinitely more important than literature, art, politics, or in fact anything in the world."

Adrian and Denis told the *Times* that they had every expectation of hearing from their father after death. "Of course, my father fully believed that when he passed over he would continue to keep in touch with us. All his family believe so, too," Adrian said. He added, "My mother and my father's devotion to each other at all times was one of the most wonderful things I have ever known."

Two days later, at the Royal Albert Hall in London, an overflow crowd estimated at eight thousand people attended a memorial service for the beloved author and "spiritist." There was an empty chair on the stage, between Lady Jean and Denis, with a cardboard sign on it reading "Sir Arthur Conan Doyle."

It was the only empty seat in the house.

The crowds were enormous partly because of Doyle's fame and partly because there was the widely rumored hope that Sir Arthur might actually return to speak from beyond the grave.

A diminutive medium named Estelle Roberts walked onto the stage, stood in contemplative silence for a very long time, then called out, "There are vast numbers of spirits here with us!" Then she began naming them—"There is a gentleman on the Other Side, John Martin, looking for his daughter Jane. . . . He has got your mother and your sister Mary with him." This went on for more than half an hour, at which point the medium cried, *"He is here! He is here!"*

She pointed to the empty chair between Lady Jean and Denis. Later Roberts claimed to have seen Conan Doyle, in evening dress, walk to the chair. Then Roberts announced to the multitude that she had received a transmission from Sir Arthur, the guest of honor in absentia, and strode across the stage to where

Lady Jean was sitting to deliver it to her. Just as she leaned over to speak to Lady Doyle, an overenthusiastic organist filled the auditorium with several resounding chords from the Albert Hall's giant pipe organ, completely drowning out the message.

Lady Jean never revealed what the communication from her beloved had been—if there had been one at all.

Shortly after the great dirigible R101 crashed and burned in 1930, its deceased pilot seemed to "come through" during a séance with the medium Eileen Garrett. Then the spirit of Conan Doyle came through.
CHRONICLE / ALAMY STOCK PHOTO

CHAPTER FIFTEEN
Sir Arthur, Is That You?

"At three forty-three on the afternoon of July 7th, 1930, a press agency rang me up and informed me that Sir Arthur Conan Doyle had 'come back' and manifested through a medium in the Midlands—exactly 6½ hours after the passing of the great apostle of spiritualism," the famous psychic investigator Harry Price wrote in a 1931 article for the British literary periodical *Nash's* magazine.

When the press agent asked if Price had any opinion on the matter, Price predicted that before the day was out, phone lines would be "red-hot" with reports that Sir Arthur had sent "messages" from beyond. And, in fact, within forty-eight hours of Doyle's death, Price had received reports of at least seventeen mediums—from Vancouver and Paris to New York and even Wilkes-Barre, Pennsylvania—that Sir Arthur had "come through."

Price had made his reputation debunking phony mediums and was the founder and director of the National Laboratory of Psychical Research, which was an attempt to bring the rigor of scientific methods to the study of occult phenomena. His laboratory bristled with all manner of gadgetry—ultraviolet, infrared, and X-ray equipment, galvanometers, thermographs, an array of cameras and darkroom equipment, and other paraphernalia intended to catch a fake medium in the act. (In truth, Price probably knew where to look, because in his early days he was a conjurer and magician and had also been accused of occasionally faking psychic phenomena.) Now, with the passing of Sir Arthur, Price reveled in mocking all these alleged transmissions from beyond. Most of them were preposterous, he said, even "pathetic." Some originated from two different locations at once.

And some were worse than fraudulent. Price reported, with glee, a case from Milan in which two men called on a spiritualist family with news that one of them was able to invoke the spirit of Conan Doyle and suggested holding a séance. That evening, the whole family gathered for the sitting; the medium's "manager" agreed to stay outside the séance room to ensure that there was no confederacy involved. At the end of the séance, in which the family "drank in Doyle's philosophy from the grave," and just before the lights came on, the medium excused himself. The family sat there waiting for a long time until, finally growing impatient, they left the room, only to discover that they'd been robbed blind, the medium's confederate having stripped the house and driven off in a van full of loot.

Harry Price had had an uneasy acquaintance with Conan Doyle while the famous author was still alive. In 1922, Price had exposed as a fraud a "spirit photographer" named William Hope whom Doyle believed to be genuine. In public and in private letters, the two men quarreled bitterly for years afterward. Price felt that Doyle was too credulous, too quick to believe; Doyle felt that Price's rigorous and demanding testing filtered out mediums who were genuinely gifted.

About one of their quarrels, Price wrote, "For more than half an hour we discussed the various differences between us. Doyle accused me of medium-baiting. I suggested that his great big heart was running away with him and that he was no match for the charlatans who, like giant parasites, battened on his good nature." Though he later wrote that Doyle "never really forgave me," a few months before his death Sir Arthur seemed to declare a truce, and the two men became, if not friends, at least friendlier.

It was almost three months after Sir Arthur's death, in early October 1930, that an Australian journalist named Ian Coster contacted Price about setting up a séance. Coster, who wrote for

Cosmopolitan, Collier's, and the British magazine *Nash's,* had heard of Price's reputation as a reputable psychic investigator and someone who might be able to set up a credible séance. Coster's assignment, from the editors of *Nash's,* was both simple and somewhat silly: They wanted him to see if he could have Price conduct a séance in which he tried to make contact with Conan Doyle's spirit, exactly three months after his death. That would be October 7, 1930, only a few days away.

Price agreed, but only if he could find the right medium. And the one who came immediately to mind was Eileen Garrett. Not only was Garrett highly respected, but also she had known Sir Arthur personally, and that might make establishing contact easier. Price also liked it that Garrett was not a spiritualist and was in fact not even convinced that the soul survives bodily death. "In all my years' professional mediumship I have had no 'sign,' 'test' or slightest evidence to make me believe I have contacted another world," Garrett had written.

Her own theory was that her gifts might have come from a nightmarish childhood—both her parents committed suicide—in which psychological trauma created a "split personality" that somehow created a "magnetic field" that made it appear she was contacting other worlds. "I prefer to think of the controls as principles of the subconscious," she explained. "I had, subconsciously, adopted them during the years of early training, and given them names. I respect them. But I cannot explain them."

Nevertheless, whatever the source of her gifts, according to Price, "not the slightest suspicion attaches to her name and integrity as a medium and she has achieved some brilliant successes." (More than likely, he was referring to the Hinchliffe case, among others.) Mrs. Garrett eschewed the flashier effects of some of the famous mediums—ectoplasmic hands, table tipping, spirit photography, and so on—and simply "channeled" voices of apparent discarnate spirits.

Because she was available, the séance was arranged for October 7, 1930, at three in the afternoon, in Harry Price's specially designed séance room (which he often referred to as his "laboratory"). It was designed to be as impervious to deception and fraud as possible, with windows and doors tightly sealed, and stripped bare of every object except tables, chairs, and a few other necessary things. Unlike most séances, which were conducted in very dim or red light, this one was to take place in full light. When Mrs. Garrett arrived, a bit early, nothing was said to her about the nature of the séance. When Coster arrived a few minutes later, no one told her who he was or what he wanted, only that he had requested a sitting. The only ones present for the séance were Mrs. Garrett, Harry Price, Ian Coster, and Ethel Beenham, Price's longtime secretary, who took notes in shorthand.

According to Price's later account, Mrs. Garrett sat down in a comfortable armchair and slipped into a trance state not long after Coster arrived. Her eyes closed, and she began breathing deeply. She yawned. She seemed to relax. Then she began speaking in an odd, Oriental-sounding voice.

"It is Uvani. I give you greeting, friends; peace be with you and in your life and in your household." Uvani, Garrett's "control," always announced himself with these words. After a short pause, he continued, in his usual halting, broken English. He had a visitor there, he said—an aristocratic Viennese medical man and psychic investigator named Albert Freiherr von Schrenck-Notzing. He was a friend of Harry Price's (and of Conan Doyle's) who had died a year earlier. A skeptic, he had once remarked that "hardly one medium has appeared that has not been convicted of fraud." The baron said a few things to Price, but seemingly nothing of any particular consequence. Then, abruptly, Mrs. Garrett became visibly upset, and for a moment tears streamed down her cheeks. Her voice became rushed and disjointed, full of urgency and emotion.

> "I see for the moment I-R-V-I-N-G or I-R-W-I-N," Uvani said. "He say he must do something about it . . . apologizes for coming . . . for interfering . . . seems to be anxious to speak to a lady in the body. . . . Never mind about me but do, for heavens sake, give this to them. . . .

> The whole bulk of the dirigible was entirely and absolutely too much for her engine capacity."

Then, after a short pause, the voice continued, heavy and sorrowful, speaking in broken sentences:

> Engines too heavy. It was this that made me on five occasions have to scuttle back to safety. Useful lift too small. Gross lift computed badly—inform control panel. And this idea of new elevators totally mad! Elevator jammed. Oil pipe plugged. This exorbitant scheme of carbon and hydrogen is entirely and absolutely wrong! To begin with, the demand for it would be greater than the supply.

Scribbling as fast as she could, Ethel Beenham did not understand what any of it meant. She just kept on writing it all down.

> Also let me say this: I have experimented with less hydrogen in my own dirigible, but with the result that we are not able to reach 1,000 meters. With the new carbon hydrogen you will be able to get no altitude worth speaking about. With hydrogen, one is able to do that quite easily. Greater lifting than helium. Explosion caused by friction in electric storm. Flying too low altitude and could never rise. Disposable lift could not be utilized. Load too great for long flight. Same with S.L.8. Tell Eckener . . .

It is not clear, based on Mrs. Beenham's real-time notes taken during the séance, at what point the participants began to realize what seemed to be happening. But they would realize soon enough. That morning's newspapers had been filled with the dreadful details of the crash of the British Air Ministry's dirigible R101, which had gone down in flames in the woods near the French town of Beauvais two days earlier, at two in the morning on October 5. Of the fifty-four people on board, forty-eight were killed, including its captain, Flight Lieutenant H. Carmichael Irwin. The enormous airship, the largest flying craft in the world with an interior volume of five and a half million cubic feet, had been on its maiden voyage, from London to India, when it foundered and went down in an electrical storm.

This strange, disjointed, disembodied voice, filled with sorrow as well as technical detail—could it be the voice of the R101's captain, Irwin, coming through?

> Cruising speed bad and ship badly swinging. Severe tension of fabric, which is chafing. Starboard strakes started. . . . Airscrews too small. Fuel injection bad and air pump failed. . . . Bore capacity bad. . . . It had been known to me on many occasions that the bore capacity was entirely inadequate to the volume of the structure. This I had placed again and again before engineer, without being able to enlarge capacity of diesel twin-valve. . . . At inquiry to be held later, it will be found that the superstructure of the envelope contained no resilience, and had far too much weight in envelope. The added middle section was entirely wrong. Too short trials. No one knew the ship properly. . . . Two hours tried to rise but elevator jammed. Almost scraped the roofs at Achy.

Mrs. Beenham, writing as fast as she could in shorthand, took down "Irwin's" melancholy monologue, consisting almost entirely of technical details. Several things were remarkable about this. First, it was well-known that Mrs. Garrett was so unsophisticated about technology that she did not even drive a car and knew nothing of engineering or aeronautics. And second, "Irwin" was providing such a wealth of detail that the session contained what Conan Doyle and Price had always sought—"evidential" facts that could be independently verified.

As the séance unfolded, no one in the room yet knew what

"strakes" were, what "S.L.8" meant, who "Eckener" might be, or what "scraped the roofs at Achy" could possibly mean. (Therefore this did not appear to be telepathic communication of facts from someone in the room to the medium.) It was only later, when Harry Price began investigating, that he learned "Eckener" was the name of the German designer of the *Graf Zeppelin*. "S.L.8" turned out to be the name of a design series of German dirigibles. "Strakes" referred to a continuous line of planking or plates running from stem to stern of a ship. It was a nautical term, but because many of the men of the R101 crew, including Captain Irwin, were former navy men, it made sense that the term was used. "Almost scraped the roofs at Achy" was tougher. There was no town called "Achy" on the Michelin map of France or any of the atlases Price consulted. The name was not mentioned in any of the newspaper accounts of the crash. It was only later, when he found a large-scale flying map such as Captain Irwin might have used, that Price saw the place-name Achy—really, not much more than a railroad crossing—about twelve miles from Beauvais and directly on the R101's fateful path. Later accounts revealed that the doomed airship had precipitously dipped, to perhaps less than three hundred feet above the ground, in that area.

In fact, it later turned out that this session with Eileen Garrett contained so much technical detail that Harry Price shared the séance report with Will Charlton, a supply officer at Cardington, where R101 had been built and tested. After studying this report, Charlton declared it an "amazing document," containing more than forty technical, and often highly confidential, details of the airship's construction as well as a harrowing narrative about what likely occurred during its final flight. Some details were known only to the builders or suppliers of the airship. For instance, the reference to the "exorbitant scheme of carbon and hydrogen," apparently a reference to upcoming experiments involving a mixture of oil fuel—"carbon"—and hydrogen, experiments still only in the planning stages at Cardington, had never been reported in the press and were known only to project team members like Irwin. The fact that the flight trials were "too short" was a concern to those working at Cardington, but unknown to the public.

The séance report was later submitted to Sir John Simon, who was in charge of the investigation into the crash. Simon found that most of the details given in the trance session tallied almost precisely with what was later found in the course of the official inquiry into the crash, whose results were not released until six months later.

Seven other séances were later held with Eileen Garrett and Major Oliver Villiers, senior assistant intelligence officer in the British Air Ministry, an expert in aeronautics and a personal friend of Irwin and the rest of the R101 crew. Other members of the crew appeared to come through, describing technical details of the crash and using expressions of speech Villiers associated with them. One voice, claiming to be the crew member Lieutenant Commander Atherstone, the first mate, claimed he had kept a secret diary to record his worries about the R101 program. When officials questioned his widow about the diary, she claimed never to have heard of it. But almost forty years later, in 1967, Mrs. Atherstone was to come forward with her husband's diary, which contained the very same concerns expressed by the supposed "Atherstone" personality in the séance.

Over the ensuing years, there were many attempts to discredit the material produced in these séances. Skeptics later pointed out that not every single thing that "Irwin" said was true; that it was theoretically possible that Garrett could have found some, though not all, of the details she mentioned in the newspapers; and that she was the only medium involved in both Price's and Villiers's séances, whereas the case would have been much stronger had three or four mediums been involved. In the early 1960s, the researcher Archie Jarman—who had known Garrett for years—investigated the case thoroughly. He knew that she often traveled by car from Calais to Paris and would have known of the tiny town of Achy. He suggested that she might have subconsciously picked this name from her own memory. But how would she have known that people in Achy later reported seeing the airship descend dangerously right over the town, a fact not reported until days after the séance? In the end, Jarman's exhaustive report took six months, ran 455 pages, with maps and blueprints, and involved interviews with aeronautical experts. Jarman concluded, "My opinion is that greater credulity is demanded to believe that Eileen obtained her obscure and specialized data by mundane means than to accept that, in some paranormal manner, she had contact with the remembering psyche of the dead Captain Irwin."

Harry Price himself was more cautious: "It is not my intention to discuss if the medium were really controlled by the discarnate entity of Irwin, or whether the utterances emanated from her subconscious mind or those of the sitters. 'Spirit' or 'trance personality' would be equally interesting explanations—and equally remarkable. There is no real evidence for either hypothesis. But it is not my intention to discuss hypotheses, but rather to put on record the detailed account of a remarkably interesting and thought-provoking experiment."

But, of course, the whole purpose of the séance that afternoon of October 7 was to attempt to contact Sir Arthur Conan Doyle, now dead for three months.

It was now nearly four o'clock in the afternoon, and "Uvani" seemed to be growing weary when he announced the presence of someone else. "An elderly person here saying that there is no reason in the world why he attend you, but he has got here an SOS sent out to him, to be precise, five days ago." It had been five days earlier when Price phoned the medium to set up the séance.

Uvani described the person who was waiting to speak to Price: "He is tall, rather heavy of stature, feet rather bad, jolly, great of heart, deep blue eyes, a drooping moustache, strong chin, dominating, courageous, stubborn, heart of a child . . . amusing, and at times very difficult. . . . Has almost a threefold personality." According to Price, this was a remarkably accurate description of Conan Doyle—not just his physical presence, but his innermost nature.

Then the medium's voice changed suddenly, shifting to a British lilt with a bit of a Scottish burr on the *r*'s.

"Here I am. Arthur Conan Doyle. Now how am I going to prove it to you?" Speaking very rapidly, as Doyle was inclined to do, the voice went on to say, "I, myself, did not recognize the difficulty there would be in getting through this wall or 'density' that stands between us. . . . I would like you to know my location—that I am in a nebulous belt lying outside the earth's surface." He went on to say, "I shall be most happy if anything I can say from this side helps you to understand the blackness on your side and the intricacies and difficulties of communicating. The difficulties are stupendous."

The two men talked about their recent dispute.

"It was your fault that we disagreed," the voice said.

"We were working with the same object in view, but in different ways. I am trying to arrive at the truth," Price replied.

"I always had my eye on you, and you used to watch me like a cat watching a bird in a cage!" "Doyle" said.

After a time, the two men good-naturedly agreed to shake hands over the matter. The Doyle voice, with some amusement, observed that "most people think I made a great deal of money out of spiritualism by beating the big drum, but I realized there was very little money in the whole business. Many of my friends said 'You are a stout old dog—it must bring you in a tidy income!' "—but that, he said, was entirely untrue. In fact, his devotion to the cause of spiritualism, his extensive lecture tours, his short-lived psychic bookshop, and so on had actually cost him a small fortune, not to mention the stress and inconvenience of international travel. In fact, according to his biographer John Dickson Carr, Doyle spent 250,000 pounds promoting the cause of spiritualism (several million dollars in today's money).

Price asked which of Doyle's fictional characters he liked best.

Without hesitation, he answered "Rodney Stone," hero of a little-known novel of the same name, a coming-of-age story about a Sussex lad taken to the big city, set in the world of the bare-knuckle boxing of the day. He made no mention of Sherlock Holmes at all.

When Price inquired about the nature of his current condition, "Doyle" replied, "When I say I am living in a world considerably like the one I have left, people will be surprised. I find myself doing many of the things which I did there. I am living in a world as dark as that which I left, more's the pity. It is a country where pain is forever ended; where emotion is born a thousand times stronger; where inspirations reach me easier. . . . I understand that it tends to confirm the theory of reincarnation and the soul goes through many phases. . . . I am still 'material,' and so long as I am material, I feel myself the man I was on earth."

Price thanked "Doyle" for having written a letter to the *Evening Standard,* about a month before his death, applauding the work of Price's organization and its efforts to scientifically study paranormal phenomena. "Do you still think the scientific investigation of [psychic] phenomena is necessary?" Price asked.

"I cannot help thinking, my dear Price," the voice replied, "that after many years' study of spiritualism, I have definitely come to the conclusion that before you get a sane, sound, sensible man to take hold of the thing and lead it to our goal, which is world knowledge, you need the most rigorous care from the scientific point of view. It is far more difficult to establish a fact than it is to advertise an illusion."

Indeed.

NOTES

The reader will notice here that this book has not been footnoted down to the tiniest detail, in academic fashion. That's because it aspires to be a jolly romp, rather than a scholarly treatise. While raising the profound questions inherent in this material, we aimed to favor high spirits, delicious speculations, and compelling scenes and characters. Hence, the authors have footnoted only direct quotations, major factual details, and other key specifics.

PROLOGUE: THE INFINITE STRANGENESS OF LIFE

1 **"There is a rush and roar"**: Lachtman, *Sherlock Slept Here,* 66.

2 **"ghost machine"**: www.paranormal-encyclopedia.com, s.v. "Thomas Edison and the Ghost in the Machine."

3 **"I came of age at 80 degrees north latitude"**: Doyle, *"Dangerous Work,"* journal of the whaling ship S.S. *Hope,* entry from May 22, 1880.

3 **"never loses his temper"**: Houdini, *Magician Among the Spirits,* 139.

4 **simply called himself "Conan Doyle"**: Ibid.

5 **"The subject of psychical research"**: Doyle, *New Revelation,* 13.

5 **"In the presence of an agonized world"**: Ibid., 39.

5 **"infinitely the most important thing"**: Ibid., 97.

CHAPTER ONE: INTO THE UNKNOWN

9 **"Only a week from Shetland"**: This and all quotations from the logbook of the S.S. *Hope* are from the annotated reprint Doyle, *"Dangerous Work."*

9 **a fellow student named Currie**: Doyle, *Memories and Adventures,* 29.

11 **a fierce feud**: Ibid., 5.

12 **"My real love for letters"**: From an interview first published in the *New York World,* July 28, 1907.

14 **"to his family he was becoming"**: Carr, *Life of Sir Arthur Conan Doyle,* 9.

15 **"they are more weird"**: Lamond, *Arthur Conan Doyle, a Memoir,* 9.

16 **"Nothing can exceed"**: Doyle, *Memories and Adventures,* 15.

18 **"Well, my man"**: Ibid., 20.

CHAPTER TWO: "MISTER SPLITFOOT, DO AS I DO!"

This account of the story of the Fox sisters is based on several sources, both contemporary and archival. Chief among them are E. E. Lewis's *Report of the Mysterious Noises* (1848); E. W. Capron's *Modern Spiritualism;* the journalist Reuben Davenport's *Death-Blow to Spiritualism;* Leah Underhill's *Missing Link in Modern Spiritualism;* Robert Dale Owen's classic *Footfalls on the Boundary of Another World;* Conan Doyle's much later (1926) account in *The History of Spiritualism;* Miriam Buckner Pond's *Time Is Kind;* and two good more recent books, Barbara Weisberg's *Talking to the Dead* and Nancy Stuart's excellent *The Reluctant Spiritualist.*

24 **At other times, Mrs. Fox later reported**: Capron, *Modern Spiritualism,* 6; Owen, *Footfalls on the Boundary of Another World,* 285.

24 **"On March 30th we were disturbed all night"**: Capron, *Modern Spiritualism,* 6.

25 **"I advise you not to say a word"**: Owen, *Footfalls on the Boundary of Another World,* 287.

25 **"Now do this just as I do"**: Ibid., 41.

27 **"That rude room"**: Doyle, *History of Spiritualism,* 63.

27 **"on the night of March 31st, 1848"**: From Wallace's critique of

Mesmerism, Spiritualism, &c., Historically and Scientifically Considered (1877), by William B. Carpenter.

28 **"On Sunday morning, the second of April"**: Owen, *Footfalls on the Boundary of Another World,* 145.

29 **Lucretia Pulver told this story**: Stuart, *Reluctant Spiritualist,* 14.

30 **"sit under the bedroom window"**: Ibid.

30 **"believed him to be a man"**: Ibid., 16.

31 **"One day about two o'clock, P.M."**: Capron, *Modern Spiritualism,* 38.

31 **"completely broken down"**: Stuart, *Reluctant Spiritualist,* 27.

32 **"the sun shone brightly"**: Underhill, *Missing Link in Modern Spiritualism,* 34.

32 **"Oh, that dreadful sound!"**: Owen, *Footfalls on the Boundary of Another World,* 58.

33 **"I was particular to tell the agent"**: Underhill, *Missing Link in Modern Spiritualism,* 35.

33 **"Can it be possible?"**: Ibid., 37.

34 **"I can't pray"**: Ibid., 45.

35 **"He was much disappointed"**: Capron, *Modern Spiritualism,* 60.

36 **"Dear friends, you must proclaim these truths"**: Underhill, *Missing Link in Modern Spiritualism,* 49.

37 **"MY DEAR CHILDREN"**: Ibid., 51.

38 **"This proposition was met"**: Capron, *Modern Spiritualism,* 93; Underhill, *Missing Link in Modern Spiritualism,* 62.

39 **"the citizens of Rochester"**: Stuart, *Reluctant Spiritualist,* 50.

39 **"She is a very interesting and lovely young lady"**: Underhill, *Missing Link in Modern Spiritualism,* 63.

40 **"I know it is true"**: Ibid.

40 **"were not altogether right"**: Capron, *Modern Spiritualism,* 93.

41 **"conclusively shown [the sounds] to be produced"**: Doyle, *History of Spiritualism,* 82.

41 **"we shall not stir from this room"**: Underhill, *Missing Link in Modern Spiritualism,* 69.

42 **"I cannot have you go without me"**: Doyle, *History of Spiritualism,* 71.

43 **"So long as the public"**: Ibid., 82.

44 **"This infantile explanation"**: Richet, *Thirty Years of Psychical Research,* 28.

44 **"great souls from Atlantis"**: Godwin, *Upstate Cauldron,* chap. 12.

CHAPTER THREE: THE SPIRITUAL WILDFIRE

47 **their first visitor was Horace Greeley**: Cadwallader, *Hydesville in History,* 49.

47 **Two nights later, they conducted**: This account was given in full detail in the June 8, 1850, edition of the *New-York Tribune.*

49 **"They have prepared me for this hour"**: Cadwallader, *Hydesville in History,* 50.

50 **"Most advised a maximum"**: Braude, *Radical Spirits,* 20.

50 **"In five years it has spread like wild-fire"**: Fornell, *Unhappy Medium,* 35.

50 **"The dear spirits"**: Braude, *Radical Spirits,* 17.

51 **"wise mentor at the elbow"**: Doyle, *History of Spiritualism,* 87.

51 **"Again we are asked how a spirit can rap"**: Capron and Barron, *Explanation and History of the Mysterious Communion with Spirits,* 79.

52 **describes a private party in London**: Winter, *Mesmerized,* 145.

53 **Dickens was quite pleased**: Kaplan, *Dickens and Mesmerism,* 70–90.

54 **"The spirits of our departed friends"**: Dods, *Spirit Manifestations,* 75–83.

55 **"It would be difficult to determine"**: Hardinge, *Modern American Spiritualism,* 55.

55 **no more than 15 percent of Americans**: Kramnick and Moore, *Godless Constitution,* 17.

56 **When the suffragist Lucy Stone**: Braude, *Radical Spirits,* 90.

56 **"born and baptized"**: Ibid., 59.

57 **Dissident Quakers supplied the critical mass**: Ibid., 57.

57 **Susan B. Anthony would travel every summer**: Ibid., 196.

58 **Most other prominent abolitionists**: Moore, *In Search of White Crows,* 71; Godwin, *Upstate Cauldron,* 149.

59 **Left to fend for himself**: Gauld, *Founders of Psychical Research,* 16–17.

59 **On July 25, 1855, the poet**: This account of an 1855 séance with Robert and Elizabeth Barrett Browning at the Rymer home is woven from four sources: Porter's *Through a Glass Darkly,* esp. 50; Doyle's *Edge of the Unknown;* Home's memoir, *Incidents in My Life,* 106; and Browning's *Letters to Her Sister,* 218.

CHAPTER FOUR: THE INVENTION OF SHERLOCK HOLMES

Though much has been written about Doyle's early years, this chapter is primarily drawn from Doyle's own recollections, in his autobiography and spiritualist writings.

66 **But he soon discovered that Budd's "practice"**: Doyle, *Memories and Adventures.*
67 **"As long as I was thoroughly unsuccessful"**: Ibid., 57, 90.
68 **"No man could have a more gentle"**: Ibid., 65.
68 **"I had ceased to butt my head"**: Ibid., 656.
69 **"in an intelligent Force"**: Doyle, *New Revelation,* 15.
69 **"I found myself, like many young medical men"**: Doyle, *Memories and Adventures,* 77.
69 **"each man in his egotism"**: Doyle, *New Revelation,* 15.
70 **"I had said that the flame could not exist"**: Ibid., 35.
70 **"I had always sworn by science"**: Ibid., 36.
71 **"I am afraid the only result"**: Doyle, *Memories and Adventures,* 79.
71 **"I read the book with interest"**: Doyle, *New Revelation,* 17.
71 **The Europeans could not claim**: Ibid., 29, 30.
74 **"Mrs. Fox Kane"**: This anecdote of Maggie Kane's last days is from R. G. Pressing, *Rappings That Startled the World* (Lily Dale, N.Y.: Dale News, 1942), 75–76.
75 **"appropriately enough, through the dead letter office"**: Doyle, *New Revelation,* 21.
75 **"I was still a skeptic"**: Ibid., 23.
75 **"what proof was there"**: Ibid., 28.
76 **It was the first time he would go public**: Doyle, *Memories and Adventures,* 80.
76 **"a great root book"**: Doyle, *New Revelation,* 32.
77 **In a grainy black-and-white Movietone film**: "Sir Arthur Conan Doyle, 1930," Fox Movietone News Story 6-962.
80 **"weak as a child and as emotional"**: Doyle, *Memories and Adventures,* 91.

CHAPTER FIVE: THE SCIENCE OF THE UNSEEN

83 **James Hyslop, was hounded out of his faculty position**: Blum, *Ghost Hunters,* 247–48.

84 **"We are ill equipped for the investigation"**: Oppenheim, *Other World,* 332.

84 **"Above all, *he could discern the value*"**: Lamond, *Arthur Conan Doyle, a Memoir,* 270.

84 **"Each honest inquiry can only strengthen"**: Doyle, *Spiritualism and Rationalism,* 141, in the Cambridge Scholars edition.

85 **"I had been brought up deaf"**: Hare, *Experimental Investigation,* 38.

85 **"The result was not as he expected"**: Alfred Russel Wallace, *The Scientific Aspect of the Supernatural,* 34. All of Wallace's writings are collected on the excellent Web pages of Charles H. Smith, a professor and science librarian at Western Kentucky University (people.wku.edu/charles.smith/).

85 **"The brave report"**: Doyle, *History of Spiritualism,* 1:138.

86 **"From the hour of the Hare report"**: Doyle, *Spiritualism and Rationalism,* 137.

87 **"Aunt Sara said she wasn't dead"**: Blum, *Ghost Hunters,* 97; Tymn, *Resurrecting Leonora Piper,* 2.

88 **In a trance, she got up from her chair**: Blum, *Ghost Hunters,* 98; Tymn, *Resurrecting Leonora Piper,* 3; Gauld, *Founders of Psychical Research,* 252.

88 **Notably, all this took place in broad daylight**: Tymn, *Resurrecting Leonora Piper,* 98.

89 **"I feel as if something were passing"**: Piper, *Life and Work of Mrs. Piper,* 67.

90 **Then she asked about a dead child**: Blum, *Ghost Hunters,* 100.

90 **James submitted a brief account**: Gauld, *Founders of Psychical Research,* 253.

90 **In late 1884, Hodgson went to Madras, India**: Blum, *Ghost Hunters,* 83–91.

91 **Alfred Russel Wallace was especially peeved**: Ibid., 119.

91 **Phinuit claimed to be a French doctor**: Tymn, *Resurrecting Leonora Piper,* 18; Gauld, *Founders of Psychical Research,* 252.

91 **"Phinuit began, after the usual introduction"**: Gauld, *Founders of Psychical Research,* 254.

91 **Phinuit said she was standing right there**: Tymn, *Resurrecting Leonora Piper,* 20.

93 **Hodgson said nothing**: Blum, *Ghost Hunters,* 135.

93 **Hodgson didn't even know his sister was expecting**: Tymn, *Resurrecting Leonora Piper,* 21.

93 **James tried to make light of it**: Piper, *Life and Work of Mrs. Piper,* 45.
93 **Hodgson . . . was becoming obsessed**: Blum, *Ghost Hunters,* 142–43.
94 **"It happens that an uncle"**: Gauld, *Founders of Psychical Research,* 255–57.
94 **"I took every precaution"**: Tymn, *Resurrecting Leonora Piper,* 46.
96 **And in his *Proceedings* report**: Ibid., 65.
96 **All this was true, and it was way past telepathy**: Ibid., 66.
96 **Pellew took over Mrs. Piper's body**: This conversation (p. 468) and many other particulars are found in Holt, *On the Cosmic Relations.*
97 **Phinuit was speaking and George was writing with one hand**: Tymn, *Resurrecting Leonora Piper,* 75, citing Lodge, *Survival of Man,* 251.
98 **"He was a very Saul"**: Doyle, *History of Spiritualism,* 2:75.
98 **Hyslop said the ghost of his father**: Blum, *Ghost Hunters,* 245.
99 **"keeping up a conversation"**: Doyle, *History of Spiritualism,* 2:83.
99 **In 1909, G. Stanley Hall**: His cruelty to Mrs. Piper is documented in Blum, *Ghost Hunters,* 303 ff; Tymn, *Resurrecting Leonora Piper,* 182; and in her daughter's biography, Piper's *Life and Work of Mrs. Piper,* 173–75.
100 **In 1925, Sir William Barrett**: Tymn, *Resurrecting Leonora Piper,* 191.

CHAPTER SIX: "SOME SPLENDID STARRY NIGHT"

103 **He was just shy of thirty-eight**: Carr, *Life of Sir Arthur Conan Doyle,* 101.
104 **"I tried never to give Touie a moment's unhappiness"**: Ibid., 175–77.
104 **A year after Touie's death**: Booth, *The Doctor and the Detective,* 267.
104 **Though he generally wrote**: Carr, *Life of Sir Arthur Conan Doyle,* 177.
105 **"My dear fellow":** Ibid., 171.
105 **"You know, Arthur, it would be strange"**: Ibid., 172.

106 **Sir Arthur's nephew Oscar Hornung**: Lycett, *Man Who Created Sherlock Holmes,* 385.

106 **"The Bowmen," by the Welsh author Arthur Machen**: The story of the Angels of Mons is retold in several places, including in "Smoke Without Fire: A Re-examination of the Angels of Mons," militaryhistoryonline; "Angels of Mons," firstworldwar.com; and Arthur Machen's 1915 book *The Bowmen and Other Legends of the War.*

108 **"Now Lodge, while we are not here as of old"**: Lodge, *Raymond,* 90.

109 **"the reference is to Horace's account"**: Ibid., 91.

109 **"TELL FATHER I HAVE MET SOME FRIENDS OF HIS"**: Ibid., 98.

109 **"a man, a writer of poetry"**: Ibid., 100.

110 **"I have met hundreds of friends"**: Ibid., 99.

110 **"is particular that I should tell you this"**: Ibid., 105.

111 **The photograph arrived in Oliver Lodge's mailbox**: Ibid., 109.

111 **It appears to have been sometime**: Booth, *The Doctor and the Detective,* 312.

112 **"In spite of occasional fraud"**: Item by A. Conan Doyle, *Light,* Nov. 4, 1916.

113 **In 1916, during the Battle of the Somme**: Details in Lycett, *Man Who Created Sherlock Holmes,* 390, 399.

114 **"He was a very perfect man"**: Booth, *The Doctor and the Detective,* 311.

114 **"on the whole, Evan Powell may be said"**: Doyle, *History of Spiritualism,* II, 210.

115 **He had given many sittings**: *Psychic Science,* July 1925.

115 **After Doyle's lecture that night**: Conan Doyle described this key séance with Evan Powell in "A Wonderful Experience," *Two Worlds,* Dec. 19, 1919, and in "A Wonderful Séance," *Light,* Dec. 27, 1919. The full text of these items can be found in the *Arthur Conan Doyle Encyclopedia,* arthur-conan-doyle.com. A description of the séance also occurs in Daniel Stashower's biography, *Teller of Tales,* 346. Stashower writes that Doyle had described the séance in a letter to Oliver Lodge and later repeated it many times over the years.

117 **"universal sorrow and loss"**: Doyle, *Memories and Adventures,* 387.

118 **"I have clasped materialized hands"**: Ibid., 393, 394.
119 **"Spiritualism has been for me"**: Doyle, *New Revelation,* 103.

CHAPTER SEVEN: THE SAINT PAUL OF SPIRITUALISM

121 **all twenty-four hundred tickets were sold out**: Doyle to his mother (before the event), Feb. 1920, in Lellenberg, Stashower, and Foley, *Life in Letters,* 663.
121 **"a combative and aggressive spirit"**: Doyle, *Psychic Experiences,* 117.
121 **"Someone has called me"**: Lellenberg, Stashower, and Foley, *Life in Letters,* 656.
121 **"I go into battle"**: Ibid., 665.
122 **"This is a serious debate"**: All quotations are taken from *Verbatim Report of a Public Debate on "The Truth of Spiritualism."*
123 **"Those who discharge promptly"**: Greeley, *Autobiography,* 239.
123 **"When the whole world is living vividly"**: Doyle, *Wanderings of a Spiritualist,* 64.
125 **"in short snip-snap sentences"**: Doyle, *Spiritualism and Rationalism,* 151.
125 **that's just how Joseph McCabe died**: *Oxford Dictionary of National Biography.*
126 **"who had passed over"**: Doyle, *Wanderings of a Spiritualist,* 5.
126 **"big arresting presence"**: Ibid., 31.
126 **At the start of his first speech in Sydney**: *Sydney Morning Herald,* Nov. 16, 1920, 9.
127 **"A wise spirit control"**: Doyle, *Wanderings of a Spiritualist,* 42.
128 **"So amazing a phenomenon"**: Doyle, *History of Spiritualism,* 2:214–15.
128 **Wallace requested a sunflower**: Alfred Russel Wallace, *A Defence of Modern Spiritualism* (Boston: Colby and Rich, 1874), 646.
128 **"Almost at once he breathed very heavily"**: Doyle, *Wanderings of a Spiritualist,* 46–48.
129 **"I had an Indian nest"**: Ibid., 128.
129 **There, in the archives**: *Stanford Magazine,* May/June 2000 and Sept./Oct. 2012.
130 **"Who was the greatest medium-baiter"**: Doyle, the opening words of "The Riddle of Houdini," in *Edge of the Unknown.*

131 **"What religion could there be in a jumping table"**: Doyle, *Our American Adventure,* 10 (Cambridge Scholars ed.).

131 **He'd been answering that question**: Cf. *Daily Chronicle,* Feb. 20, 1919.

131 **"Unselfishness, that is the keynote"**: Doyle, *New Revelation,* 195.

132 **"When I said that the average human being"**: Doyle, *Our American Adventure,* 17.

133 **He said most of the Bible was worse than worthless**: Doyle, *Vital Message,* esp. 123 (Cambridge Scholars ed.).

133 **"the sweetest soul that ever trod"**: Lamond, *Arthur Conan Doyle, a Memoir,* 230.

133 **"One thing that can safely be said of Paul"**: Doyle, *Wanderings of a Spiritualist,* 38.

133 **"When we translate Bible language"**: Doyle, *Vital Message,* 164.

133 **"Don't tell me, Daddy"**: Doyle, *Land of Mist,* 19.

134 **"The differences between various sects"**: Doyle, *Vital Message,* 135.

134 **an eighth principle, recognizing Jesus**: Lamond, *Arthur Conan Doyle, a Memoir,* 233.

134 **In the last days of his life, infighting**: Lycett, *Man Who Created Sherlock Holmes,* 460.

134 **"so scanty that I cannot bring myself"**: Gibson and Green, *Letters to the Press,* 301.

134 **American spiritualists were no better**: Moore, *In Search of White Crows,* esp. 42–46.

135 **"So soon as they become satisfied"**: *Banner of Light,* Dec. 11, 1869, cited in ibid., 69.

135 **It had a print run of fewer than a thousand copies**: Lycett, *Man Who Created Sherlock Holmes,* 458.

CHAPTER EIGHT: AN EMBARRASSMENT OF FAIRIES

137 **"either the most elaborate and ingenious hoax"**: Doyle, *Coming of the Fairies,* 3.

137 **"If I myself am asked"**: "Fairies Photographed: An Epoch-Making Event Described by A. Conan Doyle," *Strand Magazine,* Dec. 1920.

138 **"I was up the beck alone"**: Cottingleyconnect.org.uk/fairies.shtml.

139 **"Elsie and I are friendly with the beck fairies"**: Ibid.

140 **"The fact that two young girls"**: Paul Smith, "The Cottingley Fairies: The End of a Legend," in *The Good People: New Fairylore Essays,* ed. Peter Narváez (Lexington: University Press of Kentucky, 1997), 371–405.

140 **"quiet, well-balanced and reserved"**: Doyle, *Coming of the Fairies,* 10.

141 **"throw [this news] into literary shape"**: Ibid.

141 **As other critics later pointed out**: Ibid., 11.

142 **"This bracket and plant are opposite my daily seat"**: Baker, *Doyle Diary,* 48.

142 **"These two negatives are entirely genuine"**: Doyle, *Coming of the Fairies,* 25, 31.

143 **Kodak declined to warrant the genuineness of the images**: Cottingleyconnect.org.uk; Doyle, *Coming of the Fairies,* 17, 19.

143 **"impressed me favourably"**: Doyle, *Coming of the Fairies,* 19.

143 **"entirely uninspired, and bore no possible resemblance"**: Ibid., 33.

144 **"most observers of fairy life have reported"**: Ibid., 32.

144 **"Poor Sherlock Holmes—Hopelessly Crazy?"**: Baker, *Doyle Diary,* xix.

144 **"on the evidence I have no hestitation"**: Doyle, *Coming of the Fairies,* 49.

145 **"The wonderful thing has happened"**: Ibid., 59.

145 **In a second article for *The Strand***: Arthur Conan Doyle, "The Evidence for Fairies," *Strand Magazine,* March 1921.

145 **"No contrast could well be more marked"**: Doyle, *Coming of the Fairies,* 115.

146 **"I've told you they're photographs"**: Cottingleyconnect.org.uk.

147 **"It was a wet Saturday afternoon"**: Ibid.

CHAPTER NINE: THE STRANGEST FRIENDSHIP IN HISTORY

148 **"If ever there was a whole-hearted believer"**: Ernst and Carrington, *Story of a Strange Friendship,* 31.

150 **"This is to certify that Mr. Harry Houdini"**: Ibid., 76.

151 **"I have always been a good boy, have I not?"**: Ernst and Carrington, *Story of a Strange Friendship,* 26.

152 **It was, he later said, his most difficult escape**: Wikipedia, s.v. "Harry Houdini."

152 **Houdini's onstage marvels were so remarkable**: www.paranormal-encyclopedia.com, s.v. "Harry Houdini".

154 **"I have always wondered"**: Ernst and Carrington, *Story of a Strange Friendship,* 44.

154 **"Houdini, you know more about myself"**: Ibid., 49.

154 **"was a great master of his profession"**: Ibid., 16.

154 **"In a long life which has touched"**: Doyle, *Edge of the Unknown,* 11.

154 **"comes automatically to the mind"**: Houdini, *Magician Among the Spirits,* 140.

155 **"Until Thursday is over"**: Ernst and Carrington, *Story of a Strange Friendship,* 137, 132.

155 **"A retinue of rogues"**: Ibid., 34.

155 **"he has refused to discuss"**: Houdini, *Magician Among the Spirits,* 141.

156 **"I see that you know a great deal"**: Ernst and Carrington, *Story of a Strange Friendship,* 51.

156 **"the fervor with which [Houdini] carried on"**: Ibid., 41.

157 **"the most home-like home"**: Ibid., 122.

157 **Doyle was convinced that the study**: Sandford, *Houdini and Conan Doyle,* 104.

158 **"Houdini produced what appeared to be an ordinary slate"**: This remarkable demonstration, described several places, is described best in Carrington and Ernst, *Story of a Strange Friendship,* 245–50.

159 **"Sir Arthur thinks that I have great mediumistic powers"**: Houdini, *Magician Among the Spirits,* 159, 165.

159 **From under his chair, he pulled out a picture**: Sandford, *Houdini and Conan Doyle,* 134.

160 **"The method in which Houdini"**: Doyle, *Edge of the Unknown,* 33, 34.

160 **"Smilingly, my good little wife said"**: Houdini, *Magician Among the Spirits,* 150–51.

161 **"Sir Arthur tried to quiet her"**: Ibid., 152.

161 **"It was a singular scene"**: Sandford, *Houdini and Conan Doyle,* 137.

161 **"I *always* read my beloved son's mind"**: Houdini, *Magician Among the Spirits,* 154.
162 **"he looked up at me and I was amazed"**: Doyle, *Edge of the Unknown,* 34.
162 **"The Spirits have directed you"**: Sandford, *Houdini and Conan Doyle,* 138.
162 **"walking on air ever since"**: Doyle, *Edge of the Unknown,* 33.
163 **"There is a man here"**: Houdini, *Magician Among the Spirits,* 155.
163 **"Trusting you will accept"**: Ibid., 158.
164 **"in case of my death"**: Carrington and Ernst, *Story of a Strange Friendship,* 176.

CHAPTER TEN: SEX, LIES, AND SÉANCES

167 **On the steamy summer night**: Most of the details in this chapter come from unpublished real-time notes of this séance, August 25, 1924, and personal correspondence from Dr. Le Roi Crandon to Conan Doyle, on file in the Arthur Conan Doyle archive housed at the marvelous Harry Ransom Center, University of Texas at Austin.
167 **"too attractive for her own good"**: Tietze, *Margery,* xxi, 9.
170 **"a loud merry whistle"**: Ibid., 23.
171 **"I have said many times"**: Houdini, *Magician Among the Spirits,* 270.
172 **Walter was intrigued enough**: Tietze, *Margery,* 3.
172 **"deep and frivolous, superficial and solemn"**: Ibid., 9.
173 **At the conclusion of the sitting**: Ibid., 16.
173 **"was able to produce an extraordinary spectrum"**: Ibid., 19.
174 **"what amazing things people are willing to believe"**: Ibid., 25.
175 **"ANNOUNCING $5,000 FOR PSYCHIC PHENOMENA"**: Ibid., 33.
177 **"We continue to sit for the Scientific American Committee"**: Le Roi Crandon to Doyle, Ransom Center.
177 **"I am Houdini!"**: "Mina Crandon & Harry Houdini: The Medium and the Magician," Historynet.com.
177 **"has collected every lie and innuendo"**: Crandon to Doyle, Ransom Center.
178 **"I see that you are on the Scientific American Committee"**: Houdini, *Magician Among the Spirits,* 159.

178 **One early "medium" was a man from Wilkes-Barre**: For this and the descriptions of other applicants to the *Scientific American* challenge, see Sandford, *Houdini and Conan Doyle,* 163–67.
179 **" 'Margery' Passes All Psychic Tests"**: Harry Houdini, *"Margery" the Medium Exposed* (1924); Houdini, *Magician Among the Spirits,* 159.
179 **"regarded himself as the hub"**: Bird, *"Margery" the Medium,* 405.
180 **"in building up a new stage personality"**: Ibid., 408.
180 **"at this moment it looks"**: Crandon to Doyle, Ransom Center.
180 **"She's forced open the cabinet with her shoulders!"**: Details and quotations from séance notes, taken August 25, 1924, Ransom Center archive.

CHAPTER ELEVEN: HOUDINI CHEATS . . . AGAIN

Nearly all of the detail here comes from séance notes, and private letters from Le Roi Crandon and Dr. McDougall, at the Arthur Conan Doyle archive at the Ransom Center.

186 **"In Majesty Death Comes"**: Tietze, *Margery,* 152.
189 **"messiahs to a half million"**: Sandford, *Houdini and Conan Doyle,* 213.
190 **"Oh, this is terrible!"**: Tietze, *Margery,* 52.
193 **"I wish it here recorded"**: Ibid., 53.
194 **"Collins smiled wryly"**: Ibid.
194 **"He just materialized out of nowhere"**: Sandford, *Houdini and Conan Doyle,* 213.
196 **"Dudley claimed there were no fewer"**: Tietze, *Margery,* 156.
196 **And a new analysis found that the match**: Ibid., 161.
196 **One problem with this story**: Sandford, *Houdini and Conan Doyle,* 215.
196 **"None of the evidence offered"**: Houdini, *Magician Among the Spirits,* 270.
197 **"I am convinced that no snap judgement"**: Tietze, *Margery,* 58.
198 **"My decision is, that everything which took place at the séances"**: Ibid., 60.
199 **But how did Walter whistle?**: Dr. Crandon's research is given in full detail in his chapter "The Margery Mediumship," in Murchison, *Case for and Against Psychical Belief,* 65–109.

CHAPTER TWELVE: "WE HAVE JUST BEGUN TO FIGHT!"

203 **"the 'slickest' ruse I have ever encountered"**: Houdini's pamphlet can be found online at pbs.org, *"Margery" the Medium Exposed*. The pamphlet goes on to explain, with diagrams, how he believed he'd caught Margery ringing the bell box with her foot.

204 **"regarded a major part of his duties"**: Bird, *"Margery" the Medium,* 405.

204 **"while an ordinary investigator"**: Houdini, *"Margery" the Medium Exposed.*

205 **"abandoned all pretense at judicial consideration"**: Bird, *"Margery" the Medium,* 409.

205 **"Well, gentlemen, I've got her"**: Ibid., 413.

210 **"I have never on any occasion detected"**: Polidoro, *Final Séance,* 154, 155.

210 **On two occasions, Walter's voice and Margery's voice**: Bird, *"Margery" the Medium,* 462.

211 **"I was waiting for you to ask that"**: Ibid., 477.

211 **One summer day in 1926**: J. B. Rhine and Lousia E. Rhine, "One Evening's Observation on the Margery Mediumship," *Journal of Abnormal and Social Psychology* 21, no. 4 (Jan.–March 1927).

211 **"Could this man be expected"**: Polidoro, *Final Séance,* 202, 203.

212 **"J. B. Rhine Is an Ass"**: Ibid., 203.

212 **"completely won over"**: Sandford, *Houdini and Conan Doyle,* 214.

213 **"will turn out to be the most extraordinary mediumship"**: Crandon to Lodge, Ransom Center archive.

CHAPTER THIRTEEN: A DEATH FORETOLD

217 **"Do the Spirits Return?"**: www.wildabouthoudini.com.

218 **"HOUDINI CHALLENGES LOCAL SOOTHSAYERS!"**: Sandford, *Houdini and Conan Doyle,* 202.

219 **"I am Houdini, and you are a fraud!"**: Ibid., 197.

219 **"Men like McDougall and Conan Doyle"**: Ibid., 216.

219 **Earlier that year, Houdini had testified**: Alicia Puglionesi, "In 1926, Houdini Spent 4 Days Shaming Congress for Being in Thrall to Fortune-Tellers," Atlas Obscura, Oct. 11, 2016, atlasobscura.com.

226 **"When November comes around"**: Sandford, *Houdini and Conan Doyle,* 207.

220 **"You won't live 'til Halloween!"**: "Mina Crandon & Harry Houdini."

221 **"many cases where [he had] escaped"**: Sandford, *Houdini and Conan Doyle,* 198.

221 **Later that night, after the performance**: Polidoro, *Final Séance,* 203–8. Other accounts of Houdini's tragic last days can be found at "The Death of Houdini," www.thegreatharryhoudini.com; "Harry Houdini," biography.com; and "Harry Houdini Dies After Operations," *New York Times,* Nov. 1, 1926.

223 **"I know for a fact that Houdini knew"**: Fulton Oursler letter to Arthur Conan Doyle, Harry Ransom Center.

224 **"I greatly admired him"**: Polidoro, *Final Séance,* 205.

225 **"Sweetheart, when you read this"**: Ibid., 208.

225 **"I thank you for your kind letter"**: Ernst and Carrington, *Story of a Strange Friendship,* 212.

226 **"If, as you believe, he had psychic power"**: Ibid., 214.

226 **"Two days before he went to his beloved mother"**: "Breaking the Houdini Code," Victorzammit.com.

227 **"The most important thing upon earth"**: Ernst and Carrington, *Story of a Strange Friendship,* 227.

228 **"I think the mirror incident shows"**: Ibid., 229.

231 **It was pointed out that the "secret" code**: "The Day Houdini (Almost) Came Back from the Dead," *Skeptical Inquirer,* March/April 2012.

231 **It's not clear what caused her to change her mind**: "Breaking the Houdini Code."

232 **"Both read the Bible day and night"**: William Blake, *"The Everlasting Gospel."*

CHAPTER FOURTEEN: THE LION IN WINTER

235 **In 1928, he calculated his and Lady Jean's net worth**: Lycett, *The Man Who Created Sherlock Holmes,* 452.

235 **Though he had lost Kingsley**: Doyle, *Memories and Adventures,* 236.

236 **Doyle sometimes wrote forty or more letters a day**: Carr, *Life of Arthur Conan Doyle,* ix, 276.

237 **"I couldn't revive him if I would"**: This famous comment was made in a letter to an unnamed friend.

237 **"Me? These crowds have nothing to do with me"**: Carr, *Life of Arthur Conan Doyle,* 274.

237 **"Wherever I go, there are two great types"**: Ibid.

237 **"Thank God that book is done!"**: Doyle to Smith, in ibid., 276.

238 **"I wish I could do as you wish"**: Carr, *Life of Arthur Conan Doyle,* 277.

238 **"I am in a position to do it"**: Quoted in obituary, *New York Times,* July 8, 1930.

238 **"Why do you go on hammering at proof"**: Carr, *Life of Arthur Conan Doyle,* 278.

239 **"We would beg the most orthodox reader"**: Doyle, *Pheneas Speaks,* 4.

240 **"A great light shall shine"**: Sandford, *Houdini and Conan Doyle,* 151.

240 **"a period of terrific natural convulsions"**: Personal correspondence, Ransom Center archive.

241 **In March 1927, Doyle sent a confidential memo**: Doyle to Lodge, Ransom Center.

242 **"I have moments of doubt"**: Sandford, *Houdini and Conan Doyle,* 221.

243 **But the hope of glory was heady**: This long account of the last flight of Captain Hinchliffe was based on several sources, including Fuller, *Airmen Who Would Not Die;* Jayne Baldwin, *West over the Waves: The Final Flight of Elsie Mackay* (Wigtown: GC Books, 2008); croydonairportcalling.blogspot.com; and "Loss of Hinchcliffe [*sic*] and Miss Elsie Mackay: A Spiritualist Message," *Sunday Express,* July 8, 1928, found at trove.nla.gov.au.

245 **"CAN YOU HELP A MAN WHO WAS DROWNED"**: Fuller, *Airmen Who Would Not Die,* 49–53.

248 **He described the interior of their house perfectly**: Ibid., 104.

249 **"MY BODY HAS WASHED NEAR JAMAICA"**: Ibid., 98.

251 **"When I talk about this subject"**: "Sir Arthur Conan Doyle, 1930," Fox Movietone News Story 6-962.

251 **"I have broken down badly"**: Doyle to Ernst in Sandford, *Houdini and Conan Doyle,* 250.

252 **"creator of Sherlock Holmes"**: Obituary, *New York Times,* July 8, 1930.

253 **"There are vast numbers of spirits"**: Sandford, *Houdini and Conan Doyle,* 254.

CHAPTER FIFTEEN: SIR ARTHUR, IS THAT YOU?

This account is based on the following sources.

An account by the journalist Michael Prescott, michaelprescott .freeservers.com/r-101.html, tells the story of Eileen Garrett's remarkable séance in the "laboratory" of Harry Price. This narrative includes a discussion of the various alternative theories that have been offered to explain away Garrett's detailed description of the R101 disaster. Additional details were found on the Harry Price Web site, harrypricewebsite.co.uk. This material, under "Eileen Garrett," is the complete text from chapter 6 of Price's book *Leaves from a Psychist's Case-Book* (London: Gollancz, 1933).

www.harrypriceweb site.co.uk/Séance/Garrett/leaves-r101.htmO.

A more detailed retelling of this story occurs in Fuller, *Airmen Who Would Not Die* (now out of print). Also, for a richer understanding of Harry Price himself, we used Morris, *Harry Price.*

BIBLIOGRAPHY

Ackroyd, Peter H. *A History of Ghosts*. With Angela Narth. New York: Rodale Press, 2009.

Baker, Michael. *The Doyle Diary: The Last Great Conan Doyle Mystery*. New York: Paddington Press, 1978.

Barkas, Thomas P. *Outlines of Ten Years' Investigations into the Phenomena of Modern Spiritualism*. London: Frederick Pitman, 1862.

Barnes, Julian. *Arthur & George*. New York: Vintage International, 2005.

Bird, James Malcolm. *"Margery" the Medium*. London: John Hamilton, 1925.

Blum, Deborah. *Ghost Hunters: William James and the Search for Scientific Proof of Life After Death*. New York: Penguin Press, 2006.

Booth, Martin. *The Doctor and the Detective: A Biography of Sir Arthur Conan Doyle*. New York: Thomas Dunne Books, 2000.

Braude, Ann. *Radical Spirits: Spiritualism and Women's Rights in Nineteenth-Century America*. 2nd ed. Bloomington: Indiana University Press, 2001.

Browning, Elizabeth Barrett. *Letters to Her Sister*. Edited by Leonard Huxley. London: J. Murray, 1931.

Cadwallader, M. E. *Hydesville in History*. Chicago: Progressive Thinker, 1917.

Capron, E. W. *Modern Spiritualism: Its Facts and Fanaticisms, Its Consistencies and Contradictions*. Boston: Bela Marsh, 1855.

Capron, E. W., and Henry Barron. *Explanation and History of the Mysterious Communion with Spirits*. Auburn, N.Y.: Capron and Barron, 1850.

Carr, John Dickson. *The Life of Sir Arthur Conan Doyle*. New York: Harper, 1949.

Chase, Warren. *Forty Years on the Spiritual Rostrum*. Boston: Colby & Rich, 1888.

Cheroux, Clement, Andreas Fischer, Pierre Apraxine, Denis Canguilhem, and Sophie Schmit. *The Perfect Medium: Photography and the Occult*. New Haven, Conn.: Yale University Press, 2004.

Clark, Uriah. *Plain Guide to Spiritualism*. Boston: William White, 1863.

Cooke, Ivan. *The Return of Arthur Conan Doyle*. Liss, Hampshire, U.K.: White Eagle Publishing Trust, 1963.

Crawford, William Jackson. *The Reality of Psychic Phenomena*. New York: E. P. Dutton, 1918.

Davenport, Reuben Briggs. *The Death-Blow to Spiritualism: Being the True Story of the Fox Sisters, as Revealed by Authority of Margaret Fox Kane and Catherine Fox Jencken*. New York: G. W. Dillingham, 1888.

Dods, John Bovee. *Spirit Manifestations Examined and Explained*. New York: DeWitt & Davenport, 1854.

Doyle, Arthur Conan. *Arthur Conan Doyle's Book of the Beyond*. Hampshire, U.K.: White Eagle Publishing Trust, 2003. First published as *Thy Kingdom Come*, 1933.

———. *The Coming of the Fairies*. 1922. Middletown, Del.: Forgotten Books, 2007.

———. *The Complete Sherlock Holmes*. Garden City, N.Y.: Doubleday, 1930.

———. *"Dangerous Work": Diary of an Arctic Adventure*. Edited by Jon Lellenberg and Daniel Stashower. London: British Library, 2012.

———. *The Edge of the Unknown*. New York: G. P. Putnam's Sons, 1930.

———. *The History of Spiritualism*. London: Jonathan Clowes, 1926.

———. *The Land of Mist*. New York: George H. Doran, 1926.

———. *The Lost World*. 1912. New York: Dover, 1998.

———. *Memories and Adventures*. Boston: Little, Brown, 1924.

———. *The New Revelation*. New York: George H. Doran, 1918.

———. *Our African Winter*. 1929. Newcastle upon Tyne: Cambridge Scholars, 2009.

———. *Our American Adventure*. New York: George H. Doran, 1923.

———. *Psychic Experiences*. New York; G. P. Putnam's Sons, 1925.

———. *Through the Magic Door*. 1907. N.p.: HardPress, 2010.

———. *The Vital Message*. New York: George H. Doran, 1919.

———. *The Wanderings of a Spiritualist*. New York: George H. Doran, 1921.

Edmonds, John Worth, and George T. Dexter. *Spiritualism*. New York: Partridge & Brittan, 1853.

Ernst, Bernard M. L., and Hereward Carrington. *Houdini and Conan Doyle: The Story of a Strange Friendship.* 1933. New York: Benjamin Blom, 1972.

Flammarion, Camille. *The Unknown.* New York: Harper & Bros., 1900.

Fornell, Earl Wesley. *The Unhappy Medium.* Austin: University of Texas Press, 1964.

Fuller, John G. *The Airmen Who Would Not Die.* G. P. Putnam's Sons, 1979.

Funk, Isaac K. *The Psychic Riddle.* New York: Funk & Wagnalls, 1907.

———. *The Widow's Mite and Other Psychic Phenomena.* 3rd ed. New York: Funk & Wagnalls, 1911.

Gauld, Alan. *The Founders of Psychical Research.* London: Routledge & Kegan Paul, 1968.

Gibson, John Michael, and Richard Lancelyn Green, eds. *The Unknown Conan Doyle: Letters to the Press.* London: Secker & Warburg, 1986.

Godwin, Joscelyn. *Upstate Cauldron: Eccentric Spiritual Movements in Early New York State.* Albany: State University of New York Press, 2015.

Goldfarb, Russell, and Clare Goldfarb. *Spiritualism and Nineteenth-Century Letters.* Cranbury, N.J.: Associated University Presses, 1978.

Greeley, Horace. *The Autobiography of Horace Greeley; or, Recollections of a Busy Life.* New York: E. B. Treat, 1872.

Grosso, Michael. *The Man Who Could Fly: St. Joseph of Copertino and the Mystery of Levitation.* Lanham, Md.: Rowman & Littlefield, 2016.

Gurney, Edmund, Frederick W. H. Meyers, and Frank Podmore. *Phantasms of the Living.* New York: E. P. Dutton, 1918.

Hagerty, Barbara Bradley. *Fingerprints of God: The Search for the Science of Spirituality.* New York: Riverhead Books, 2009.

Hardinge, Emma. *Modern American Spiritualism: A Twenty Years' Record of the Communion Between Earth and the World of Spirits.* New York: published by the author, 1870.

Harrold, Robert. *Cassadaga.* Miami, Fla.: Banyan Books, 1979.

Higham, Charles. *The Adventures of Conan Doyle.* New York: W. W. Norton, 1976.

Hill, J. Arthur. *Spiritualism: Its History, Phenomena, and Doctrine.* New York: George H. Doran, 1919.

Holt, Henry. *On the Cosmic Relations.* Boston: Houghton Mifflin, 1915.

Home, D. D. *Incidents in My Life.* New York: A. K. Butts, 1874.

Houdini, Harry. *A Magician Among the Spirits.* New York: Harper & Brothers, 1924.

Hudson, Thomas Jay. *A Scientific Demonstration of the Future Life.* Chicago: A. C. McClurg, 1895.

Hyslop, James. *Contact with the Other World.* New York: Century, 1919.

———. *Science and a Future Life.* Boston: Herbert H. Turner, 1905.

Jacobs, Joseph, ed. *Celtic Fairy Tales.* New York: G. P. Putnam's Sons, 1923.

———. *More Celtic Fairy Tales.* New York: G. P. Putnam's Sons, 1900.

James, William. *The Varieties of Religious Experience.* New York: Modern Library, 1902.

Jones, Kelvin. *Conan Doyle and the Spirits.* Wellingborough, U.K.: Aquarian Press, 1989.

Kaplan, Fred. *Dickens and Mesmerism.* Princeton, N.J.: Princeton University Press, 1975.

Korbon, Gregg. *Beyond Reason: Lessons from the Loss of a Gifted Child.* New York: iUniverse, 2009.

Kramnick, Isaac, and R. Laurence Moore. *The Godless Constitution.* New York: W. W. Norton, 1997.

Lachtman, Howard. *Sherlock Slept Here.* Santa Barbara, Calif.: Capra Press, 1985.

Lamond, John. *Arthur Conan Doyle, a Memoir.* London: John Murray, 1931.

Laszlo, Ervin. *The Immortal Mind: Science and the Continuity of Consciousness Beyond the Brain.* Rochester, Vt.: Inner Traditions, 2014.

Lellenberg, Jon, Daniel Stashower, and Charles Foley, eds. *Arthur Conan Doyle: A Life in Letters.* New York: Penguin Press, 2007.

Lodge, Sir Oliver. *Raymond; or, Life and Death.* New York: George H. Doran, 1916.

———. *The Survival of Man: A Study in Unrecognized Human Faculty.* New York: George H. Doran, 1909.

Lycett, Andrew. *The Man Who Created Sherlock Holmes.* London: Weidenfeld & Nicolson, 2007.

Mather, Cotton. *The Wonders of the Invisible World: Being an Account of the Tryals of Several Witches Lately Executed in New-England.* London, 1693.

Moore, R. Laurence. *In Search of White Crows: Spiritualism, Parapsychology, and American Culture.* New York: Oxford University Press, 1977.

Morris, Richard. *Harry Price: The Psychic Detective.* Gloucestershire, U.K.: Sutton, 2006.

Murchison, Carl, ed. *The Case for and Against Psychical Belief.* Worcester, Mass.: Clark University, 1927.

Murphy, Gardner, and Robert Ballou. *William James on Psychical Research.* New York: Viking Press, 1960.

Myers, F. W. H. *Human Personality and Its Survival of Bodily Death.* London: Longman's, Green, 1903.

Oppenheim, Janet. *The Other World: Spiritualism and Psychical Research in England, 1850–1914.* Cambridge, U.K.: Cambridge University Press, 1985.

Owen, Alex. *The Darkened Room: Women, Power, and Spiritualism in Late Victorian England.* Chicago: University of Chicago Press, 1989.

Owen, Robert Dale. *Footfalls on the Boundary of Another World.* Philadelphia: J. B. Lippincott, 1860.

Piper, Alta L. *The Life and Work of Mrs. Piper.* London: Kegan Paul, 1929.

Polidoro, Massimo. *Final Séance: The Strange Friendship Between Houdini and Conan Doyle.* Amherst, N.Y.: Prometheus Books, 2001.

Pond, Mariam Buckner. *Time Is Kind: The Story of the Unfortunate Fox Family.* New York: Centennial Press, 1947.

Porter, Katherine H. *Through a Glass Darkly: Spiritualism in the Browning Circle.* Lawrence: University of Kansas Press, 1958.

Price, Harry. *Fifty Years of Psychical Research: A Critical Survey.* London: Longman's, Green, 1939.

Prince, Walter Franklin. *Noted Witnesses for Psychic Occurrences.* New Hyde Park, N.Y.: University Books, 1962.

Redmond, Christopher. *Welcome to America, Mr. Sherlock Holmes.* Toronto: Simon & Pierre, 1987.

Richet, Charles. *Thirty Years of Psychical Research.* Translated by Stanley De Brath. London: W. Collins & Sons, 1923.

Roach, Mary. *Spook: Science Tackles the Afterlife.* New York: W. W. Norton, 2005.

Rosenberg, Samuel. *Naked Is the Best Disguise: The Death & Resurrection of Sherlock Holmes.* Indianapolis: Bobbs-Merrill, 1974.

Sage, Michel. *Mrs. Piper and the Society for Psychical Research.* Translated by Noralie Robertson. London: R. Brimley Johnson, 1903.

Sandford, Christopher. *Houdini and Conan Doyle: The Great Magician and the Inventor of Sherlock Holmes.* London: Duckworth Overlook, 2011.

Stashower, Daniel. *Teller of Tales.* New York: Henry Holt, 1999.

Straughan, Roger. *A Study in Survival: Conan Doyle Solves the Final Problem.* Winchester, U.K.: O Books, 2009.

Stuart, Nancy Rubin. *The Reluctant Spiritualist: The Life of Maggie Fox.* Orlando, Fla.: Harcourt, 2005.

Tietze, Thomas R. *Margery.* New York: Harper & Row, 1973.

Tymn, Michael. *Resurrecting Leonora Piper.* Guildford, U.K.: White Crow Books, 2013.

Underhill, A. Leah. *The Missing Link in Modern Spiritualism.* New York: Thomas R. Knox, 1885.

Verbatim Report of a Public Debate on "The Truth of Spiritualism" Between Sir Arthur Conan Doyle and Joseph McCabe. London: Watts, 1920. Available online at Hathitrust.org.

Volk, Steve. *Fringeology: How I Tried to Explain Away the Unexplainable.* New York: HarperOne, 2011.

Weisberg, Barbara. *Talking to the Dead: Kate and Maggie Fox and the Rise of Spiritualism.* San Francisco: HarperSanFrancisco, 2004.

Winter, Alison. *Mesmerized: Powers of Mind in Victorian Britain.* Chicago: University of Chicago Press, 1998.

Unpublished Sources

Harry Ransom Center, University of Texas at Austin.

Letters, manuscripts, and real-time notes from séances, in this superb collection of Arthur Conan Doyle material, specifically detailed in the notes.

INDEX

Note: Kinship terms are in relation to Arthur Conan Doyle.